# Your Birthday, *Your Card*

By Robert Lee Camp

SOURCEBOOKS, INC.
NAPERVILLE, ILLINOIS

Published by Sourcebooks, Inc.
P.O. Box 4410, Naperville, Illinois 60567-4410
(630) 961-3900
Fax: (630) 961-2168
www.sourcebooks.com

Library of Congress Cataloging-in-Publication Data

Camp, Robert (Robert L.)
  Your birthday, your card : the secrets of life, love and destiny in a deck of playing cards / by Robert Lee Camp.
    p. cm.
  1. Fortune-telling by cards. 2. Fortune-telling by birthdays. I. Title.
  BF1878.C275 2008
  133.3'242—dc22

                          2008018834

        Printed and bound in the United States of America.
          DR 10 9 8 7 6 5 4 3 2 1

# Dedication

This book is dedicated to our wonderful existence. Here we live, on this beautiful green and blue marble, perfectly suspended in space, a marvel of simplicity and complexity, all the while guided by its cycles and the cycles of neighboring planets and stars. May we always be grateful for the wonderful world that we live upon and for this sacred science, which reveals the intimate details of our destiny here.

# Contents

# Introduction

In 1987, a friend handed me an old book called *Sacred Symbols of the Ancients* and asked my opinion of it. I had just started studying astrology a few years earlier, and she thought this book might interest me. I looked up my birthday in the back of the book and discovered that I was a Queen of Diamonds Birth Card, and then read a chapter all about me that was based upon this card. I was stunned by the accuracy of what I read: There before me was a description of my life, so clear and concise, describing just how my life had been up to that point. It was not a flattering interpretation by any means—it pointed out my faults as well as my gifts and told how my particular life path was one of the most difficult. I thought it was a rather negative interpretation, but I could not deny that it was accurate.

I could not understand how the system in that book could be so accurate. Astrologers need a person's birthday, including the year, time, and place of birth, in order to make an analysis. *Sacred Symbols of the Ancients* only used the day and month of my birth— nothing more. And, to add to the mystery, I discovered there are eight birthdays that all have my same card. How is it possible to have eight birthdays in a year that all have the same basic description—an accurate description? To someone studying astrology, this was impossible—a complete mystery. I had to find out how it was done. I searched and searched for more books on this fascinating system, but I could find none. Slowly I gave up trying.

Then, two years later, I moved to Los Angeles, and within two weeks, I met the man who was to become my teacher in the cards, Arnie Lein. He introduced me to the rest of this amazing system, how monthly and yearly predictions could be made and how analyses of relationships are done. Shortly after I studied with him, he passed away. I was lucky to have known and studied with him, as I knew I had found something special. This was, in my estimation, the fabled 'Book of Destiny'—the book that held the secrets to each person's special destiny. I could not believe that this amazing system was so unknown to most people. At that time, I made a commitment to bring this knowledge to the attention of the world.

Within six months I had written my first book. And I have been writing more books and bringing this system to the world's attention ever since.

In the intervening years, I have performed analyses for thousands of people. I have looked at their personalities, their relationships, and their past, present, and future. The cards have never been wrong. I like to say that "'the cards never lie.'" That has been my experience over and over again, and I think you will discover the same!

This book will give you a fun and quick peek at this ancient and valuable knowledge. Here you can find out what your Birth Card is and what that says about you. You will learn about some of your unique characteristics in many areas of your life, such as work, health, relationships, and more. Every Birth Card is unique and has its own distinct characteristics. Our Birth Card is our karmic package, the sum total of characteristics that we were born with that allow us to fulfill our destiny in this lifetime. It is amazing, really. We can even take an infant and know a lot about him or her, regardless of who their parents are or how their childhood may unfold. Just a birthday is all we need to know to find the pattern someone is born into.

I hope you enjoy this book and that you share it with your friends. It is a lot of fun to discover who you are and the traits that make up your birthday.

# Chapter One

## The Fascinating Truth about Playing Cards

Most people have never stopped to wonder about the many interesting things associated with a regular deck of playing cards. Why, for instance, are there fifty-two cards in a deck? Why four suits? What do these suits represent, if anything? Where did the playing cards come from? I would like to share with you some interesting connections that our cards have with our world, and reveal to you why they are actually a calendar system that is intimately connected to our life here on Earth.

### The Deck of Cards Is Our Calendar

Let's examine some of the things playing cards and the calendar we use today have in common. First of all, there are four suits of thirteen cards each, totaling fifty-two cards, plus a Joker. Let's begin with the number 52. What else is there fifty-two of that is common knowledge? Well, there are fifty-two weeks in a year. Now, in numerology, we reduce numbers by adding their digits. If we reduce the number 52 we get $5 + 2 = 7$— the number of days in a week, and the number of visible planets. Seven is a very magical number in many ways and is considered the most spiritual number. It is also used extensively in many mystical traditions, including the Bible. Fascinating, isn't it? We can imagine that sometime in our ancient past, man discovered that a full year comprised something in the neighborhood of 365 days and nights. Looking into the heavens, they also noticed the sun, moon, and five other visible 'objects'; objects we now know are planets circling our sun. Taking their combined number, 7, and dividing the number of days in a year by it, they came up with fifty-two cycles in a year that we now call weeks. The wise ones realized that this number had much more significance and used these simple facts as a springboard for more advanced study.

Once again, taking the numerology of the cards, we assign numeric values to each of the cards. The Aces are 1, the Twos, 2, and so forth until we get to the Jack. The Jack is given the value of 11, the Queen, 12, and the King 13. Now, if we add up all the number values of every card in the deck, what do you guess will be the result? This means four times thirteen for the four Kings plus four times twelve for the four Queens, etc. What would be the resulting total of every card in the deck? Did you guess 365? Well, that's pretty close. The total actually comes to 364. We know that there are 365 and 1/4 days in a year, so what happened to the other day and a quarter? There is also another card in the deck that we haven't counted yet, and that is the Joker. And guess what? The Joker's value is exactly that of one and one quarter, which brings the total value of the deck of cards to exactly equal the number of days in a year. The twelve court cards in the deck represent the twelve months in the year and the twelve signs of our zodiac. The Joker's value of one and one quarter comes from the fact that he is 'all the four suits plus himself.' He stands apart as a unique balancing element in the scheme of the cards and the many card personalities.

These numeric values alone should convince the average person that there is more to a deck of cards than meets the eye. In fact, our deck of cards originated as a tool used to make calculations and estimations of time and the movements of Earth and the other planets surrounding our sun. Using the most advanced techniques, a deck of cards has been used to calculate the exact movement of the planets in our solar system. The closer we look at a deck of cards, the more fascinating they become. Every aspect of their construction and design has significance and pertinence to the world we live in.

## The Seasons and Their Corresponding Suits

Let's look now at the four suits. Playing cards are symbols, and everything about them symbolizes something. The suits have just as much meaning as the numbers. What do you imagine they represent? If you guessed that the suits represent the four seasons and the four elements (water, air, earth, and fire), you are right again. All these sets of four things are connected, as anyone who studies the Tarot or astrology will tell you. There is a suit for each season and element. Before we examine the suits and their meanings more closely, I suggest you look up your Birth Card in the chart at the end of the book. Just see which card is listed for your birthday—that is your Birth Card. The suit of your Birth Card will reveal something about your life and personality.

The first season of the year is spring. Animals are bearing their young, April showers are bringing a riot of colorful flowers, love is in the air, and life is erupting everywhere. In the first season of our life, we are surrounded by the love and caring of our parents and family. This season, so filled with love and life-giving rain, is represented by the suit of Hearts, which is the element of water and would be the suit of Cups in the Tarot. Heart Cards represent love and relationships. If your personal Birth Card is of the Hearts suit, you are a person whose main form of expression and whose personal karma is worked out through the vehicle of relationships and family. In addition, if you are a Heart, you are essentially childlike in your nature, and you relate well to children—you may even work with them. Hearts are the children of the deck, regardless of their physical age. Hearts are fond of beauty and pleasure, and sometimes over-indulgent in them.

The next season is summer, and during the summer season of life, love and family no longer surround us. Instead, we find ourselves occupied by school, books, and knowledge. In this season, we leave the love and tears of childhood behind and turn our attention to more educational pursuits. The suit that corresponds to summer is Clubs, which is of the air element. This is the same as the Swords suit in the Tarot. Clubs represent the status of our mind and mental pursuits, acquisition of knowledge, and communications. Those who are born in the suit of Clubs work with ideas, points of view, and the ability to communicate. For them, the idea and concept of a person or thing is often just as important as the thing itself. Clubs are the eternal college students, usually eager to learn new things and interested in the details of life.

In the autumn season, we are harvesting the fruits or our efforts, reaping the riches we have sown in the soil of our lives. It is in the autumn season of life that we generally accumulate wealth and property. Diamonds represent this third season, and they coincide with the element of earth and the suit of Pentacles in the Tarot. The most common meaning of Diamonds is money, though on a deeper level, they represent what we most value in life. Those born as a Diamond Card work out their karma with money and values. Diamonds are the adults of the deck, and Diamond children do not like being treated as anything other than adults.

It is in the winter season that death and transformation reign supreme. After the harvest, winter sets in, and much of what was born in the spring dies away. In the winter season of life, we prepare for, and eventually experience, our own death. Health concerns become more prominent, as well as our interest in our spiritual life. Though the shadow of the gravedigger's spade is ever present on our minds, so too is the promise of a new spiritual life. This promise, like a phoenix rising from the ashes, makes the winter suit, the suit of Spades, the most powerful suit. This transformative quality of the last period of our life connects Spades to the element of fire and the suit of wands in the Tarot. Spades are a more complicated suit than the others in some ways. They represent work and health on a basic, material level, but on a deeper level, they represent spirituality and the condition of our inner 'fire.' The symbol of the spade is as much that of an acorn as it is the shovel. Secrets lie hidden within this tiny seed, and secrets are another meaning of this card. Those born as Spade Cards usually have a very strong materialistic nature or a very spiritual nature, sometimes both. In any case, they are very hard-working people. Spades are the old people of the deck, often showing advanced wisdom and maturity at an early age. They usually focus much of their attention on the perfection of their work.

Note:
There is considerable discussion among both Tarot users and people who use this system about the assignment of the suits and elements. Many will disagree with the research I have done; these are the associations that fit best for me. But you do not need to agree with me to gain the benefits of this system.

## The Fascinating Ace of Spades

If you get out a deck of cards right now and look through them, you will notice that the Ace of Spades is much different than the other Aces in the deck. First of all, it has a much larger symbol in the center of the card. Secondly, on many decks, you will find that the center Spade symbol has been ornately decorated, often very beautifully. Usually manufacturers will place their company name on this card somewhere. Do you know why the Ace of Spades is so different? Most of the manufacturers don't even know, but it is because the Ace of Spades is the card that represents The Order of the Magi and the secret societies of old. It is the one card, above all others, that represents the secrets that are there to be discovered by studying the cards in-depth.

In our system, the Ace of Spades represents secrets as well. It is the card that represents the science of the cards. The Ace of Spades has always been a symbol of death as well. It is likened to a single bullet that ends our life. Many cultures have used this card in film and literature as a death symbol. It holds true here as well. The Ace of Spades is one of the more powerful symbols for personal transformation, and in some cases, physical death.

## The Little Book of the Seven Thunders

Now that we have learned a little about the fascinating links that the cards have to our world, let's look a bit at the history of our cards. Consider this verse from the Bible:

> And when the Seven Thunders had uttered their voices, I was about to write; but I heard a voice from heaven saying unto me, "Seal up those things, uttered by the Seven Thunders, and write them not."
> And I took the little book out of the Angel's hand and devoured it; and to my taste it was sweet as honey; but as soon as I had devoured it, it became bitter unto my inside.
> And he said unto me "You must prophecy again before many peoples and nations and tongues and kings."

> *Revelations, 10:4, 10, and 11*

The first known book ever published about this system of divination and self-understanding is *The Mystic Test Book*, by Olney Richmond, originally published in 1893. Mr. Richmond was at that time the Grand Master of a secret society known as The Order of the Magi. He claimed that his order was instructed, since the days of Egypt, to keep the secrets of the cards alive and protected until the proper time for their revelation to the world. Olney Richmond claimed that the above passage from Revelations, if translated with awareness of the subtleties of spiritual discernment, reveals that the "little book" mentioned is the book of our same fifty-two cards. According to Mr. Richmond, these passages clearly indicate their mission to keep their secrets hidden from the reach of the common man until the time was right. Whether or not this is true, it is interesting to note that Richmond's book was the first to reveal any of these secrets. No other books have been found with any similar materials prior to that time.

In his book, Richmond explains how the cards must have originated in Atlantis, since all major civilizations claim their invention, and then he explores many other facets of the cards that are both fascinating and amazing. I've read his book several times and used the cards for many years, and I still haven't begun to understand some of the topics in that book. I will say, however, that based on what I have learned so far, it is clear to me that if we were to completely understand their numbers and meanings, we would have a tool that could easily give us specific information about almost any area of life or science. *The Mystic Test Book* is a fascinating book that can still be purchased at some metaphysical bookstores and online.

One other interesting fact Richmond discusses is that over the years, card manufacturers have tried unsuccessfully to print cards with different faces on the Queens, Kings, and Jacks. Even today, if you go into some of the larger game stores, you will find a host of other kinds of playing cards. Some will have characters of various shapes and sizes, some will have the faces of famous people on them, and the like. At any rate, if you ask any card manufacturer, they will tell you that these variations of cards never sell that well. Richmond claims that the reason the other variations of cards do not sell is that decks of cards have a mystical potency, which maintains the integrity of their original design. For this reason, he says, the other cards never sell. Olney says that the members of their order were instructed never to deface, alter, or otherwise change the cards in any way. I personally recommend that when you choose a deck of playing cards, choose cards that are of the original design, and avoid cards that are different. This includes cards that have the large numbers and the reduced faces. Stick with the old standbys.

I hope that I've stimulated your interest in our not-so-common deck of cards. Now we will begin to learn more about you and your place in the cards. As we uncover more of the secrets that lie within the cards, keep in mind that the science you are now learning has been around a long time and has many connections to the past.

This book is pretty straightforward. You look up the birthday of anyone you want to know more about and find out what their Birth Card and Planetary Ruling Card are from the list of birthdays in the back of the book. Then, you read about those two cards. That's really all there is to it. But I will provide some additional information here that can make your study more enjoyable and interesting. First about our Birth Card and Planetary Ruling Card, which you can determine by looking at the chart on page 14.

## Birth and Planetary Ruling Cards

Each birthday of the year is associated with one of the 53 cards in a deck. From the A♥ to the K♠ to the Joker, there are 53 distinct personality types. This Birth Card is the primary symbol of our karma for this lifetime. That karma is the accumulated pattern that we are born under. It is amazing, really, that we each have such distinguishable and unique traits, symbolized by the Birth Card and Planetary Ruling Card. The Birth Card is the first and foremost of our symbols. It is our essence. It also represents a gift of some sort. We are always able to access the high side of that card and usually do so often. This process is for the most part unconscious. We just act out this card without reflecting on what we are doing or why. We can make our actions more conscious and deliberate, but it takes a while. And even then, we will usually act out from this primary symbol of who we are. However, when some people read about their Birth Card, they do not completely relate to the description. Most of these people are identify more with their Planetary Ruling Card.

The Planetary Ruling Card is a card that is derived from your Birth Card and your astrological Sun Sign. It is not who we really are, like the Birth Card is, but instead it is an indicator of who we identify with and think that we are. This belief— that we are this card—can make the Planetary Ruling Card extremely important. First of all, most of us identify more with our Planetary Ruling Card than with our Birth Card. Secondly, we usually exaggerate the qualities of our Planetary Ruling Card much more than our Birth

Card. For example, someone who is a King Birth Card may be strong-willed and bossy at times, but a person whose Planetary Ruling Card is a King is much more likely to be that way all the time. They will appear much stronger, dominating, or bossy than someone whose Birth Card is a King.

When you look up your birthday or the birthday of someone you want to study, be sure to read the descriptions of both cards to get the whole picture, and make sure you keep in mind the identification with and exaggeration of the Planetary Ruling Card.

## Leos and Scorpios—Exceptions to the Rule

Leos do have both a Birth Card and Planetary Ruling Card, but they are the same card! Since Leos are ruled by the Sun, their Planetary Ruling Card is a Sun Card, or Birth Card, as well. Essentially, Leos are a double influence of their Birth Card. This creates a more dramatic and striking example of their personality. Leos are among the best examples of cards to study, because they exemplify the traits so clearly and distinctively. They are more dramatic and unforgettable examples of their cards, and I have learned a lot by watching them.

Scorpios are ruled by two planets, Mars and Pluto. For this reason, they have two Planetary Ruling Cards. Each has a purpose and each is significant. However, for most uses, the first Planetary Ruling Card, the one associated with Mars, is the one we notice being emphasized in their personality. The second Planetary Ruling Card for Scorpios is their Phoenix card. Usually a Scorpio person will not show those traits until after age forty-five, when they have made some of the necessary transformations. Remember, they are the sign of death and rebirth. When you see an "&" sign between two cards, it is always a Scorpio birthday. The first one listed is the Mars Planetary Ruling Card and the one you should focus on more.

## Born on the Cusp

Around the 21st of each month, the Sun moves from one sign to the next. This varies from month to month and from year to year, producing a possible three-day span during which someone's Sun Sign is in question. For example, anyone born from May 20th through May 22nd could be either a Taurus or a Gemini. For those born on a cusp, this book does not state for certain which cards pertain to them. So when you see the word "or" between two cards listed beside a birthday in the Birth Card and Planetary Ruling Card Chart, it means it is a cusp birthday. The first card listed would be for the person who is the sign of the previous period. In our example, most of May is Taurus and then changes to Gemini somewhere between the 20th and 22nd each year. The first card displayed would be for those who are Taurus Sun Signs, and the second one for those who are Gemini. In order to know for sure what your Sun Sign is, you will have to have an astrological chart done. The easiest and least expensive way to do this is to go to www.astro.com. You can do a free chart there. All you need is your birthday, birthplace, and birth time. Once you know your Sun Sign, you can study that birthday's cards with the assurance that you are accurate.

## Time of Birth

Most people do not know what time they were born, at least not by heart. But this can be important. If you were born around midnight, let's say within thirty minutes, there is a good chance that your actual birthday was the day before or the day after the recorded birth. This could give you an entirely different Birth Card and Planetary Ruling Card. Why is this so? For many reasons, really, but the biggest reason is that the card system is based upon what we call "true solar time." This is also called sundial time, since it is the time that it really was at the place of your birth. And know this— it is the time it was at the place of your birth that counts, not the time it was in Greenwich, England. It is always the local time that counts.

If you were born during a month that daylight savings was being observed, your true solar time of birth was an hour earlier than what was recorded on your birth certificate. So, if you were born at 12:45 a.m. in July 4th of 1966 in New York City, your actual real birthday was 11:45 p.m. on July 3rd. Naturally, that can make a huge difference. The rule of thumb here is that if your birth time was within an hour of midnight, there is the possibility of discrepancy in your date of birth. If your Birth Card just doesn't fit you, this may be the reason. The actual process of calculating the exact true solar time of birth is somewhat complex and requires not only the date and time of birth, but also the location. If your birthday is in question, you can send an email to info@7thunders.com, and we will send you instructions on how to calculate your true solar time of birth.

## Best Marriages, Hottest Sex

As you read each card's description, you will see a list of cards denoting which other cards are best for marriage or with whom you will have the hottest sex. I need to point out here that these are not complete lists by any means. But for the most part, the cards listed are ones that are commonly found in couples with those characteristics.

Marriage is a complex subject. People get married for many reasons. However, I have found that a good majority of marriages have a special connection called the Moon connection. This is fully described in my book *Love Cards*, but here I list the cards with which each card has this important connection. You will find that most people of a certain card will marry someone of one of the cards listed here. Do keep in mind that you should be looking at two lists of cards— the one for your Birth Card and the one for your Planetary Ruling Card, too! When you combine both lists, you get a pretty long list of people with whom you have the Moon connection. There is a lot more to the story, and you can read more about that in *Love Cards* if you like, but this will give you a good starting point.

The hottest sex comes from the Mars connection, which is also described in depth in Love Cards. Mars is the attraction that often draws people together. However, this is not the only sexual connection, just the most common. Again, look at the list for both your Birth Card and Planetary Ruling Card.

The lists given in both categories are not exhaustive. And there are some exceptions. But for a good starting point and for having lots of fun with this system, these are perfect. I hope you enjoy them.

## Marriageability

This book will help you find out something about your basic nature when it comes to love and relationships. I have coined a term for this book: "marriageable." Some cards are very marriageable, and others are not. Essentially, being marriageable means the ability to create and sustain a long-term committed relationship. Some unmarriageable cards can get married but are not able to sustain it, or end up cheating. Some cards are serial monogamists—they get married, but it never lasts long, and they then quickly remarry. There is room for lots of variety here. But being unmarriageable means that there are parts of your personality that make long-term commitment difficult, or in some cases, impossible. This is not a judgment of any kind. Life allows for a variety of expressions. Some people just do not think that marriage is all that important anyway!

This evaluation comes from my nearly twenty years of experience watching people and their Birth Cards. It is by no means conclusive. In other words, just because you are listed as being un-marriageable does not mean you cannot get married or make commitments. But for most people with cards that are not that marriageable, this will be true. Also, it is important to know that if you are willing to look at the factors that govern your marriageability and work on them, you can have a long term committed relationship. No one is excluded. But your card will have a certain unconscious way of being in relationship. It can be changed, but only by the conscious intentional effort of the individual. Chapter Four, "The Marriageability Factor," gives a lot more information about it.

# Birth Card and Planetary Ruling Card Chart

## January

| | BC | PRC | | BC | PRC |
|---|---|---|---|---|---|
| 1 | K♠ | 5♣ | 17 | 10♦ | 5♥ |
| 2 | Q♠ | K♣ | 18 | 9♦ | 4♥ |
| 3 | J♠ | 10♦ | 19 | 8♦ | 10♠ |
| 4 | 10♠ | 7♦ | 20 | 7♦ | 2♥ |
| 5 | 9♠ | 4♣ | 21 | 6♦ | A♥ or A♦* |
| 6 | 8♠ | 3♣ | 22 | 5♦ | K♣ |
| 7 | 7♠ | 4♦ | 23 | 4♦ | 10♣ |
| 8 | 6♠ | 3♥ | 24 | 3♦ | 9♣ |
| 9 | 5♠ | K♥ | 25 | 2♦ | 10♦ |
| 10 | 4♠ | A♥ | 26 | A♦ | 7♣ |
| 11 | 3♠ | J♣ | 27 | K♣ | 6♣ |
| 12 | 2♠ | 10♣ | 28 | Q♣ | 7♦ |
| 13 | A♠ | 9♣ | 29 | J♣ | 4♥ |
| 14 | K♦ | 8♣ | 30 | 10♣ | 10♠ |
| 15 | Q♦ | 7♣ | 31 | 9♣ | 4♣ |
| 16 | J♦ | 6♣ | | | |

## February

| | BC | PRC | | BC | PRC |
|---|---|---|---|---|---|
| 1 | J♠ | 8♠ | 17 | 8♦ | 5♣ |
| 2 | 10♠ | 5♠ | 18 | 7♦ | K♥ |
| 3 | 9♠ | 2♦ | 19 | 6♦ | A♥ |
| 4 | 8♠ | 3♠ | 20 | 5♦ | K♣ or J♦* |
| 5 | 7♠ | 2♠ | 21 | 4♦ | 8♣ |
| 6 | 6♠ | A♣ | 22 | 3♦ | 9♣ |
| 7 | 5♠ | K♦ | 23 | 2♦ | 8♣ |
| 8 | 4♠ | Q♦ | 24 | A♦ | 5♣ |
| 9 | 3♠ | 9♦ | 25 | K♣ | 6♠ |
| 10 | 2♠ | 8♦ | 26 | Q♣ | 5♠ |
| 11 | A♠ | 9♦ | 27 | J♣ | 4♦ |
| 12 | K♦ | 6♦ | 28 | 10♣ | 5♣ |
| 13 | Q♦ | 5♦ | 29 | 9♣ | 2♦ |
| 14 | J♦ | 6♠ | | | |
| 15 | 10♦ | 3♣ | | | |
| 16 | 9♦ | 4♦ | | | |

## March

| | BC | PRC | | BC | PRC |
|---|---|---|---|---|---|
| 1 | 9♠ | J♠ | 17 | 6♦ | Q♦ |
| 2 | 8♠ | 9♥ | 18 | 5♦ | J♦ |
| 3 | 7♠ | 8♥ | 19 | 4♦ | 8♦ |
| 4 | 6♠ | Q♣ | 20 | 3♦ | 9♠ or 7♦* |
| 5 | 5♠ | 6♥ | 21 | 2♦ | 8♠ or 6♦* |
| 6 | 4♠ | 5♥ | 22 | A♦ | 3♣ |
| 7 | 3♠ | 7♥ | 23 | K♣ | 4♦ |
| 8 | 2♠ | K♠ | 24 | Q♣ | 3♦ |
| 9 | A♠ | 2♥ | 25 | J♣ | 2♦ |
| 10 | K♦ | 4♠ | 26 | 10♣ | 3♥ |
| 11 | Q♦ | Q♠ | 27 | 9♣ | K♥ |
| 12 | J♦ | Q♥ | 28 | 8♣ | 10♥ |
| 13 | 10♦ | 3♣ | 29 | 7♣ | J♣ |
| 14 | 9♦ | 2♥ | 30 | 6♣ | 10♣ |
| 15 | 8♦ | 3♥ | 31 | 5♣ | 7♥ |
| 16 | 7♦ | K♦ | | | |

## April

| | BC | PRC | | BC | PRC |
|---|---|---|---|---|---|
| 1 | 7♠ | J♦ | 17 | 4♦ | 6♣ |
| 2 | 6♠ | 8♦ | 18 | 3♦ | 7♦ |
| 3 | 5♠ | 9♠ | 19 | 2♦ | 6♦ |
| 4 | 4♠ | 8♠ | 20 | A♦ | 3♣ or 5♥* |
| 5 | 3♠ | 5♦ | 21 | K♣ | 4♦ or 4♥* |
| 6 | 2♠ | 6♠ | 22 | Q♣ | 5♣ |
| 7 | A♠ | 5♦ | 23 | J♣ | 7♦ |
| 8 | K♦ | 2♦ | 24 | 10♣ | K♠ |
| 9 | Q♦ | 3♠ | 25 | 9♣ | 2♥ |
| 10 | J♦ | 2♠ | 26 | 8♣ | 4♠ |
| 11 | 10♦ | A♦ | 27 | 7♣ | Q♠ |
| 12 | 9♦ | K♦ | 28 | 6♣ | Q♥ |
| 13 | 8♦ | A♦ | 29 | 5♣ | A♠ |
| 14 | 7♦ | 9♣ | 30 | 4♣ | J♠ |
| 15 | 6♦ | 10♦ | | | |
| 16 | 5♦ | 9♦ | | | |

## May

| | BC | PRC | | BC | PRC |
|---|---|---|---|---|---|
| 1 | 5♠ | 9♣ | 17 | 2♦ | 8♣ |
| 2 | 4♠ | 10♦ | 18 | A♦ | 5♥ |
| 3 | 3♠ | 7♣ | 19 | K♣ | 4♥ |
| 4 | 2♠ | 6♣ | 20 | Q♣ | 5♣ or 10♠* |
| 5 | A♠ | 7♣ | 21 | J♣ | 7♠ or 9♦* |
| 6 | K♦ | 4♣ | 22 | 10♣ | K♠ or 8♦* |
| 7 | Q♦ | 3♣ | 23 | 9♣ | 9♠ |
| 8 | J♦ | 4♣ | 24 | 8♣ | 6♦ |
| 9 | 10♦ | A♥ | 25 | 7♣ | 5♦ |
| 10 | 9♦ | 2♣ | 26 | 6♣ | 6♠ |
| 11 | 8♦ | 3♥ | 27 | 5♣ | 3♦ |
| 12 | 7♦ | J♥ | 28 | 4♣ | 2♦ |
| 13 | 6♦ | 10♥ | 29 | 3♣ | 3♠ |
| 14 | 5♦ | J♣ | 30 | 2♣ | K♣ |
| 15 | 4♦ | 8♥ | 31 | A♣ | Q♣ |
| 16 | 3♦ | 7♥ | | | |

## June

| | BC | PRC | | BC | PRC |
|---|---|---|---|---|---|
| 1 | 3♠ | 9♥ | 17 | K♣ | J♦ |
| 2 | 2♠ | 8♥ | 18 | Q♣ | 10♠ |
| 3 | A♠ | 7♥ | 19 | J♣ | 9♦ |
| 4 | K♦ | 6♥ | 20 | 10♣ | 8♦ |
| 5 | Q♦ | 5♥ | 21 | 9♣ | 9♠ |
| 6 | J♦ | 4♥ | 22 | 8♣ | 6♦ or J♠* |
| 7 | 10♦ | 8♠ | 23 | 7♣ | 9♥ |
| 8 | 9♦ | 7♠ | 24 | 6♣ | 8♥ |
| 9 | 8♦ | K♠ | 25 | 5♣ | 10♠ |
| 10 | 7♦ | 5♠ | 26 | 4♣ | 6♥ |
| 11 | 6♦ | 4♠ | 27 | 3♣ | 5♥ |
| 12 | 5♦ | Q♠ | 28 | 2♣ | 7♠ |
| 13 | 4♦ | 2♠ | 29 | A♠ | 3♥ |
| 14 | 3♦ | A♠ | 30 | K♥ | 2♥ |
| 15 | 2♦ | J♠ | | | |
| 16 | A♦ | Q♦ | | | |

* denotes cusp birthdates—see page 10 for full explanation.

# Birth Card and Planetary Ruling Card Chart

## July

| | BC | PRC | | BC | PRC |
|---|---|---|---|---|---|
| 1 | A♠ | 3♦ | 17 | J♣ | Q♠ |
| 2 | K♦ | K♥ | 18 | 10♣ | Q♥ |
| 3 | Q♦ | A♦ | 19 | 9♣ | J♥ |
| 4 | J♦ | K♣ | 20 | 8♣ | J♠ |
| 5 | 10♦ | 10♥ | 21 | 7♣ | 9♥ |
| 6 | 9♦ | J♣ | 22 | 6♣ | 8♥ |
| 7 | 8♦ | 10♣ | 23 | 5♣ | 10♠ or 5♣* |
| 8 | 7♦ | 7♥ | 24 | 4♣ | 4♣ |
| 9 | 6♦ | 8♣ | 25 | 3♣ | 3♣ |
| 10 | 5♦ | 7♣ | 26 | 2♣ | 2♣ |
| 11 | 4♦ | 4♥ | 27 | A♣ | A♣ |
| 12 | 3♦ | 5♣ | 28 | K♥ | K♥ |
| 13 | 2♦ | 4♣ | 29 | Q♥ | Q♥ |
| 14 | A♦ | A♥ | 30 | J♥ | J♥ |
| 15 | K♣ | 2♣ | 31 | 10♥ | 10♥ |
| 16 | Q♣ | A♣ | | | |

## August

| | BC | PRC | | BC | PRC |
|---|---|---|---|---|---|
| 1 | Q♦ | Q♦ | 17 | 9♣ | 9♣ |
| 2 | J♦ | J♦ | 18 | 8♣ | 8♣ |
| 3 | 10♦ | 10♦ | 19 | 7♣ | 7♣ |
| 4 | 9♦ | 9♦ | 20 | 6♣ | 6♣ |
| 5 | 8♦ | 8♦ | 21 | 5♣ | 5♣ |
| 6 | 7♦ | 7♦ | 22 | 4♣ | 4♣ or 2♦* |
| 7 | 6♦ | 6♦ | 23 | 3♣ | 3♣ or 3♠* |
| 8 | 5♦ | 5♦ | 24 | 2♣ | K♣ |
| 9 | 4♦ | 4♦ | 25 | A♣ | Q♣ |
| 10 | 3♦ | 3♦ | 26 | K♥ | K♦ |
| 11 | 2♦ | 2♦ | 27 | Q♥ | 10♣ |
| 12 | A♦ | A♦ | 28 | J♥ | 9♣ |
| 13 | K♣ | K♣ | 29 | 10♥ | 10♦ |
| 14 | Q♣ | Q♣ | 30 | 9♥ | 7♣ |
| 15 | J♣ | J♣ | 31 | 8♥ | 6♣ |
| 16 | 10♣ | 10♣ | | | |

## September

| | BC | PRC | | BC | PRC |
|---|---|---|---|---|---|
| 1 | 10♦ | 8♠ | 17 | 7♣ | 5♦ |
| 2 | 9♦ | 7♠ | 18 | 6♣ | 6♠ |
| 3 | 8♦ | K♠ | 19 | 5♣ | 3♦ |
| 4 | 7♦ | 5♠ | 20 | 4♣ | 2♦ |
| 5 | 6♦ | 4♠ | 21 | 3♣ | 3♠ |
| 6 | 5♦ | Q♠ | 22 | 2♣ | K♣ or J♦* |
| 7 | 4♦ | 2♠ | 23 | A♣ | Q♣ or 10♠* |
| 8 | 3♦ | A♠ | 24 | K♥ | 6♥ |
| 9 | 2♦ | J♠ | 25 | Q♥ | 8♦ |
| 10 | A♦ | Q♦ | 26 | J♥ | 9♠ |
| 11 | K♣ | J♦ | 27 | 10♥ | 8♠ |
| 12 | Q♣ | 10♦ | 28 | 9♥ | 5♦ |
| 13 | J♣ | 9♦ | 29 | 8♥ | 6♠ |
| 14 | 10♣ | 8♦ | 30 | 7♥ | 5♠ |
| 15 | 9♣ | 9♠ | | | |
| 16 | 8♣ | 6♦ | | | |

## October

| | BC | PRC | | BC | PRC |
|---|---|---|---|---|---|
| 1 | 8♦ | 3♥ | 17 | 5♣ | A♠ |
| 2 | 7♦ | J♥ | 18 | 4♣ | J♠ |
| 3 | 6♦ | 10♥ | 19 | 3♣ | 9♥ |
| 4 | 5♦ | J♣ | 20 | 2♣ | J♦ |
| 5 | 4♦ | 8♥ | 21 | A♣ | 10♠ |
| 6 | 3♦ | 7♥ | 22 | K♥ | 6♥ |
| 7 | 2♦ | 8♣ | 23 | Q♥ | 8♦, or K♠ & 5♣* |
| 8 | A♦ | 5♥ | 24 | J♥ | 9♥, or 2♥ & 2♣* |
| 9 | K♣ | 4♥ | 25 | 10♥ | A♥ & 3♠ |
| 10 | Q♣ | 5♣ | 26 | 9♥ | Q♠ & K♣ |
| 11 | J♣ | 7♥ | 27 | 8♥ | Q♥ & A♣ |
| 12 | 10♣ | K♠ | 28 | 7♥ | J♥ & K♣ |
| 13 | 9♣ | 2♥ | 29 | 6♥ | J♠ & 10♣ |
| 14 | 8♣ | 4♥ | 30 | 5♥ | 9♥ & 9♦ |
| 15 | 7♣ | Q♠ | 31 | 4♥ | 8♥ & 8♦ |
| 16 | 6♣ | Q♥ | | | |

## November

| | BC | PRC | | BC | PRC |
|---|---|---|---|---|---|
| 1 | 6♦ | 10♦ & 5♥ | 17 | 3♣ | 7♣ & 7♠ |
| 2 | 5♦ | 9♦ & 4♥ | 18 | 2♣ | 4♥ & 6♣ |
| 3 | 4♦ | 6♣ & K♠ | 19 | A♣ | 5♣ & 5♠ |
| 4 | 3♦ | 7♦ & 2♥ | 20 | K♥ | 4♣ & 4♥ |
| 5 | 2♦ | 6♦ & A♥ | 21 | Q♥ | K♠ & 5♣ |
| 6 | A♦ | 3♣ & Q♠ | 22 | J♥ | 2♥ & 2♦ |
| 7 | K♣ | 4♣ & Q♥ | 23 | 10♥ | A♦ |
| 8 | Q♣ | 3♦ & J♥ | 24 | 9♥ | J♣ |
| 9 | J♣ | 2♣ & 2♠ | 25 | 8♥ | 10♣ |
| 10 | 10♣ | 3♥ & 3♦ | 26 | 7♥ | 9♣ |
| 11 | 9♣ | K♥ & J♠ | 27 | 6♥ | 8♣ |
| 12 | 8♣ | 10♥ & Q♦ | 28 | 5♥ | 7♣ |
| 13 | 7♣ | J♣ & J♦ | 29 | 4♥ | 6♣ |
| 14 | 6♣ | 10♣ & Q♣ | 30 | 3♥ | 5♣ |
| 15 | 5♣ | 7♥ & 9♠ | | | |
| 16 | 4♣ | 8♣ & 8♠ | | | |

## December

| | BC | PRC | | BC | PRC |
|---|---|---|---|---|---|
| 1 | 4♦ | 6♠ | 17 | A♣ | 3♦ |
| 2 | 3♦ | 5♠ | 18 | K♥ | 2♦ |
| 3 | 2♦ | 4♠ | 19 | Q♥ | 3♥ |
| 4 | A♦ | 3♠ | 20 | J♥ | K♥ |
| 5 | K♣ | 2♠ | 21 | 10♥ | A♦ or Q♦* |
| 6 | Q♣ | A♠ | 22 | 9♥ | J♣ or 9♦* |
| 7 | J♣ | K♣ | 23 | 8♥ | 8♦ |
| 8 | 10♣ | A♣ | 24 | 7♥ | 9♠ |
| 9 | 9♣ | K♦ | 25 | 6♥ | 6♦ |
| 10 | 8♣ | 10♦ | 26 | 5♥ | 5♦ |
| 11 | 7♣ | 9♦ | 27 | 4♥ | 6♣ |
| 12 | 6♣ | 8♦ | 28 | 3♥ | 3♦ |
| 13 | 5♣ | 7♦ | 29 | 2♥ | 2♦ |
| 14 | 4♣ | 6♦ | 30 | A♥ | 3♠ |
| 15 | 3♣ | 5♦ | 31 | Joker | |
| 16 | 2♣ | 4♦ | | | |

The suit of our Birth Card reveals a lot about us, and if we spend some time examining those people we know of the various suits, we find many patterns emerging that help us to better understand ourselves and the mysteries of our world.

The four suits in a deck of cards are associated with the four seasons, the grand cycle of birth, growth, maturity, and death. Hearts are spring, Clubs are summer, Diamonds are fall, and Spades represent winter. The four suits also represent the four seasons of life. Hearts, the suit of love and family, represent our childhood. Clubs, the suit of knowledge and ideas, represent our adolescent school years, lasting until we graduate from college and have completed our vocational training. Diamonds, the suit of money and values, represent adulthood and the time of amassing our fortune in the world. Finally, Spades, the suit of work, health, and spirituality, represent our final years on the planet as we prepare for the life hereafter.

Just knowing this much can tell you a lot about people by their Birth Card. We might say that Hearts are eternally youthful and childlike. Hearts enjoy children and are excellent school teachers. They retain their youthful nature their entire life. In one sense, they never grow old. On the negative side, these folks may retain a certain immaturity as well. Clubs are the eternal high-school or college student. They are always inquisitive and interested in new ideas or ways of looking at things. They are avid talkers and are always learning new things in their lives. They also love to read, more than any other suit in the deck. A Club is never too old to go back to school, where they usually find a great deal of satisfaction. On the negative side, a Club can be overly attached to their own ideas and take what they or others say too seriously.

Diamonds are the adults of the deck. For this reason, they usually do not like it when people try to tell them what to do, especially if they feel they are being treated like a child. This would never do for a Diamond. By the same token, a Diamond may take on an adult or parent role in their relationships and associations. They want to be seen as mature and responsible for the most part to retain this adult image. Diamonds put special emphasis on the accumulation of value and will be the first to tell you about the importance of having a good job or occupation. They will also try to help you commercialize your skills and abilities, one of the major occupations of the Diamond period of our life. Spades can be seen as eternal old people. Even children and babies who are Spades seem to have that 'wise look' upon their face. Spade people tend to relate best to older people, at the least to those people who act more mature and responsible. Spades are the workers of the deck and tend to have strong wills. They also can be the most spiritually oriented people in the deck, but this is not the rule.

Just from knowing the connections with the seasons, we can see how the vibration of a particular suit translates into personality traits that can be identified in the people we know. However, there are more subtle manifestations of the suits that we can explore, some of which are connected to these same seasons, and others to the elements that go with the seasons. We can also learn a lot about each of the suits by studying the King and Queen of each suit as role models for the suit in general.

 *Hearts*

People who are of the Heart suit act young and look young, too. They can be dramatic and entertaining. Hearts is the suit of love, youth, children, romance, relationships, and artistic expression. Astrologically, this would tend to associate those of the Hearts suit with the sign of Leo and the fifth house. This is also the suit of sensual pleasure and delight. Hearts have special affinity for the subjects just listed. Hearts women can be the ideal romantic partner or wife. They can also be overly interested in sensual pleasure and turn towards the lazy and self-indulgent side of their suit. Any person of the Heart suit runs the risk of becoming overly infatuated with the romantic, sexual, or pleasurable side of their personality.

It is said that every Heart, at some point in their life, makes romance or having a child the major focus of their life to the exclusion of all other things. By diving deeply into the things associated with their suit, they hope to learn about themselves and their inner natures. This obsessive behavior will take over for a while, until they learn to find a balance between those sides of their personality and the other considerations of a healthy lifestyle. Still, we can find many Hearts that are focusing much of their life energy on these topics with great success. Many become famous artists, actors and actresses, or musicians. Others are the playboys and playgirls of the deck. On the negative side, many of those who abuse children are Heart cards. These are people whose obsession with children has found expression in an unhealthy manner.

Since the suit of Hearts relates to childhood, there are other connections that we can see in Hearts people. Our childhood is where we develop our basic personality and where we achieve a certain level of self-esteem. We might say that Hearts are related to self-esteem in many important ways. The Hearts person can give acceptance and acknowledgment of our value as a human being, the very same things that parents give their children in the first years of life. By the same token, a Hearts person can withhold acknowledgment if they want to hurt or control us in some way. These are the levels of communication that they most often work through. We might say that acknowledgment, acceptance, and approval are their domain. Any Hearts person may choose to use or abuse their power—it is up to the individual how it is manifested in their life.

## Clubs

Clubs also retain a certain youthfulness in their countenance. Like an eternal college or high-school student, they retain a certain curiosity about life, people, and new situations. They are most interested in ideas, methods of communications, the quality of their own thoughts and ideas, and in making a mark on the world with these thoughts and ideas. To a Club, the idea is as good as the thing itself. The word is as good as the action. The intention is as good as the deed. A Club will tend to take you on your word and take your words seriously, sometimes to a fault. One of the major challenges that all Clubs must face at some point in their life is to separate what others say from who they really are and what they do.

Clubs are searching for the truth in all things, and this truth does help guide them through the maze of experiences that life has to offer. For example, a Club person who has all the facts about certain experiences in childhood may be able to quickly recover from emotional injuries inflicted by a parent. In this manner, a Club person's energy is superior to a Heart person's energy.

To further explain, a Hearts person who is, for whatever reason, not in a loving mood, may use the withholding of affection and approval to try and manipulate or hurt us. However, the beauty of the Club person's energy is that when we know the truth about ourselves—that is, if they know that they are loving and wonderful inside—no assault from a Hearts person may touch them. One might say that mental truth, represented by Clubs, can overcome emotional injury, represented by Hearts. The tools that Hearts use on others, to either get their way or to try and hurt them, are only effective if the other person is not whole in his inner child. Clubs energy can rise above these areas by seeing the facts and truth of the situations.

Every person of any suit will be tempted to abuse the qualities of their suit from time to time. When they do, they will manifest the negative side of that suit. Clubs will abuse the facts and truth at times when they are under emotional distress. A Club, for example, could use against you something you had said earlier, much as an attorney would use your words in court after you have been sworn under oath. Another Club malady is that of trying to get at the truth of a situation based solely upon the facts and whatever their definition of fairness is, without taking into account their own feelings. Often their conclusions exclude their own emotional involvement, which can often be at the real root of the situation. Sometimes focusing on the facts can be a means of avoiding one's feelings.

A Club is interested in the details, facts, and reasons why a certain thing happened. However, reasons do not always make up for a person's actions. If someone hurts our feelings and then gives us good reasons for hurting us, it does not make it okay. It is a challenge for the Club to learn that the spoken word is not always the final truth about something. Oftentimes, people's actions speak louder than their words.

Knowing the details of every situation is generally a basic need for Clubs people. If you are dating or married to one, you have to get used to the fact that you need to tell them all the details of a situation, not because they don't trust you, but because it is one of their basic needs.

Likewise, a Club may take what you say to heart a little too often. They can identify strongly with their ideas, and if you shoot down their idea, they may feel you are shooting them down. To fight these sorts of irrational reactions, we need only to understand that all of us are identified somewhat with the suit of our Birth Card, and to realize that it has both a liability and a benefit. In this case, the benefit is the power that the Clubs person has in his speech and expression, and in his dedication to learning. The negative is that Clubs sometimes cannot separate themselves from their own beliefs and thoughts, that they are not their ideas.

One last comment about Clubs is that many of them have issues centered around freedom and individuality. Like the wind that is connected with their element, air, they want to be able to move freely and come and go as they please. For many of them, this independent nature makes relationships difficult. They often see relationships as restricting their freedom in some way. Being so strongly identified with their ever-changing minds can preclude the possibility of a happy relationship. This is not true of all Clubs, of course, but we can see some of these elements in a great majority of its natives.

## Diamonds

We Diamonds are big spenders. I say we, because I am a Q♦ Birth Card myself. All of us identify with our values and our possessions to some extent. As mentioned earlier, we are the adults of the deck and dislike being treated as children, being bossed around, or patronized. We are the ones who are always asking how much things cost. To us, everything has a value, if not an actual price on it. I used to say in my presentations that if you are married to a Diamond, you have a price on your head. Because we are so closely associated with values, we are constantly exploring what everything in our life is worth and not worth, both on a personal level and a more universal level as we observe the goings on in the world.

Diamonds develop techniques to get their needs met in childhood. These often center around Skinnerian psychology, the concept of "instrumental learning" and the "token economy." In short, this philosophy states that we do everything to either get a reward or to avoid punishment. Pavlov's dog is what we are, or so this point of view states. Thus we can be manipulated by being offered pleasurable or valued things or altered by exposure to things we do not like, as in the case of shock treatment and punishment. We are the greatest salespeople and the easiest targets for salespeople. It is the task of every Diamond person to arrive at a higher set of values if he or she is ever to attain peace of mind.

Every Diamond person, at some stage in his life, is likely to try and make the acquisition of money and property his most important and cherished goal. This is how we learn about ourselves. It is by attaining this "pile of money" that Diamonds realize just how meaningless it is and learn that true happiness requires more than money. Still, even after the lesson is learned, Diamonds like money and enjoy spending and shopping, two of their favorite activities.

When a Diamond is feeling bad, he will often want to go out and spend some money, just as a Club might want to read a book. Buying something is often just the remedy for their blues. Of course, this doesn't always work, and in some cases, it is actually a bad idea. A Diamond is more likely than any other suit to spend so much money that they lose their own sense of financial security. When Diamonds spend, we like to get quality items. Remember that we are concerned with the value of things. To purchase something of low quality often means undermining ourselves. However, purchasing quality usually means spending more for things, and this can develop into a vicious cycle that leaves a Diamond feeling worried about money most of the time.

Diamonds make the best salespeople because they know how to bring out the value of things to others. Most of the advertising we see is created by Diamond people. Many salespeople are Diamonds. Once Diamonds believe in something, they are the best promoters in the deck.

Diamonds will also try and use your values to control you, just as Hearts and Clubs will try and use the qualities of their suits. Diamond energy, or values, is superior to that of Hearts and Clubs only from the standpoint that our truth (Clubs) is really based upon what we want (Diamonds or values). My teacher, Amrit Desai, would often say that whatever we want in our lives, our minds will try to make up good reasons why we should have it. This illustrates what I feel is a truth about life and the distinctions and relationships between the suits. Most facts that are presented in this world have some motive or reason for being presented when they are presented. This motive or reason is usually found within the values of the person who is presenting them. A Diamond person who is clear about his or her values would never be influenced by anyone else's truth or philosophy, or emotional factors (a Heart's), either.

Let's take some examples to illustrate this. Someone who smokes cigarettes will have some sort of philosophy or belief structure that makes smoking okay for them. They might tell you, "I have known lots of people who smoked every day of their lives and lived to be ninety," "Smoking is great, it doesn't bother me at all," "Many famous people smoke cigarettes," or other statements like that. Clearly, their truth supports their smoking. Take this same person just after he or she has decided to quit smoking, and they will present you an entirely different philosophy.

I was a celibate for five years while living in a Yoga ashram with my teacher, Amrit Desai. During that time we learned all the ancient philosophies about the benefits of celibacy. There were many truths about celibacy that we learned, and practically recited, daily in order to stick to our vow. Among them were things like, "Only a celibate can reach the highest stages of Yoga and meditation," and "Sex destroys the spirit of a person, his creativity, and his chances for liberation." Then, I got married and began having sex. All those beliefs came to haunt me, making me feel guilty, and causing me to believe that I was a bad person for having sex. Later, I discovered an entirely new set of beliefs that actually supported having sex and being married. I literally changed my beliefs just as I would change a set of clothes to adapt to weather conditions.

This illustrates how values are stronger than beliefs. For every belief and truth you may find, there is another one, probably one that seems exactly opposite that also exists and is just as true for the person who believes it as your truth is for you. This is what Diamonds, and Clubs to a lesser extent, are here to learn. Since Diamonds and Clubs make up approximately 66 percent of our population, it is not surprising that values are such a predominant part of our culture. The United States, a J♦, exemplifies much of the value-based motivations and activities that characterize this day and age.

## Spades

The Spade person, being associated with the last suit in the deck, operates in a much different manner than the other suits. In some ways, they have the ability to rise above the concerns of the other three suits. It is through the application of their willpower that they can be untouched by the manipulations of the other three suits.

Spades are workers, concerned with getting the job done. They tend to be as interested in the quality of their work as they are in how much money they will make from it. The Spade is the craftsman who takes pride in his or her work, or the laborer who drudges through life and never rises above the mire of slavery. The boss who is a Spade can be ruthless and hard driving. They will expect you to work for what you get just as they have had to do.

Spades is the suit of wisdom and experience, traits associated with the older generation. Spades tend to relate to people who are older or more mature. They tend to have a more mature outlook on life. Most Spade birth dates fall in the winter between January and April. They represent that last period of life when we prepare for our own death and transformation. This tends to associate Spades with the sign of Scorpio, the sign of death, sex, and power. Spades are powerful people with strong wills. Spades are called the most powerful and strongest suit in the deck. For this reason, many Spade people have power issues to deal with in relationships. Power struggles and control issues will surface in their lives until they find some resolution of their inner struggles in these areas. They won't like anyone's attempt to control them, and they will try and maintain control of their life and relationships as much as possible.

Their powerful wills can make them impervious to the manipulations of other suits. But they are only able to maintain this high place if they themselves have learned to acknowledge the qualities of the three suits that precede them. Spades are said to contain within themselves all the other suits. If they refuse to acknowledge any aspect of another suit within themselves, they, too, can fall prey to the challenges and difficulties faced by the other suits. For example, as powerful as they are, Spades can have tremendous challenges in the area of relationships. It seems that the relative distance between the Hearts and Spades (three suits apart) makes dealing in those areas somewhat foreign to them. According to most Spades, working and performing one's job well are more important than catering to human relationships and emotional needs. This is not to say that Spades cannot have a good marriage or love life. It is simply a common challenge for those of this suit.

Spades possess the opportunity to align themselves to the will of God, and by so doing, achieve the highest form of expression. This involves a process of surrender of their wills to the higher will. When they do turn their attention away from their work and careers long enough to realize that they also possess a great spiritual reserve, they can tap into a huge reservoir of spiritual understanding that can benefit both themselves and everyone with whom they come in contact. They represent souls on the stepping-off point, where matter touches spirit. By their example, we can share in their wisdom and be lifted to new heights.

# Chapter Four

## The Marriageability Factor

Many cards are what I term "unmarriageable." These cards represent people who, for one reason or another, have great difficulty with the concept of commitment. There are many cards that fall into this category, listed at the end of the chapter. Before you turn to the list, however, I must say that even though these cards are typically unable or unwilling to make commitments, there are exceptions (though, in my own experience, I have found few exceptions at most). The only exceptions I have found to these unmarriageable cards fall into two categories:

1. They are over fifty-five years of age and come from the tradition that dictated that when you got married, you stayed married. These exceptions are becoming fewer each year. These are the people who got married in the thirties, forties, and fifties. Not too many of them are around (or available for marriage!) these days.

2. People who are keenly aware of their emotional problems and have made a personal commitment to work on them, using their relationships as a tool for their personal growth. Though this sounds like a goal that many would aspire to, in reality there are very few people who are doing this. Not many people have experienced enough pain to make their spiritual growth a full-time job. But there are a few. And these are the unmarriageables that become marriageable.

In the table "Marriageability of the Cards" on page 29, I list each card in the deck, how unmarriageable it probably is, and the probable factors that could lead to commitment problems. Next to the Birth Card is a number from one to ten. Ten represents the most unmarriageable influences possible, and one the least. This means the people with the highest numbers are the ones least likely to make any sort of commitments in personal relationships. All the cards with rankings above five are highly suspect.

## Marriageability of Each Card

A lower ranking means people of that card are more marriageable, and a higher ranking means they're less marriageable and have more problems with commitment. An interesting point to consider is that people whose Sun Sign is a fixed sign, such as Taurus, Aquarius, and Scorpio, are generally better at commitment than the mutable signs (Gemini, Sagittarius, Virgo, and Pisces) and the cardinal signs (Cancer, Libra, Capricorn, and Aries). Leos are fixed, but often they love romance so much that their lives become a string of new love affairs.

The most common factors associated with unmarriageability are:

1. The Three-Energy influence. This makes a person become bored easily with one relationship while at the same time bringing a lot of uncertainty and fear about getting enough affection. This person may never make a commitment or may practice what they call 'serial monogamy.' In serial monogamy, the person makes commitments, but they never last very long. Within a year or two, they find reasons to break off their relationships and go on to someone new. These people have a lot of fear related to getting enough affection. Instead of facing that fear and dealing with it firsthand, they try to keep a steady supply of romantic partners on hand so that they never have to feel the abandonment that is within them. Many of them profess how much they want to get married and complain about how they always seem to attract men or women who are unable to make commitments. These people often fall in love with married people because with a married person, they themselves will never have to make any sort of commitment. These people actually have some of the strongest fears about love. Their minds are usually quite well developed and they go around and around trying to understand love without feeling their emotions. They just don't want to feel the fear that is so strong within them. Often, strong Three-energy results in confusion over sexual preferences as well.

2. The Five-Energy influence. People with strong Five-energy, and of course that includes all of the Five Birth Cards, are here to express their personal freedom and to gather up as many different kinds of personal experiences as they can over the duration of their lives. To most Five people, marriage is seen as a cage that will restrict their freedom to explore new experiences. Freedom is such a strong theme for a Five that

they may believe marriage would be like taking away their reason for living. They will have relationships, and many of them will last a long time. But they have to find a way to maintain these relationships while avoiding the M-word. In many cases, it is the concept or sound of it that they fear the most. Five people are often in conflict within themselves. Part of them wants the security and comfort that a long-term relationship brings, while the other part is constantly fighting to break free of anything seen as a confinement. This inner conflict is very painful for some and reflects itself in the quality of their relationships—which are usually shallow at best.

3. The Saturn/Venus influence. In this scenario, which is experienced by a great many cards, the person comes into this life with a karmic debt to pay in the area of relationships. Often they were extremely uncaring in their previous lifetimes and hurt the feelings of others by being so inconsistent and freewheeling in areas of love. Because of their lack of awareness of how much their actions cause pain in others, they make a date to come back in this lifetime to see what it is like to be on the receiving end of such treatment. These people are often hurt very deeply by a love relationship early in their life. The hurt is felt so keenly that they choose to close up their emotions almost completely. In many cases, they make an unspoken vow to never let anyone get close enough to hurt them again. In doing so, they cut themselves off from any chance of emotional fulfillment. These people have relationships but never allow anyone to get close to them. Emotionally, they are dead—they never feel much joy or pain in love. Commitment to them has no meaning. They usually resign themselves to quasi-relationships with people in categories one and two listed above.

4. The Neptune influence. With these people, love is a thing of grandeur and splendor. It is the panacea for all of their problems, and if they could only find the right person, all of their troubles would be over. They inwardly know that love is the most powerful force in the universe and they see themselves as saviors of other poor souls that are without love and compassion. The thing that they will avoid at all cost is the feeling that they have hurt someone else. They often attract partners that are broken down—alcoholics, drug addicts, people who can't find jobs, and the like. They want to see their love heal and change someone, all the while completely neglecting their own personal needs as if they are some angel who has no needs of their own. However, those they love never

seem to change. They create heavily co-dependent relationships and feel weighed down by the burden of all of those who constantly sponge off of their energy. If they do meet the person who seems to be the one of their dreams, they usually fall head over heels and get hurt much more deeply than the average person. Like those in category three, they then choose to never open up again to anyone, just to avoid the pain they felt. Another manifestation of the Neptune influence is when the person's ideals of love are so high that they can never find a partner who is perfect enough for them.

5. The Pride influence. This combines with the other factors mentioned above and adds a distinct quality to them. This is experienced by the all of the royal cards—the Jacks, Queens, and Kings—and by other cards that have a strong connection to these royal cards. Among the others are the 8♦, 10♣, 7,♠ 8♠, and 9♠. There are others as well, but these are the main ones. These people place a lot of value upon 'looking good.' They have a certain amount of pride in themselves and never want to appear to lower themselves in any way. Part of lowering oneself would be to show fear or insecurity. Therefore, these people have a particular aversion to showing their vulnerable sides to their partners. This being the case, they never allow a free exchange of love in their personal relationships. They can give to their partner, but they may have difficulty in receiving, especially if that receiving requires them to drop their pride and ask for help.

6. The Power influence. These people have a certain amount of charm and magnetism that make it easy for them to find new partners for love. Because of this, they can always find someone new if their current relationship gets to be a bother. In most cases, they will choose to leave their current relationship and start a new one rather than face the problems that come up. This is especially true when the problems that arise start to show them their own faults and weaknesses. With so much power at their disposal, they have usually made it a habit to blame everyone else for problems that arise in this area. This inclination to lay blame on others is closely linked to the pride influence just mentioned—many cards that have one of these also has the other. And why should they ever consider a real commitment when it is so easy for them to just find someone to take your place?

In these words, from the beginning of the Book of John, we get the very essence of the Aces. Above all else, the Ace represents the most primary of

## Marriageability of the Cards (lower means more marriageable)

A higher ranking means less Marriageable and more problems with commitment

| Birth Card Ranking | Factors Involved | Birth Card Ranking | Factors Involved |
|---|---|---|---|
| A♥ – 5 | 1 | A♣ – 5 | 1, 4 |
| 2♥ – 5 | 4 | 2♣ – 2 | |
| 3♥ – 7 | 1 | 3♣ – 10 | 3, 4, 5 |
| 4♥ – 5 | 4 | 4♣ – 5 | 2 |
| 5♥ – 7 | 1, 2 | 5♣ – 10 | 2 |
| 6♥ – 2 | | 6♣ – 2 | |
| 7♥ – 5 | 3 | 7♣ – 4 | 1 |
| 8♥ – 7 | 6 | 8♣ – 4 | 3, 6 |
| 9♥ – 5 | 4 | 9♣ – 4 | 4 |
| 10♥ – 3 | 1 | 10♣ – 9 | 1, 5, 6 |
| J♥ – 3 | 4 | J♣ – 4 | 2 |
| Q♥ – 3 | 4 | Q♣ – 9 | 1, 2, 3, 5 |
| K♥ – 6 | 5, 6 | K♣ – 5 | 4, 5 |

| Birth Card Ranking | Factors Involved | Birth Card Ranking | Factors Involved |
|---|---|---|---|
| A♦ – 6-10* | 1, 2 | A♠ – 7 | 3, 4 |
| 2♦ – 2 | | 2♠ – 4 | 1, 4 |
| 3♦ – 8 | 1, 3 | 3♠ – 6 | 1, 4 |
| 4♦ – 5 | 3 | 4♠ – 2 | 2 |
| 5♦ – 8 | 2, 4 | 5♠ – 5 | |
| 6♦ – 5 | 3 | 6♠ – 5 | 3 |
| 7♦ – 5 | 3 | 7♠ – 4 | 5 |
| 8♦ – 7 | 1, 3 | 8♠ – 6 | 1, 5 |
| 9♦ – 4 | 1 | 9♠ – 5 | 5 |
| 10♦ – 7 | 1, 2, 3 | 10♠ – 2 | |
| J♦ – 7 | 2, 4, 5 | J♠ – 6 | 6, 5 |
| Q♦ – 8 | 1, 2, 3, 5, 6 | Q♠ – 2 | |
| K♦ – 5 | 1, 5 | K♠ – 5 | 2, 3, 5 |

• *A♦ men are the ones with the higher numbers. In general I would rank A♦ men at an 8 or 9 and the women at a 4 or 5.
• Rankings under 3 are people that typically have fairly good marriage karma and less difficulty with commitment.

# Chapter Five

### Written in the Cards—The Personalities, Lives, and Loves of Each of the 52 Cards

In this chapter, you will find a separate description for each of the fifty-two-card personalities and the Joker (who is all cards and no card at once). This is where you will discover the traits that make up each of the individual Birth Card personalities. This is also where you can look up the relationship connections between any card and all the other cards in the deck.

Each Birth Card has a name or phrase that is used to make a quick identification of its common character traits. Some of these names are flattering and others are not. I have endeavored to use the more positive names for the cards while at the same time bring out some of the more challenging natures of the cards in the descriptions. Some cards commonly have very difficult lives. But they also have a good side that can be accessed by its possessor. One always has the opportunity to turn around the negatives and make them a shining success. Therefore, these descriptions present both the positive and negative sides of each of the cards. I leave it up to you to decide how the individual is accessing those potentials.

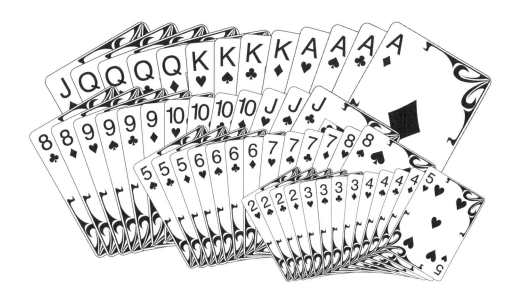

# The Aces

"In the beginning was the Word, and the Word was with God, and the Word was God"

the masculine, creative principal, the Word that calls forth things into being. In Genesis, we see God creating the heavens and the Earth, all by simply saying it was so ( "and God said…and lo and behold…came into being."). The world we know is made up of a huge matrix of masculine and feminine energies, interacting and evolving and yet always staying in balance. All masculine energy is a part of God's creative force, whereas feminine energy is the fertile, receptive force of God. We might say that all of our creating ultimately comes from the mind of God, and those of us who are creative are vessels for His ideas. Who else puts all these ideas into our minds? All Aces, regardless of their gender, will have a somewhat masculine nature, either physically or just as part of their personality, and they will reflect this masculine, creative principle in their lives.

Aces know all about creating and manifesting. Their lives are a constant chain of one creation after another. They exemplify the creative force and are conduits of many new ideas and projects. One might say that they are constantly receiving input from some higher force to go forth and create something new. They love new beginnings and they love to see their ideas materialize. Seeing, hearing, tasting, or touching something they have created brings them great pleasure. It is part of their birthright to bring many things into being which were not there before. This brings them the greatest satisfaction and the greatest challenge.

Aces are not usually known for their patience. With so much to accomplish in this lifetime and so little time to do it, they hardly have any time to waste standing in line or waiting for others to finish their sentences. They are bubbling over with the desire to make something happen. It is not in their nature to wait for something to happen. If they seem a little short with you, it is because they have something important that they want to get done—not that they don't like you.

However, they can also be charming and caring. It is a paradox that the cards that often feel the need to be by themselves also have a great longing for the perfect mate or companion. They also excel at communications for the most part. Their lives are often an endless flow of phone calls, e-mail, and letters. They are surrounded by people most of the time. Don't be fooled by this appearance, however. Aces are individuals above all else. They need time to themselves to explore who they are on a basic level. Being an Ace means being self-absorbed to a certain degree, and many of them can be categorized as loners. It is an Aries energy. Aries is the first sign in the zodiac, and people of this sign are known to be self-engrossed. Nothing means anything in their life if it is not contributing something to them in a tangible way. If their relationship with you has outlived its ability to give them something they want or need, you may be history.

The A♥ personifies the 'Search for Self' in more ways than the other Aces, though they all have undertaken this search in one way or another. Their suit tells us in which basic area of life they emphasize this search. A♥ people search for themselves in their relationships. This includes not only lovers and mates, but family and friends as well. The A♣ searches for his or her own meaning through the books they read and things they learn in other ways. Like the A♥, they, too, seek the perfect love relationship that will fulfill their deep yearnings for completion. The A♦ finds conflict between their driving ambition and the desire for companionship and marriage. They cannot seem to have both at the same time. Like all Diamonds, they tend to value themselves based upon what they have or how successful they are financially. They seek to acquire or attain something that is so valuable that it will make them the valuable person that they want to be. The A♠ person usually has difficulties in love that make finding happiness seem impossible. They often abandon the idea completely and let all of their passion express itself in their work and careers. Perfection in their work, either through quality or quantity, is their means of finding the love for themselves that they seek. They are considered one of the most ambitious cards in the entire deck.

In all cases, the hidden motive for the Aces is self-acceptance. However, since there is so much masculine energy being expressed as action and accomplishment, they seek to find themselves in the reflection of their accomplishments instead of just stopping and looking within. Hopefully they will love what they have created and complete the circle, discovering that what they were looking for is already within them. They are the prodigal sons and daughters seeking to come home.

# Ace of Hearts

You are the Ace of Hearts! You are one of the rarest of the cards in a deck—only one birthday has your Birth Card. And you have the distinction of being the first card in the deck. Therefore, like a young seed that has just sprouted, you enter this world and this life full of passion and enthusiasm, ready to grow and achieve many things. There is so much to explore and to realize. Your ambition drives you to achievement, and even though you are a Heart and primarily concerned with love matters, your career might be even more important. Your ambition can bring you success in most any area you choose, but you also have a good deal of artistic and creative ability. At the very least, your life will have many facets to it—you will achieve the variety of expression that you seek. But even the variety will never sway you from achieving your goals. Life is a series of goals accomplished for the Ace of Hearts. And each one brings you a sense of validation and self-worth that nothing else can replace.

You are a loner in some ways, but you can be very sociable, too. You need your alone time, but when the occasion calls for mixing it up, you are well versed. The strong creative drive of the A♥ often makes for a strong romantic drive, and one

# Ace of Hearts

that cannot be fulfilled by one person. Often people of your card get married once and for a long time. But once they end that relationship, they prefer to remain single and have lovers instead. And there are some A♥ that will never marry for the same reason. When you do marry, you like someone of financial means. You probably would not even date someone who wasn't somewhat well-to-do.

Passion is an important ingredient in the recipe of success—and because you have so much of it, your success is assured. You may spend some time deciding which path is best for you and find one that you can truly hone in on for a sustained period of time. But once you do, the sky is the limit!

**Some of the best A™ marriages happen with:**
K♠, 2♥, A♣, A♦, 8♠, K♣, 9♥, 7♦, 3♣, and 4♦

**The hottest sex happens with:**
4♥, 10♠, J♠, 10♣, Q♣, 10♦, 5♥, 4♦

**Your marriageability is:**
Questionable, but only because you may never choose it.

**Affirmation for you:**
I am the embodiment of passion and ambition. I am here to accomplish as much as I can and express my abundant creativity.

| Famous A♥ Birth Card people | |
|---|---|
| Rudyard Kipling | 12/30/1865 |
| Bo Diddley | 12/30/1928 |
| Sandy Koufax | 12/30/1935 |
| Joseph Bologna | 12/30/1938 |
| Michael Nesmith | 12/30/1942 |
| Davy Jones | 12/30/1945 |
| Patti Smith | 12/30/1946 |
| Meredith Vieira | 12/30/1951 |
| Tracey Ullman | 12/30/1959 |
| Heidi Fleiss | 12/30/1965 |
| Jay Kay | 12/30/1969 |
| Tiger Woods | 12/30/1975 |
| Meredith Monroe | 12/30/1977 |
| Tyrese | 12/30/1978 |
| Eliza Dushku | 12/30/1980 |

# Ace of Clubs

You are the Ace of Clubs! Though your suit is Clubs, the suit of information and communication, you are equally a Heart, the suit of Love. For you, knowledge and love go hand in hand. This usually means that you have a love of knowledge, and you are a perpetual student of love. A♣ are known to be collectors of books, information, and teachings of all sorts. An A♣ friend of mine has so many books in his apartment that you can hardly get through his living room. Though he may be an extreme example, most A♣ never lose their natural mental curiosity and desire to learn new things. This curiosity and desire to learn is a good thing, since this card is also considered fairly fixed in nature. A♣ can be pretty stubborn sometimes. The new things you learn help to broaden your perspective.

But love is also a major topic for your life. You are intimately connected with the Lover's Card, the 2♥. This means that you are seeking the ideal relationship, and that relationship is extremely important to you. But we are not talking about just any kind of relationship. This is soul mate stuff here. The A♣ wants to find that special someone whom they have loved in past lives and

# Ace of Clubs

who is their perfect lover and romantic partner. They are very particular about this. They will know who it is when they meet them. Before they do, A♣ are often quite promiscuous. Perhaps they see their many romantic engagements as a course of study in their life-long pursuit of love knowledge. It is not really marriage that you seek, but you would marry the person of your dreams if you wanted that.

You are highly intelligent and enjoy the company of other intelligent people. You enjoy social occasions but also need lots of time to yourself. You have creative gifts and those can be employed in a variety of professions for success (see Walt Whitman, Alfred Noble, Norman Vincent Peale, and Leonard Bernstein for examples). Your mother is probably a major figure in your life and is, or was, powerful and high strung.

**Some of the best A♣ marriages happen with:**
Q♣, 10♠, 4♥, 7♦, 8♣, 3♣, and Q♥

**The hottest sex happens with:**
5♣, 4♣, J♥, 8♦, 8♠, 6♦, and 9♣

**Your marriageability is:**
Very good. Usually, if you are married, it is because this is the right person.

**Affirmation for you:**
Through knowledge and love I discover my true identity and seek to express the beauty I behold inside.

| Famous A♣ Birth Card people | |
|---|---|
| Indira Gandhi | 11/19/1917 |
| Leonard Bernstein | 8/25/1918 |
| George Wallace | 8/25/1919 |
| Mickey Rooney | 9/23/1920 |
| Roy Campanella | 11/19/1921 |
| Denholm Elliot | 5/31/1922 |
| Norman Lear | 7/27/1922 |
| Prince Ranier | 5/31/1923 |
| Monty Hall | 8/25/1923 |
| Vincent Canby | 7/27/1924 |
| Joyce Randolph | 10/21/1925 |
| John Coltrane | 9/23/1926 |
| Whitey Ford | 10/21/1928 |
| Marilyn Beck | 12/17/1928 |
| Clint Eastwood | 5/31/1930 |
| Robert Evans | 6/29/1930 |
| Sean Connery | 8/25/1930 |
| Ray Charles | 9/23/1930 |
| Bob Guccione | 12/17/1930 |
| Larry King | 11/19/1933 |
| Jim Hutton | 5/31/1934 |
| Regis Philbin | 8/25/1934 |
| Cal Ripken Sr. | 12/17/1935 |
| Harmon Killebrew | 6/29/1936 |
| Dick Cavett | 11/19/1936 |
| Tommy Steele | 12/17/1936 |

# Ace of Clubs

| | | | | |
|---|---|---|---|---|
| Peter Yarrow | 5/31/1938 | | Elvis Costello | 8/25/1954 |
| Romy Schneider | 9/23/1938 | | Carol Leifer | 7/27/1956 |
| Ted Turner | 11/19/1938 | | Carrie Fisher | 10/21/1956 |
| Manfred Mann | 10/21/1940 | | Tim Burton | 8/25/1958 |
| Judy Sheindlin | 10/21/1942 | | Mike Mills | 12/17/1958 |
| Calvin Klein | 11/19/1942 | | Jason Alexander | 9/23/1959 |
| Paul Butterfield | 12/17/1942 | | George Bell | 10/21/1959 |
| Sharon Gless | 5/31/1943 | | Tamara De Treaux | 10/21/1959 |
| Joe Namath | 5/31/1943 | | Chris Elliot | 5/31/1960 |
| Julio Iglesias | 9/23/1943 | | Allison Janney | 11/19/1960 |
| Gary Busey | 6/29/1944 | | Lea Thompson | 5/31/1961 |
| Little Eva | 6/29/1945 | | Sharon Lawrence | 6/29/1961 |
| Paul Petersen | 9/23/1945 | | Billy Ray Cyrus | 8/25/1961 |
| Rollie Fingers | 8/25/1946 | | Meg Ryan | 11/19/1961 |
| Lux Interior | 10/21/1946 | | Amanda Donohoe | 6/29/1962 |
| Richard Lewis | 6/29/1947 | | Jodie Foster | 11/19/1962 |
| Carlos Santana | 6/29/1947 | | Karl Mueller | 7/27/1963 |
| Betty Thomas | 7/27/1947 | | Brooke Shields | 5/31/1965 |
| Mary Kay Place | 9/23/1947 | | Claudia Schiffer | 8/25/1970 |
| Peggy Fleming | 7/27/1948 | | Ani DiFranco | 9/23/1970 |
| Tom Berenger | 5/31/1949 | | Jade Jagger | 10/21/1971 |
| Dan Dierdorf | 6/29/1949 | | Abe Cunningham | 7/27/1973 |
| Maureen McGovern | 7/27/1949 | | Giovanni Ribisi | 12/17/1974 |
| Gene Simmons | 8/25/1949 | | Milla Jovovich | 12/17/1975 |
| Bruce Springsteen | 9/23/1949 | | Colin Farrell | 5/31/1976 |
| Benjamin Netanyahu | 10/21/1949 | | Jeremy Miller | 10/21/1976 |
| Gregory Harrison | 5/31/1950 | | Jonathan Rhys Meyers | 7/27/1977 |
| Rob Halford | 8/25/1951 | | Jason Michael Zimbler | 7/27/1977 |
| Wanda Hutchinson | 12/17/1951 | | Jaimee Foxworth | 12/17/1979 |
| Brent Mydland | 10/21/1952 | | Bart Simpson | 12/17/1979 |
| Colin Hay | 6/29/1953 | | Sean Timothy McEnroe | 9/23/1987 |
| Charlotte Caffey | 10/21/1953 | | Benjamin Storm Keough | 10/21/1992 |

# *Ace of Diamonds*

You are the Ace of Diamonds! Don't you love knowing you are an Ace? You are charming, personable, and extroverted for the most part, unafraid to start a conversation with anyone. You do enjoy your private time, however, and you are one of the few cards that actually needs time to yourself on a regular basis. You are passionate in many ways, but especially about making money and business. They say that if you want to get something done, give it to a busy person. Well, that would be you—you are always busy doing so many things. You are also artistically inclined. Many people of your birthday make a lot of money with talents in this area. You can also work several jobs or professions at once, another of your God-given gifts. There really is not just one area you can do best in, because you are versatile. You can basically make a success of anything you really want to do. And the "want" part is critical. You are desire incarnate. If you don't want it, it is not important, and the things you will always do best at are the ones you desire the most.

You have a business/passionate side, but you also have a strong compassionate side. You go out of your way to help others and like to think of yourself as being there for

# Ace of Diamonds

them when they need you. This could be why Paul Newman, a famous A♦, has contributed so much to charity. This savior mentality, however, doesn't help you much with your personal relationships. As a matter of fact, being successful in both work and love at the same time is one of your biggest challenges. When work is going well, your love life seems to drop off, and vice versa. But hey, what is life without a good challenge! If you really do want both, you can certainly have them. It might just take more effort than you initially think. If you are a male A♦, marriage may not be your best alternative. The male A♦ greatly enjoys the company of women, and there are so many women to meet! And women just love male A♦s, too. They are so charming and boyish. The female A♦ has much better chances for a successful marriage, though some of them have such independent natures that they may forego it. Traveling for love or with a loved one is one of your favorite things.

Self-confidence is something you need to develop if you are to reach all the fantastic goals and dreams you have for yourself. You are independent and definitely a self-starter and a leader. With belief in yourself, there is little you cannot accomplish. Also, realize that what you are really seeking, behind all your various jobs or occupations, is self-worth. More than any other card in the deck, you tend to measure your own worth by how much money you are making or how much success you have in business. You are truly the seeker of self-worth.

Female A♦ make the best marriages with the K♣. He will adore you and let you have your business and other interests. And he will travel with you to your various enterprises. Even the male A♦ does well with a K♣ woman. But there are other cards that do well with A♦, too. Among them are the 8♣, A♥, 5♥, 3♦, Q♦, and 5♦. Keep in mind that a lot of the cards you are most compatible with fall into the category of 'unmarriageable.' But you will run into them just the same for the lessons you both can share.

**Some of the best A♦ marriages with happen with:**
K♣, 2♦, Q♦, A♥, 8♣, 3♦, Q♣, and 5♦

# Ace of Diamonds

**The hottest sex happens with:**
4♦, 5♥, 10♦, 10♥, J♣, 3♥, 6♠, 2♠, and 3♣.

**Your marriageability is:**
Pretty bad (for men A♦) and pretty good (for females)

**Affirmation for you:**
With self-confidence I can accomplish anything. I am here to do and create many things.

| Famous A♦ Birth Card people | |
| --- | --- |
| Jeff Bridges | 12/4/1949 |
| Pamela Stephenson | 12/4/1949 |
| Helen Shaver | 2/24/1951 |
| Louise Jameson | 4/20/1951 |
| Luther Vandross | 4/20/1951 |
| Patricia Wettig | 12/4/1951 |
| Joel Silver | 7/14/1952 |
| Thomas Toop | 8/12/1952 |
| Lucinda Williams | 1/26/1953 |
| Chaka Khan | 3/22/1953 |
| Bebe Buell | 7/14/1953 |
| Amy Irving | 9/10/1953 |
| Catherine Cryer | 11/6/1954 |
| Eddie Van Halen | 1/26/1955 |
| Steve Jobs | 2/24/1955 |
| Lena Olin | 3/22/1955 |
| Yun-Fat Chow | 5/18/1955 |
| Laurie Metcalf | 6/16/1955 |
| Maria Shriver | 11/6/1955 |
| Paula Zahn | 2/24/1956 |
| Bruce Greenwood | 8/12/1956 |

# Ace of Diamonds

| | | | | |
|---|---|---|---|---|
| Stephanie Zimbalist | 10/8/1956 | | Richard Grieco | 3/22/1965 |
| Teresa Ganzel | 3/22/1957 | | Billy Zane | 2/24/1966 |
| Lori Singer | 11/6/1957 | | Matthew Fox | 7/14/1966 |
| Ellen DeGeneres | 1/26/1958 | | Robin Goodridge | 9/10/1966 |
| Dan Castellaneta | 9/10/1958 | | Rebecca Schaeffer | 11/6/1967 |
| Chris Columbus | 9/10/1958 | | Guy Ritchie | 9/10/1968 |
| Jennifer Tilly | 9/10/1958 | | Kelly Rutherford | 11/6/1968 |
| Clint Howard | 4/20/1959 | | Matt Damon | 10/8/1970 |
| Bob Griffin | 12/4/1959 | | Ethan Hawke | 11/6/1970 |
| Colin Firth | 9/10/1960 | | Jay-Z | 12/4/1970 |
| Wayne Gretzky | 1/26/1961 | | Tupac Shakur | 6/16/1971 |
| Roy Hay | 8/12/1961 | | Pete Samprass | 8/12/1971 |
| Michelle Shocked | 2/24/1962 | | Elvis Stojko | 3/22/1972 |
| Sir Mix-A-Lot | 8/12/1963 | | Carmen Electra | 4/20/1972 |
| Randy Johnson | 9/10/1963 | | Thandie Newton | 11/6/1972 |
| Lauren Bettette | 11/6/1964 | | Ryan Phillippe | 9/10/1974 |
| Chelsea Noble | 12/4/1964 | | Sean Lennon | 10/8/1975 |
| Marisa Tomei | 12/4/1964 | | Reese Witherspoon | 3/22/1976 |
| Kristin Davis | 2/24/1965 | | Joey Lawrence | 4/20/1976 |

# Ace of Spades

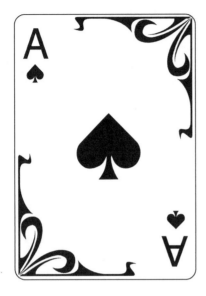

You are the Ace of Spades! Yours is the card of mystery and secrets. Traditionally, it is the card of death, but it's really the card of transformation. For you, life is a series of transformations—the person you are today is not who you were yesterday, nor who you will be tomorrow. Your life is a series of chapters, and often one chapter bears no resemblance to the one that came before. This is the first card in the suit of work, and one of the most ambitious. Regardless of your gender, your work and career will be very important in your life. And it will often compete with your desire for love—and usually win out in the end. You are ambitious and passionate and will not rest until you make a name for yourself or accomplish many great goals. Work to you is a passion and also a solace. You will turn there when other areas of your life become excessively challenging.

Relationships are challenging prospects for the Ace of Spades; you have a fairly large amount of work to do in this area. Most A♠ are very sensitive emotionally, have fears of abandonment and betrayal, and really have to learn to love unconditionally. They dream of a perfect love, the perfect lover with whom they feel a

# Ace of Spades

strong, past-life link. But usually, due to their past-life karma, their dream loves turn into loss and heartbreak. Look at Princess Diana, Jennifer Aniston, and Pamela Anderson as examples. A♠ often end up with the 2♣—this is one of the unique pairings that you'll find occur with unusual frequency. Male A♠s keep their sensitive sides hidden from others, but it is there just the same. They would rather stay busy in their work, a place where they are more comfortable and less threatened. All A♠ can choose to work on themselves and can heal the inner insecurity and sensitivity if they choose. However, the passion of the Ace for their work often keeps them too busy to give much attention to that area.

This brings up another important facet of this card. The A♠ is considered the most spiritual card in the deck. However, it is also the most materially passionate. All A♠ have untold riches inside, spiritual resources that could provide all the answers and anything else they would ever need to be happy. But only a few of them ever take a look inside to find it. It is like the story of the man who travels around the entire earth looking for a precious diamond, only to discover it buried in his backyard when he returns, many years later.

A♠ are drawn to humanitarian work and have compassion for the suffering of others. They make great counselors, and no matter what line of work they are in, they end up helping those around them in numerous ways.

**Some of the best A♠ marriages happen with:**
2♠, K♣, K♦, 3♦, 6♥, 7♥, 8♥, and 7♠

**The hottest sex happens with:**
2♥, 4♠, 4♥, 3♣, 10♦, 10♠, 5♠, and 10♥

**Your marriageability is:**
Slightly below average. You could have it, but you have to be willing to work at it.

**Affirmation for you:**
Turning within I discover my inner wealth. I am here to accomplish many goals and to prove my worth in the world.

# Ace of Spades

| Famous A♠ Birth Card people | |
|---|---|
| Robert Stack | 1/13/1919 |
| Eva Gabor | 2/11/1920 |
| Ravi Shankar | 4/7/1920 |
| Gwen Verdon | 1/13/1925 |
| Tony Curtis | 6/3/1925 |
| Leslie Nielsen | 2/11/1926 |
| Ann B. Davis | 5/5/1926 |
| Colleen Dewhurst | 6/3/1926 |
| Allen Ginsberg | 6/3/1926 |
| Pat Carroll | 5/5/1927 |
| James Garner | 4/7/1928 |
| Frances Sternhagen | 1/13/1930 |
| Leslie Caron | 7/1/1931 |
| Tina Louise | 2/11/1934 |
| Mary Quant | 2/11/1934 |
| Yuri Gagarin | 3/9/1934 |
| Burt Reynolds | 2/11/1936 |
| Mickey Gilley | 3/9/1936 |
| Larry McMurtry | 6/3/1936 |
| Jerry Brown | 4/7/1938 |
| Francis Ford Coppola | 4/7/1939 |
| David Frost | 4/7/1939 |
| Sally Quinn | 7/1/1941 |
| Twyla Tharp | 7/1/1941 |
| Tammy Wynette | 5/5/1942 |
| Curtis Mayfield | 6/3/1942 |
| Richard Moll | 1/13/1943 |
| Bobby Fischer | 3/9/1943 |
| Michael Palin | 5/5/1943 |
| Julia Phillips | 4/7/1944 |
| Gerhard Shroder | 4/7/1944 |
| Robin Trower | 3/9/1945 |
| Deborah Harry | 7/1/1945 |
| Suzi Quatro | 6/3/1950 |
| Michael Kinsley | 3/9/1951 |
| Fred Schneider | 7/1/1951 |

# Ace of Spades

| | | | | |
|---|---|---|---|---|
| Dan Aykroyd | 7/1/1952 | | Russell Crowe | 4/7/1964 |
| Jackie Chan | 4/7/1954 | | Brian Bosworth | 3/9/1965 |
| Tony Dorsett | 4/7/1954 | | Mike Gordon | 6/3/1965 |
| Jay McInerney | 1/13/1955 | | Pamela Anderson | 7/1/1967 |
| Christopher Darden | 4/7/1956 | | Jennifer Aniston | 2/11/1969 |
| Ibrahim Hussein | 6/3/1958 | | Hideki Irabu | 5/5/1969 |
| Scott Valentine | 6/3/1958 | | Emmanuel Lewis | 3/9/1971 |
| Barbie | 3/9/1959 | | Missy Elliot | 7/1/1972 |
| Kato Kaelin | 3/9/1959 | | Tina Yothers | 5/5/1973 |
| Linda Fiorentino | 3/9/1960 | | Orlando Bloom | 1/13/1977 |
| Julia Louis-Dreyfus | 1/13/1961 | | Liv Tyler | 7/1/1977 |
| Princess Diana | 7/1/1961 | | Brandy Norwood | 2/11/1979 |
| Kevin Mitchell | 1/13/1962 | | Kelly Rowland | 2/11/1981 |
| Sheryl Crow | 2/11/1962 | | Danielle Fishel | 5/5/1981 |
| Penelope Ann Miller | 1/13/1964 | | Bow Wow | 3/9/1987 |
| Juliette Binoche | 3/9/1964 | | Jessica Dubroff | 5/5/1988 |

# The Twos

In the number Two, the drive and passion of the Ace finds its complement and balance. Sexual energy in males and females finds balance in being with someone who is a complement to themselves. It is this balance, achieved by finding our counterpart, that Twos are all about. Our world is a play of duality, far more than most of us realize. Everything in our life is really nothing more than a mish-mash of opposites blended together in different amounts to create all the textures of color, feeling, sounds, and ideas that we call our living universe. Twos have a natural understanding of the laws of balance and harmony. They seek to create balance in their own lives and in the lives of those around them. They are forever seeking their complement as much as the Ace is seeking to create something new. It is as a part of a successful relationship that Twos find satisfaction. If their relationships suffer, they usually suffer as well. They have a hard time separating themselves from their relationships.

Many Twos are accused of being afraid of being alone, but this is just one way of looking at it. We could just as easily say that the Aces are afraid of balance and stasis, or that they are afraid that they will not create anything new. Twos create relationships with others. They bond with us and make us feel that we are a part of their lives. In the process, we feel accepted and wanted. We find we have a place in their lives, a home of sorts. Twos can be the very best at making us feel at ease and cared for.

However, the Two might make us feel smothered and manipulated as well. If a Two person is not aware of their deep drive for completion with others, they may try to tell themselves the opposite and execute most of their actions subconsciously. On the surface they may pretend to be aloof and uncaring. They may act as though they don't need anyone and that they would be just as happy alone as with a partner. Nothing could be further from the truth. No matter what they say or how they act, one of their primary motives is to find this completion. If it is not acknowledged openly and honestly, it can deviate into unhealthy emotional patterns and all sorts of undesirable behavior. All Twos are smart, and they can create elaborate intellectual defenses against anyone trying to find out their true needs and motives. They can be the best and worst arguers. They are the best arguers because their explanations and conclusions seem impenetrable. You may never win an argument with one of them. They are the worst arguers because they deprive themselves of so much by building strong walls around themselves and alienating those around them.

Many Twos go to extremes in love, often alternating between long periods of having no one and then falling head over heels. When they do fall in love in this manner, it is usually with someone who does not deserve such love or someone who cannot return it. Their zeal and enthusiasm tries to make up for what their partner is lacking. Unfortunately, who their partner really is wins out in the end, and their high hopes fall far and fast. The pain of such lessons explains why many Twos avoid love for such long time periods. Humans will usually do more to avoid pain than we will to pursue pleasure.

Intelligent and often physically beautiful, Twos seem to have everything one would want for happiness. But until they reach inside themselves to see and accept who they really are, their patterns of unhappiness will continue. Their eternal tug of war between being in a relationship and out of a relationship will continue. Their desperate needs for friendship and affection, love and touching, will go unfulfilled. The happy Two is the one who accepts his or her needs for a complementary relationship and goes about creating it. Why not just admit how important people and love are up front? Then they can accept this part of themselves and stop pretending to be something they are not, along with all the deviant behaviors that go along with it. In accepting, there comes a sort of freedom and peace. And as a special bonus, when they accept themselves just the way they are, they are no longer bound to be or act in that certain way. They are now free to choose to be one way or the other. The conscious Two understands and accepts their Two-ness in a way that allows them the freedom to manifest it the way they like, instead of being compelled into addictive behavior patterns. They find union in a loving and conscious way.

# Two of Hearts

You are the Two of Hearts! Yours is the "sweetheart card," the card of the love affair, sex, and romance. And for better or worse, your life is mostly about relationships, both personal and professional. Just as the A♥, only one birthday has your card, so you are a rare expression. Your life path is a fortunate one, and many good things will come to you without struggle. No one's life is perfect, but you have more than most to be grateful for.

You are very intelligent and business-minded. And in business, you are relationship-oriented. Many 2♥ end up going into business with their partners. All in all, you would rather work with others than alone, and your high intelligence guarantees success in whatever field you choose. Twos have the kind of minds that can analyze and make sense of business areas, such as the stock market, and profit from them. You also have a love of learning and will always be reading new books and taking in new knowledge in various ways. This habit alone keeps you young, but most Hearts always remain like children anyway. Age is a state of mind, and Hearts never grow old.

Love is by far the most important thing to you in the world. It is not your easiest area, however. You have such a pure

# *Two of Hearts*

energy for the love affair that marriage could seem irrelevant. You are unique in your attitudes towards love and marriage. You may marry, for sure, but it is generally not an important requirement for you. What is important is that you are in love with your partner and that you feel a strong romantic and sexual connection with them. Even so, you will usually be most attracted to those of financial power or high reputation.

You can be very fixed and regimented about financial obligations. On the other hand, you may sometimes be lackadaisical about them. Responsibility around money will be a topic that comes up for you again and again until you find the right approach.

Your friends and loved ones enjoy your attention and your naturally caring demeanor. You can be as charming and loving as you want, making you popular and well liked. May you find that special person, the one you were destined to love, again and again.

**Some of the best 2♥ marriages happen with:**
3♥, Q♣, A♥, K♥, 9♠, and 2♣

**The hottest sex happens with:**
5♥, K♠, 5♣, K♣, 4♦, 10♣, 6♥, 4♣, and J♥

**Your marriageability is:**
Very good.

**Affirmation for you:**
I am a living example of love and relationship. I truly care about others.

| Famous 2♥ Birth Card people | |
| --- | --- |
| Andrew Johnson | 12/29/1808 |
| Pablo Casals | 12/29/1876 |
| Inga Swenson | 12/29/1932 |
| Ed Flanders | 12/29/1934 |
| Mary Tyler Moore | 12/29/1936 |
| Ray Nitschke | 12/29/1936 |
| Jon Voight | 12/29/1938 |
| Marianne Faithfull | 12/29/1946 |
| Laffit Pincay Jr. | 12/29/1946 |
| Ted Danson | 12/29/1947 |
| Gelsey Kirkland | 12/29/1952 |
| Patsy Ramsey | 12/29/1956 |
| Paula Poundstone | 12/29/1959 |
| Dexter Holland | 12/29/1966 |
| Alexa Ray Joel | 12/29/1985 |
| Dylan Jagger Lee | 12/29/1997 |

# Two of Clubs

You are a Two of Clubs! Before you think to yourself, "Two is such a small number!" let me tell you that the Two of Clubs is one of the most intelligent and beautiful cards in the deck. There are very few 2♣ who do not possess an unusually large quantity of beauty and grace. This is a feminine card, and even the men of this card will usually be quite handsome and attractive (look at Benjamin Bratt and Scott Baio, as examples). And as for a logical mind, there are few cards that can match the 2♣, which is why so many of them are so good at whatever they do. The 2♣ mental equipment is among the finest available, making detailed distinctions of most everything and drawing logical, well thought out conclusions. You could excel at many different kinds of work. There are 2♣ who are scientists, those who are doing clerical work, and others who are performers. Look at some of the celebrities listed below and you will see what I mean—everyone from Carl Jung to Mick Jagger to Sandra Bullock and Kevin Spacey are 2♣.

The 2♣ is a people person. And being a Two, you tend to see yourself as part of a partnership or friendship. Most 2♣ do not like being alone and usually

# Two of Clubs

arrange their lives in such a way that they always have someone there to talk to. And they love to talk. Talk, talk, talk, and a little argument thrown in for good measure. With such a command over details and facts, the 2♣ can be quite a formidable opponent in that arena. This card signifies a partnership (Two) of the mind and of conversation (Clubs), and this is an integral part of your life.

All this great mental ability does not serve you as well in your personal relationships. Being a Two and being feminine also means you are very sensitive, especially to others and how they might feel about you. One of your biggest challenges will be integrating this sensitivity and tendency towards fear-based thinking into your relationships. Some of the world's most beautiful women are 2♣, and it makes me wonder how women so attractive and talented often end up with men who don't appreciate them or who are just plain losers. It all comes down to what's going on inside. For a 2♣ to really be happy, they have to be willing to admit,

face, and work with the various fears that plague them. No card is free of fears, but the 2♣ seems the most unwilling to face them. The male 2♣ seems to have an easier time of it, though I have seen some examples of 2♣ men who have lives plagued with fears of all kinds. The powerful and keen mind of the 2♣, when influenced by fear, becomes their worst enemy. 2♣ women also seem to be attracted to playboy kinds of men, represented by the J♦. These "players" have a good rap, but they rarely deliver much, other than a brief period of fun. As much as the 2♣ wants the security of a stable relationship, they need to learn to make better choices if they want to achieve the happiness they desire.

Other than the aforementioned fears, the 2♣ have a charmed life. Everything comes to them easily, and there is really no excuse for any of them to be unhappy. They are great with people, personable, caring, and highly intelligent. Work will always come to them, and they will always be successful at it, whatever it is.

# Two of Clubs

Some of the best 2♣ marriages happen with:
K♣, 2♠, K♦, 7♠, A♣, 3♣, 2♥

The hottest sex happens with:
5♣, Q♠, 8♦, K♦, 10♦, 4♠, 4♥, 2♦

Your marriageability is:
Great! Just be more discerning on who you partner up with.

Affirmation for you:
Being willing and open to embrace my fears, I have a charmed life and all my dreams come true. I am beautiful!

| Famous 2♣ Birth Card people | |
| --- | --- |
| King Henry VIII | 6/28/1491 |
| Christopher Wren | 10/20/1632 |
| Ludwing van Beethoven | 12/16/1770 |
| Jane Austen | 12/16/1775 |
| Louis Dagueere | 11/18/1787 |
| Michael Faraday | 9/22/1791 |
| George Bernard Shaw | 7/26/1856 |
| Carl Jung | 7/26/1875 |
| Bela Lugosi | 10/20/1882 |
| James Chadwick | 10/20/1891 |
| Aldous Huxley | 7/26/1894 |
| Paul Muni | 9/22/1895 |
| Noel Coward | 12/16/1899 |
| George Gallup | 11/18/1901 |
| Margaret Mead | 12/16/1901 |
| John Dillinger | 6/28/1902 |
| Gracie Allen | 7/26/1902 |
| John Houseman | 9/22/1902 |
| Mel Blanc | 5/30/1908 |
| Imogene Coca | 11/18/1908 |
| Benny Goodman | 5/30/1909 |

# Two of Clubs

| | | | | |
|---|---|---|---|---|
| Vivian Vance | 7/26/1909 | | Shari Belafonte | 9/22/1954 |
| Arthur C Clarke | 12/16/1917 | | Dorothy Hamil | 7/26/1956 |
| Jason Robards | 7/26/1922 | | Debby Boone | 9/22/1956 |
| Chen Ning Yang | 9/22/1922 | | Sinbad | 11/18/1956 |
| Art Buchwald | 10/20/1925 | | Stephan Fry | 8/24/1957 |
| Mel Brooks | 6/28/1926 | | Johnette Napolitano | 9/22/1957 |
| Tommy Lasorda | 9/22/1927 | | Steve Guttenberg | 8/24/1958 |
| Stanley Kubrick | 7/26/1928 | | Joan Jett | 9/22/1958 |
| Joyce Brothers | 10/20/1928 | | Viggo Mortensen | 10/20/1958 |
| Mickey Mouse | 11/18/1928 | | Michael Ramos | 11/18/1958 |
| Minnie Mouse | 11/18/1928 | | Kevin Spacey | 7/26/1959 |
| Mickey Mantle | 10/20/1931 | | Karla Faye Tucker | 11/18/1959 |
| Kenny Baker | 8/24/1934 | | Alison LaPlaca | 12/16/1959 |
| Keir Dullea | 5/30/1936 | | John Elway | 6/28/1960 |
| Bobby Seale | 10/20/1936 | | Cal Ripken Jr. | 8/24/1960 |
| Don Cherry | 11/18/1936 | | Elizabeth Perkins | 11/18/1960 |
| Mason Williams | 8/24/1938 | | Scott Baio | 9/22/1961 |
| Junko Tabei | 9/22/1939 | | Catherine Oxenberg | 9/22/1961 |
| Margaret Atwood | 11/18/1939 | | Craig Kilborn | 8/24/1962 |
| Brenda Vaccaro | 11/18/1939 | | Kirk Hammett | 11/18/1962 |
| Liv Ullmann | 12/16/1939 | | Benjamin Bratt | 12/16/1963 |
| Mary Jo Kopechne | 7/26/1940 | | Wynonna Judd | 5/30/1964 |
| Patty Moon | 6/28/1942 | | Tom Morello | 5/30/1964 |
| Linda Evans | 11/18/1942 | | Sandra Bullock | 7/26/1964 |
| Gale Sayers | 5/30/1943 | | Bonnie Hunt | 9/22/1964 |
| Mick Jagger | 7/26/1943 | | Seth Joyner | 11/18/1964 |
| Steven Bocho | 12/16/1943 | | Marlee Matlin | 8/24/1965 |
| Lenny Davidson | 5/30/1944 | | John Cusack | 6/28/1966 |
| Susan Sullivan | 11/18/1944 | | Owen Wilson | 11/18/1968 |
| Helen Mirren | 7/26/1945 | | Snoop Dogg | 10/20/1971 |
| Gilda Radner | 6/28/1946 | | Carmine Giovinazzo | 8/24/1973 |
| Alan Dean Foster | 11/18/1946 | | Chloe Sevigny | 11/18/1974 |
| Kathy Bates | 6/28/1948 | | Kelly Clark | 7/26/1983 |
| Billy Gibbons | 12/16/1949 | | Sam Michael Fox | 5/30/1989 |
| Tom Petty | 10/20/1950 | | | |
| Ed Harris | 11/18/1950 | | | |
| Paul LeMat | 9/22/1952 | | | |
| Kevin Nealon | 11/18/1953 | | | |
| Martha Bailey | 7/26/1954 | | | |

# Two of Diamonds

You are the Two of Diamonds! Generally, when I meet a 2♦ and tell them what their card is, they often respond with something like "'You mean I am only a Two!'" Little do they know that the Ace is lower than them or just how fortunate this Birth Card really is.

In your card, you combine a keen mind with a love of the financial. This makes you well equipped to be very successful in business. Some of the most successful stock investors I have met are 2♦. You have a knack for analyzing stocks, markets, trends, and finding patterns that can make you rich. But your keen financial mind can be applied in any business field for success, and you are slated for success in this area. However, your mental abilities can be applied in most any area for success. Thus, we find successful 2♦ in many fields of work.

This is a partnership card, for better or worse, and most of your lessons in life will come in this area. On the positive side, 2♦ like to make money with others. This makes you a great business partner. They are generally highly intelligent, but not so experienced or wise in the emotional area. This makes for challenges in personal relationships. Being so smart and successful, but often so unsuccessful in the romance and marriage department, makes

# Two of Diamonds

you question your abilities in matters of love and relationships. You generally believe that marriage is forever, a belief often derived from a religious background. So, once you are in a bad relationship, it is very hard for you to leave. Many 2♦ spend years in a bad marriage and when they finally end it, they refuse to even try again. This has to be some cosmic joke, because their very nature is to be in a partnership.

2♦ of both sexes are often very attractive. People look at you and think, "that person could have anyone they want." If the 2♦ would spend more time working on their inner needs and issues, their entire lives would be more successful and happy. All Twos have work to do concerning fear of abandonment. The 2♦ is capable of fostering incredible relationships. Some of the best 2♦ relationships happen with the 6♣. This pairing happens frequently, and these pairings always tend to do very well together!

Hidden within every 2♦ lies a special purpose: All 2♦ cards have it, but only those who take the time to look within will find it. When you do, you discover that your life has a meaning and a plan that involves bringing the people around you to a higher understanding of life.

**Some of the best 2♦ marriages happen with:**
6♣, 8♣, 3♦, A♦, 4♣, J♠, and K♣

**The hottest sex happens with:**
5♦, J♠, Q♣, 7♥, 4♥, 7♠, 6♦, 9♣, J♣, and K♠

**Your marriageability is:**
Great!

**Affirmation for you:**
I use my gifts and my love of people to join together with others for mutual reward and fun!

| Famous 2♦ Birth Card people | |
| --- | --- |
| Vivien Leigh | 11/5/1913 |
| Gig Young | 11/5/1913 |
| June Allyson | 10/7/1917 |
| Alex Haley | 8/11/1921 |
| John Backus | 12/3/1924 |
| Peter Brook | 3/21/1925 |
| Cliff Robertson | 9/9/1925 |
| Shelley Berman | 2/23/1926 |
| James Coco | 3/21/1929 |
| Doris Roberts | 11/5/1930 |
| Dean Jones | 1/25/1931 |
| Desmond Tutu | 10/7/1931 |
| Mario Cuomo | 6/15/1932 |
| Corazon Aquino | 1/25/1933 |
| Jayne Mansfield | 4/19/1933 |
| Dick Sargent | 4/19/1933 |
| Jerry Falwell | 8/11/1933 |
| Dudley Moore | 4/19/1935 |
| Jack Kemp | 7/13/1935 |
| Diana Hyland | 1/25/1936 |
| Dennis Hopper | 5/17/1936 |

# Two of Diamonds

| | |
|---|---|
| Elinor Donahue | 4/19/1937 |
| Waylon Jennings | 6/15/1937 |
| Loretta Swit | 11/5/1937 |
| Etta James | 1/25/1938 |
| Billy Williams | 6/15/1938 |
| Peter Fonda | 2/23/1939 |
| Paul Prudhomme | 7/13/1940 |
| Patrick Stewart | 7/13/1940 |
| Elke Sommer | 11/5/1940 |
| Gregory Sierra | 1/25/1941 |
| Harry Nilsson | 6/15/1941 |
| Art Garfunkel | 11/5/1941 |
| Xaviera Hollander | 6/15/1942 |
| Harrison Ford | 7/13/1942 |
| Roger McGuinn | 7/13/1942 |
| Fred Biletnikoff | 2/23/1943 |
| Joy Behar | 10/7/1943 |
| Oliver North | 10/7/1943 |
| Sam Shepard | 11/5/1943 |
| Leigh Taylor-Young | 1/25/1944 |
| Johnny Winter | 2/23/1944 |
| Jesse Winchester | 5/17/1944 |
| Erno Rubik | 7/13/1944 |
| Tim Curry | 4/19/1946 |
| Janet Lennon | 6/15/1946 |
| Cheech Marin | 7/13/1946 |
| Marilyn vos Savant | 8/11/1946 |
| Shakira Caine | 2/23/1947 |
| Peter Noone | 11/5/1947 |
| Daphne Maxwell-Redi | 7/13/1948 |
| Pamela Des Barres | 9/9/1948 |
| Ozzy Osbourne | 12/3/1948 |
| Paloma Picasso | 4/19/1949 |
| Dusty Baker | 6/15/1949 |
| Jim Varney | 6/15/1949 |
| Joe Theisman | 9/9/1949 |
| Steve Wozniak | 8/11/1950 |
| Markie Post | 11/5/1950 |
| Patricia Richardson | 2/23/1951 |
| Didi Conn | 7/13/1951 |

# Two of Diamonds

| | | | | |
|---|---|---|---|---|
| Tom Wopat | 9/9/1951 | | Adam Sandler | 9/9/1966 |
| John Mellencamp | 10/7/1951 | | Joker Berggren | 3/21/1967 |
| Brad Whitford | 2/23/1952 | | Maxim Reality | 3/21/1967 |
| Angela Cartwright | 9/9/1952 | | Toni Braxton | 10/7/1967 |
| Dave Stewart | 9/9/1952 | | Ashley Judd | 4/19/1968 |
| Vladmir Putin | 10/7/1952 | | Julia Sawalha | 9/9/1968 |
| Kathleen Sullivan | 5/17/1953 | | Thom Yorke | 10/7/1968 |
| Tico Torres | 10/7/1953 | | Brendan Fraser | 12/3/1968 |
| Jim Belushi | 6/15/1954 | | DJ Premier | 3/21/1969 |
| Yo Yo Ma | 10/7/1955 | | Ice Cube | 6/15/1969 |
| Andy Cox | 1/25/1956 | | Leeroy Thornhill | 10/7/1969 |
| Sugar Ray Leonard | 5/17/1956 | | Matthew McConaughey | 11/5/1969 |
| Bob Saget | 5/17/1956 | | Jordan Knight | 5/17/1970 |
| Brad Gillis | 6/15/1957 | | Leah Remini | 6/15/1970 |
| Cameron Crowe | 7/13/1957 | | Macy Gray | 9/9/1970 |
| Dinah Manoff | 1/25/1958 | | Puff Daddy | 11/5/1970 |
| Gary Tibbs | 1/25/1958 | | China Kanter | 1/25/1971 |
| Brad Hall | 3/21/1958 | | Lasse Johansson | 2/23/1973 |
| Sabrina Le Beauf | 3/21/1958 | | Neil Patrick Harris | 6/15/1973 |
| Gary Oldman | 3/21/1958 | | Holly Marie Combs | 12/3/1973 |
| Daryl Hannah | 12/3/1959 | | Tyra Banks | 12/4/1973 |
| George Alvarez | 1/25/1960 | | Heather Tom | 11/5/1975 |
| Hugh Grant | 9/9/1960 | | Kandi Burruss | 5/17/1976 |
| Enya | 5/17/1961 | | Will Friedle | 8/11/1976 |
| Judy Landers | 10/7/1961 | | Kevin Federline | 3/21/1978 |
| Julianne Moore | 12/3/1961 | | Amber Brkich | 8/11/1978 |
| Matthew Broderick | 3/21/1962 | | Kate Hudson | 4/19/1979 |
| Cynthia Geary | 3/21/1962 | | Anna Chlumsky | 12/3/1980 |
| Rosie O'Donnell | 3/21/1962 | | Hayden Christensen | 4/19/1981 |
| Bobby Bonilla | 2/23/1963 | | Brian Bonsall | 12/3/1981 |
| Valerie Plame | 4/19/1963 | | Tony Parker | 5/17/1982 |
| Page McConnell | 5/17/1963 | | Rocco Ritchie | 8/11/2000 |
| Helen Hunt | 6/15/1963 | | | |
| Tatum O'Neal | 11/5/1963 | | | |
| Courteney Cox | 6/15/1964 | | | |
| Lisa Bessette | 11/5/1964 | | | |
| Veronica Webb | 2/23/1965 | | | |
| Trent Reznor | 5/17/1965 | | | |
| Katarina Witt | 12/3/1965 | | | |
| Michael Britt | 6/15/1966 | | | |

# *Two of Spades*

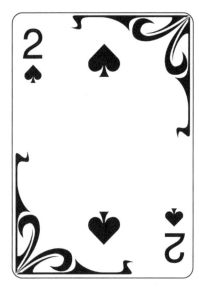

You are the Two of Spades! You are the card of friendship and, of course, your friends are important to you—much more than other cards. And friendship to you is not just talking with someone, but actually doing something with them. So, anyone who is your friend must be ready to get up and go somewhere or plan some activity. You card often manifests as working partnerships. If you look at Howard Stern, you see a great example of this. You rarely, if ever, see him alone—his entire crew, including family, friends, and coworkers, are almost always with him. Get to know any 2♠ enough and you will see how many people they stay connected to.

This is a worker card also, and you are somewhat of a perfectionist in that department. You are detail oriented and logical and really do put out very high quality work in whatever you do. A lot of the people we recognize as geniuses are 2♠. You have a command of logic and other mental operations that is far above normal. Thus, you can excel at most any line of work, but especially those where mental acuity is a basic requirement.

However, this same mental genius can get in your way when it comes to relationships. As you scrutinize the

# Two of Spades

possibility of marriage, your feelings often take a back seat to your mentality and, well, you may never get to the altar due to all the many "considerations" your mind comes up with. Actually, 2♠ are very marriageable and love being married. It is often just getting you to the alter that's tricky. The 2♠s make great husbands, wives, fathers, and mothers.

Your other challenge is health. You have a particular karma that does not allow you to abuse your body in the least. Some would call it a delicate or sensitive system, but whatever the case, your constitution will not allow the abuses most of us place upon our bodies through excesses, bad diet, or stress. You have to take care, and if you do, you will be great. Just remember that your karma will be swift and sure if you deviate from taking the highest of care with every part of your physical existence.

You inspire us all with your mental brilliance and with your desire to have us as friends. And you gather around you groups of people, all of whom feel appreciated and glad to be included in your circle of friendship.

**Some of the best 2♠ marriages happen with:**
3♠, J♦, A♠, 8♥, 4♦, 2♣, and K♣

**The hottest sex happens with:**
Q♦, 5♠, 7♣, J♠, K♥, 6♠, J♦, 10♥, A♥, and J♣

**Your marriageability is:**
Great. Why don't you just go ahead and do it?

**Affirmation for you:**
Through my circle of friends, I create community and love. I am a genius.

| Famous 2♠ Birth Card people | |
|---|---|
| Cyd Charisse | 3/8/1923 |
| Katsushige Mita | 4/6/1924 |
| Ian Paisley | 4/6/1926 |
| Leontyne Price | 2/10/1927 |
| Hosni Mubarak | 5/4/1928 |
| Andre Previn | 4/6/1929 |
| Audrey Hepburn | 5/4/1929 |
| Robert Wagner | 2/10/1930 |
| Roberta Peters | 5/4/1930 |
| Ram Dass | 4/6/1931 |
| Kreskin | 1/12/1935 |
| Sally Kellerman | 6/2/1936 |
| Merle Haggard | 4/6/1937 |
| Billy Dee Williams | 4/6/1937 |
| Roberta Flack | 2/10/1939 |
| George Will | 5/4/1941 |
| Stacy Keach | 6/2/1941 |
| Lynn Redgrave | 3/8/1943 |

# Two of Spades

| | |
|---|---|
| Michelle Phillips | 4/6/1944 |
| John Stax | 4/6/1944 |
| Paul Gleason | 5/4/1944 |
| Mickey Dolenz | 3/8/1945 |
| Carole Bayer Sager | 3/8/1947 |
| John Ratzenberger | 4/6/1947 |
| Mel Galley | 3/8/1948 |
| Peggy March | 3/8/1948 |
| Jerry Mathers | 6/2/1948 |
| Mark Spitz | 2/10/1950 |
| Kirstie Alley | 1/12/1951 |
| Rush Limbaugh | 1/12/1951 |
| Roxanne Pulitzer | 2/10/1951 |
| Jackie Jackson | 5/4/1951 |
| Marilu Henner | 4/6/1952 |
| Howard Stern | 1/12/1954 |
| Dana Carvey | 6/2/1955 |
| Pia Zadora | 5/4/1956 |
| Clive Burr | 3/8/1957 |
| Aidan Quin | 3/8/1959 |
| Randy Travis | 5/4/1959 |
| Oliver Platt | 1/12/1960 |
| George Stephanopoulos | 2/10/1961 |
| Camryn Manheim | 3/8/1961 |
| Stan Cullimore | 4/6/1962 |
| Lenny Dykstra | 2/10/1963 |
| Kathy Ireland | 3/8/1963 |
| Jeff Bezos | 1/12/1964 |
| Greg K | 1/12/1965 |
| Rob Zombie | 1/12/1966 |
| Ana Gasteyer | 5/4/1966 |
| Laura Dern | 2/10/1967 |
| Raekwon | 1/12/1968 |
| Ari Meyers | 4/6/1969 |
| Paul Rudd | 4/6/1969 |
| Zach De La Rocha | 1/12/1970 |
| Karla Homolka | 5/4/1970 |

# Two of Spades

| | | | |
|---|---|---|---|
| B-Real | 6/2/1970 | Candace Cameron | 4/6/1976 |
| Jason Hervey | 4/6/1972 | James Van Der Beek | 3/8/1977 |
| Mike Dirnt | 5/4/1972 | Jose Castellanos | 5/4/1977 |
| Melanie Chisholm | 1/12/1974 | Nikki Cox | 6/2/1978 |
| Freddie Prinze Jr. | 3/8/1976 | Lance Bass | 5/4/1979 |

# The Threes

To fully understand the nature of Threes, and of all the odd-numbered cards in the deck, one must look back at the Ace and see it as an evolutionary step out of the Zero. The Ace is the most primary of all the odd-numbered cards, and all of them reflect some of its qualities in some way. All odd-numbered cards represent a departure from the stability and evenness of the number preceding them. For the Three, this is a departure from the completion of the Two. Because the Three is the "leaving" from the Two, many of them are never satisfied with what they have, and this is especially true in their personal relationships. It is not a quality to be faulted or looked upon as a bad thing. It is just the way it is. For the Three person, this quality of leaving is basically a way of life that they must come to terms with at some point during their lives if they are to have peace and contentment.

Peace and contentment are challenges for all the odd-numbered Birth Cards. The odd numbers always represent an imbalance that is seeking balance through the creation of something else. These odd numbers are essentially masculine in nature—creative and always in motion. Whether a Three person is male or female, they will exhibit this creative drive that seeks expression. Their peace will only come through some form of action or accomplishment on the material level which will ultimately lead them back to themselves. For the Three, the urge is for self-expression and variety. They are generators of ideas, thoughts, and feelings, and they must find a suitable outlet, lest they suffer the consequence of worry and indecision.

Like Gemini sun sign people, Threes are versatile and often quite talkative. They can relate to many different kinds of people, cultures, and concepts because they are flexible. They are also quite resourceful and can come up with solutions to almost any problem that confronts them. If you need a good idea, talk to a Three. They usually have drawers full of ideas, some of which they are working on, but a multitude which they will never have the time or energy to start working on, much less follow through to completion. Art, music, and writing are excellent outlets for a Three's abundant creativity. Many of them become successful in one or more of these fields, and all of them need at least one of these outlets if they are to realize their birthright and achieve inner satisfaction. Many of them have several projects or jobs going at the same time. This gives them the variety they crave. When they start to get bored with one of the projects they are working on, they can switch to a second or third and keep going. This is a successful strategy for Threes. Otherwise, many of them go from one job to another and never complete anything, which ultimately makes them depressed and miserable. They need to see at least some of their ideas come to fruition.

Threes love romance. Astrologically, the fifth house energy is related to both creativity and self-expression, along with love affairs and romance. Three people seem to have a strong connection to this fifth house in the ways they find fulfillment. It stands to reason that those with the greatest creative gifts would also have the strongest needs for romantic involvement and sexual pleasure. Add to this the Three's natural curiosity and desire for new experiences and variety, and you can see why many Threes make great lovers but not-so-great marriage partners. They are just as likely to get bored in their relationships as they are with one of their current creative projects. They may feel like having a new affair to remedy the situation, and then jump back into your arms again when that gets boring. Though this may be a slight exaggeration, it is not an uncommon concern for Three people.

Another thing that can contribute to Threes' infidelity is their worrisome nature. Most of them, but especially the 3♣ and 3♦, are worried about not having enough (love, money, good health, etc.). Though this concern usually manifests itself as worry about finances, it can spill over into their romantic lives, too. The Three person might reason that if they have two or three lovers available to them, they will have less chance of running out of love when they need it. This can also explain why they might shy away from commitment and long-term relationships.

If you put all of these ingredients together, you can see why Threes can be very complicated people with a great potential for either happiness or unhappiness. The happiest are those who have found a place where they can express their creativity and be paid well for it. Threes are distinguished by their ideas and ability to communicate them. Many of them will make a real impact on the world with their creative gifts and will be admired for their contributions.

# Three of Hearts

You are the Three of Hearts! In you, the mind and heart are combined in a most unique way. You think a lot about love. You analyze it, study it, draw conclusions about it, and conduct experiments in order to learn more about it. Look at Dr. John Gray, author of *Men Are from Mars, Women Are from Venus*, for a good example of this. So, you are curious and always learning more about love. But your main gift is that of self-expression. Your creative gifts are abundant and must find a suitable outlet for expression. Not that this is your only area of potential expertise, but self-expression is a necessity for someone with so much to say, or sing!

You also have considerable power and drive. Women of this card do noticeably well in organizations typically dominated by males. Legal matters will usually go your way, whether you are male or female. You have a need to express, combined with the energy to work like crazy. Really nothing can stand in your way.

You will have to deal with a certain degree of uncertainty around finances. No matter how much money you have, your mind can find ways to worry about it. This is more about managing your mind than your actual financial condition. This

# Three of Hearts

is the main challenge for all Threes—to keep their active minds focused on positive expression instead of uncertainty and worry. You can overcome this if you are willing to work on it.

The 3♥ literally means creativity in love, or diversity in love. Most 3♥ will go through at least one period where there will be many partners. And there can be an uncertainty about love that shows up as a worry about not having enough love in one's life. Some 3♥ can never settle down with one person. And many are known to be bisexual. It's all part of the diversity inherent in a Three.

The ideas you generate and your self-expression are inspiring to everyone around you. We await the next thing you come up with because we delight in receiving what you give.

**Some of the best 3♥ marriages happen with:**
4♥, 2♥, 10♠, A♣, K♠, and K♣

**The hottest sex happens with:**
6♥, A♥, 3♦, 10♠, 4♥, 10♣, J♠, A♦, A♥, Q♦, 9♦, 10♦, and Q♣

**Your marriageability is:**
Questionable. Do you think you can be happy with one person?

**Affirmation for you:**
I am a creative genius.

| Famous 3♥ Birth Card people | |
|---|---|
| Jonathan Switft | 11/30/1667 |
| Mark Twain | 11/30/1835 |
| Woodrow Wilson | 12/28/1856 |
| Winston Churchhill | 11/30/1874 |
| Lucy Maud Montgomery | 11/30/1874 |
| Fatha Hines | 12/28/1905 |
| Brownie McGhee | 11/30/1915 |
| Johnny Otis | 12/28/1921 |
| Stan Lee | 12/28/1922 |
| Dick Clark | 11/30/1929 |
| G. Gordon Liddy | 11/30/1930 |
| Bill Walsh | 11/30/1931 |
| Maggie Smith | 12/28/1934 |
| Abbie Hoffman | 11/30/1936 |
| Ridley Scott | 11/30/1937 |
| Terrence Malick | 11/30/1943 |
| Edgar Winter | 12/28/1946 |
| David Mamet | 11/30/1947 |
| Dr. John Gray | 12/28/1951 |
| Mandy Patinkin | 11/30/1952 |
| June Pointer | 11/30/1954 |
| Denzel Washington | 12/28/1954 |
| Billy Idol | 11/30/1955 |
| Chad McQueen | 12/28/1960 |
| Bo Jackson | 11/30/1962 |
| Ben Stiller | 11/30/1965 |
| Patrick Rafter | 12/28/1972 |
| Mackenzie Rosman | 12/28/1989 |

# *Three of Clubs*

You are the Three of Clubs, one of the most creative and resourceful cards in the deck! This card has been called the Author's card but really is the Card of Ideas and Communications. If you are a 3♣ looking for a career direction, heed these words well. Your creative mind can be put to all sorts of useful directions. You could be an author for sure—look at Stephen King! But you can also excel at any creative pursuit. H.G. Wells, Leonard Cohen, Bill Murray, Rick Springfield, Keith Moon, and River Phoenix are all 3♣. Less obvious than your creative talents and showmanship is your innate grasp of business and a tendency to rise up to high levels in whatever direction you choose. You are one of the cards that feel very comfortable mixing it up with the rich and powerful of society. You deserve to be part of that group yourself. But creative ideas and communications are your real gift. You could make tons of money just by talking on the phone!

However, all this creativity comes at a price. Your super active mind can become your worst enemy at times. The most creative people can also be the most uncertain and worried. And life presents more than enough things to worry about.

# Three of Clubs

Money would be one area, though it is generally a misplaced worry in your case—it's your own internal sense of dissatisfaction with what you have that could lead to a heightened sense of uncertainty about your financial future. Your own mind is super active and restless. It never seems satisfied with what is, and thus your own sense of satisfaction is constantly being bombarded by new ideas, new ways of doing things, and new adventures.

This sense of dissatisfaction also affects your relationships. And though I have met successfully married 3♣s, it is considered one of the least marriageable cards, due mostly to their changeable nature and inner sense of dissatisfaction. Even when they find the ideal partner, they may seek love elsewhere. Or, as I have seen in so many of them, they find continual attractions to others who are not really available. We often like most that which we cannot have. Any 3♣ can generally get anyone they're romantically interested in—they just need to be clear about what, exactly, they want.

The life of any 3♣ is lived first and foremost in their minds. So, it is in the understanding and management of their minds that they will have the greatest personal breakthroughs in life. Everything else is very easy for them.

**Some of the best 3♣ marriages happen with:**
4♣, 3♠, 6♦, 2♣, 4♦, 6♥, and K♥

**The hottest sex happens with:**
6♣, 5♠, A♠, J♦, 7♣, 9♠, and 10♣

**Your marriageability is:**
Below average, unless you make an effort to understand yourself better.

**Affirmation for you:**
I am a creative genius. I channel that energy into success and prosperity.

| Famous 3♣ Birth Card people | |
|---|---|
| H.G. Wells | 9/21/1866 |
| Maxfield Parrish | 7/25/1870 |
| G.K. Chesterton | 5/29/1874 |
| Oswald Spengler | 5/29/1880 |
| Helen Keller | 6/27/1880 |
| J. Paul Getty | 12/15/1892 |
| Walter Brennan | 7/25/1894 |
| Lee Strasberg | 11/17/1901 |
| Bob Hope | 5/29/1903 |
| Gene Kelly | 8/23/1912 |
| Shelby Foote | 11/17/1916 |
| John F. Kennedy | 5/29/1917 |
| I.A.L. Diamond | 6/27/1920 |

# *Three of Clubs*

| | |
|---|---|
| LaWanda Page | 10/19/1920 |
| Estelle Getty | 7/25/1923 |
| Rosalie Allen | 6/27/1924 |
| Jerry Paris | 7/25/1925 |
| Rock Hudson | 11/17/1925 |
| Bob Keeshan | 6/27/1927 |
| Vera Miles | 8/23/1929 |
| Ross Perot | 6/27/1930 |
| Larry Hagman | 9/21/1931 |
| John Le Carre | 10/19/1931 |
| Robert Reed | 10/19/1932 |
| Tim Conway | 12/15/1933 |
| Barbara Eden | 8/23/1934 |
| Sonny Jurgensen | 8/23/1934 |
| Leonard Cohen | 9/21/1934 |
| Henry Lee Lucas | 8/23/1936 |
| Sylvia Browne | 10/19/1936 |
| Peter Max | 10/19/1937 |
| Fay Vincent | 5/29/1938 |
| Gordon Lightfoot | 11/17/1938 |
| Martin Scorsese | 11/17/1942 |
| Dave Clark | 12/15/1942 |
| Cheryl Crane | 7/25/1943 |
| Jim McCarty | 7/25/1943 |
| Lauren Hutton | 11/17/1943 |
| Peter Tosh | 10/19/1944 |
| Danny DeVito | 11/17/1944 |
| Lorne Michaels | 11/17/1944 |
| Tom Seaver | 11/17/1944 |
| Norma Kamali | 6/27/1945 |
| Divine | 10/19/1945 |
| Patricia Ireland | 10/19/1945 |
| John Lithgow | 10/19/1945 |
| Keith Moon | 8/23/1946 |
| Ben Vereen | 10/19/1946 |
| Martin Barre | 11/17/1946 |

# Three of Clubs

| | | | | |
|---|---|---|---|---|
| Stephen King | 9/21/1947 | | Evander Holyfield | 10/19/1962 |
| Shelley Long | 8/23/1949 | | Helen Slater | 12/15/1963 |
| Rick Springfield | 8/23/1949 | | Amy Linker | 10/19/1966 |
| Leslie Van Houten | 8/23/1949 | | Jeff Buckley | 11/17/1966 |
| Don Johnson | 12/15/1949 | | Daisy Fuentes | 11/17/1966 |
| Bill Murray | 9/21/1950 | | Sophie Marceau | 11/17/1966 |
| Julia Duffy | 6/27/1951 | | Noel Gallagher | 5/29/1967 |
| Verdine White | 7/25/1951 | | Matt LeBlanc | 7/25/1967 |
| Queen Noor al Hussein | 8/23/1951 | | Faith Hill | 9/21/1967 |
| Danny Elfman | 5/29/1953 | | Amy Carter | 10/19/1967 |
| Curtis Armstrong | 11/17/1953 | | Mo Vaughn | 12/15/1967 |
| Walter Payton | 7/25/1954 | | Blaze Bayley | 5/29/1968 |
| John Hinckley Jr. | 5/29/1955 | | Ricki Lake | 9/21/1968 |
| Isabelle Adjani | 6/27/1955 | | John Edward | 10/19/1969 |
| Iman | 7/25/1955 | | Trey Parker | 10/19/1969 |
| Paul Simenon | 12/15/1955 | | River Phoenix | 8/23/1970 |
| LaToya Jackson | 5/29/1956 | | Luke Wilson | 9/21/1971 |
| Roger Clinton | 7/25/1957 | | Liam Gallagher | 9/21/1972 |
| Jim Babjak | 11/17/1957 | | David Silveria | 9/21/1972 |
| Annette Bening | 5/29/1958 | | Melanie Brown | 5/29/1975 |
| Thurston Moore | 7/25/1958 | | Tobey Maguire | 6/27/1975 |
| Mary Elizabeth Mastrantonio | 11/17/1958 | | Louise Brown | 7/25/1978 |
| Rupert Everett | 5/29/1959 | | Kobe Bryant | 8/23/1978 |
| Heidi Bohay | 12/15/1959 | | Isaac Hanson | 11/17/1980 |
| RuPaul | 11/17/1960 | | Brad Renfro | 7/25/1982 |
| Melissa Etheridge | 5/29/1961 | | Madylin Sweeten | 6/27/1991 |
| Nancy Travis | 9/21/1961 | | Benjamin Bening-Beatty | 8/23/1994 |
| Rob Morrow | 9/21/1962 | | Sistine Rose Stallone | 6/27/1998 |

# Three of Diamonds

You are the Three of Diamonds! Your card is one of high creativity. And you can be especially good at making money at creative enterprises, such as design or art, or even performing in some manner. Many 3♦ are successful artists, actors, actresses, and authors. Creativity is especially important because if you don't find a suitable avenue for the expression of this gift, it can and will express itself as uncertainty and worry. The number Three literally means diversity. In the suit of Diamonds it means diversity in values. Another way of saying this is that you want this and you want that, often at the same time. Variety is especially important for you, as is having work that you find interesting. Anything routine or mechanical in nature would probably drive you crazy. Many people of your Birth Card will have two or more professions going at the same time. This works quite well, especially when the professions contribute to each other in some way.

What you want in life may be in flux a good bit of the time. And there can be a sense of dissatisfaction with what you have. This can make it difficult to focus in on one avenue long enough to make a success of it. But if you find the creative outlet that truly turns you on,

# Three of Diamonds

you will take a magic carpet ride to success and fulfillment.

This same sense of uncertainty and desire for variety will affect your personal relationships. Life has so much to explore, to experience, that you might feel that it's too much of a sacrifice to settle down with one person. Not that all 3♦ avoid marriage—but a great deal of them do. They do have intensely rewarding relationships, some that last for years, just without marriage. This card also has lessons to learn about relationships, about the true responsibility that is connected with romance, and sex. They dream of the ideal lover and partner. But are they willing to be the same? That is a question many 3♦ face.

Self-expression is the number one thing for all 3♦. A male 3♦ often has a powerful, commanding voice and uses that voice to command respect and success. A 3♦ has a penetrating, inquiring mind and one that is naturally drawn towards metaphysics and spiritual sciences. They find many important answers in those fields. 3♦ are deep thinkers and often uncover the most profound truths in life. Some become profound mystics.

3♦ make significant contributions to the world through their creative gifts, once they find what it is they truly want to express. And the rest of us love to enjoy what you choose to share with us.

**Some of the best 3♦ marriages happen with:**
4♦, 2♦, A♠, 7♦, and Q♣

**The hottest sex happens with:**
6♦, A♦, 7♦, 7♣, 8♦, J♥, 8♥, and 10♥

**Your marriageability is:**
Not so great. But if you get clear that you really want it, you will have it.

**Affirmation for you:**
I am a creative genius seeking the unique outlet that best expresses my ideas.

| Famous 3♦ Birth Card people | |
|---|---|
| Henry Fonda | 5/16/1905 |
| Ozzie Nelson | 3/20/1906 |
| Michael Redgrave | 3/20/1908 |
| Milton Berle | 7/12/1908 |
| Carole Lombard | 10/6/1908 |
| Burl Ives | 6/14/1909 |
| Studs Terkel | 5/16/1912 |
| Robert Motherwell | 1/24/1915 |
| Walter Cronkite | 11/4/1916 |
| Earnest Borgnine | 1/24/1917 |
| Andrew Wyeth | 7/12/1917 |
| Oral Roberts | 1/24/1918 |
| Art Carney | 11/4/1918 |

# Three of Diamonds

| | |
|---|---|
| Liberace | 5/16/1919 |
| Carl Reiner | 3/20/1922 |
| Sid Caesar | 9/8/1922 |
| Rhonda Fleming | 8/10/1923 |
| Maria Callas | 12/2/1923 |
| Grace Metalious | 9/8/1924 |
| Peter Sellers | 9/8/1925 |
| Fred Rogers | 3/20/1928 |
| Billy Martin | 5/16/1928 |
| Eddie Fisher | 8/10/1928 |
| Floyd Salas | 1/24/1931 |
| Marla Gibbs | 6/14/1931 |
| Fred Graham | 10/6/1931 |
| Ted Kennedy | 2/22/1932 |
| Patsy Cline | 9/8/1932 |
| Jerzy Kosinski | 6/14/1933 |
| Sparky Anderson | 2/22/1934 |
| Van Cliburn | 7/12/1934 |
| Bill Cosby | 7/12/1937 |
| Virna Lisi | 9/8/1937 |
| Daisy Duck | 11/4/1940 |
| Neil Diamond | 1/24/1941 |
| Britt Ekland | 10/6/1942 |
| Sharon Tate | 1/24/1943 |
| Christine McVie | 7/12/1943 |
| Domonic Barber | 10/6/1945 |
| Tex Watson | 12/2/1945 |
| Hayley Mills | 4/18/1946 |
| Donald Trump | 6/14/1946 |
| Millie Small | 10/6/1946 |
| Laura Bush | 11/4/1946 |
| Robert Mapplethorpe | 11/4/1946 |
| Gianni Versace | 12/2/1946 |
| Warren Zevon | 1/24/1947 |
| James Woods | 4/18/1947 |
| Ian Anderson | 8/10/1947 |
| Michael Des Barres | 1/24/1948 |
| Richard Simmons | 7/12/1948 |

# Three of Diamonds

| | | | | |
|---|---|---|---|---|
| Jay Thomas | 7/12/1948 | | Robin Wilson | 7/12/1965 |
| John Belushi | 1/24/1949 | | Janet Jackson | 5/16/1966 |
| Julius Erving | 2/22/1950 | | Thurman Thomas | 5/16/1966 |
| Julie Walters | 2/22/1950 | | Kathy Griffin | 11/4/1966 |
| William Hurt | 3/20/1950 | | Bryan Genesse | 3/20/1967 |
| Yakov Smirnoff | 1/24/1951 | | Riddick Bowe | 8/10/1967 |
| Cheryl Ladd | 7/12/1951 | | Mary Lou Retton | 1/24/1968 |
| Pierce Brosnan | 5/16/1952 | | Bradley Nowell | 2/22/1968 |
| Phil Kramer | 7/12/1952 | | Yasmine Bleeth | 6/14/1968 |
| Stone Phillips | 12/2/1954 | | Lucy Liu | 12/2/1968 |
| Olga Korbut | 5/16/1955 | | Tracey Gold | 5/16/1969 |
| Debra Winger | 5/16/1955 | | Steffi Graf | 6/14/1969 |
| Eric Roberts | 4/18/1956 | | Lisa Nicole Carson | 7/12/1969 |
| Mel Harris | 7/12/1956 | | Greg Eklund | 4/18/1970 |
| Spike Lee | 3/20/1957 | | Gabriella Sabatini | 5/16/1970 |
| Robert Bailey | 9/8/1957 | | Latrell Sprewell | 9/8/1970 |
| Holly Hunter | 3/20/1958 | | David Boreanaz | 5/16/1971 |
| Eric Heiden | 6/14/1958 | | Kristi Yamaguchi | 7/12/1971 |
| Kyle MacLachlan | 2/22/1959 | | David Arquette | 9/8/1971 |
| Mare Winningham | 5/16/1959 | | Michael Chang | 2/22/1972 |
| Rosanna Arquette | 8/10/1959 | | Angie Harmon | 8/10/1972 |
| Natassia Kinski | 1/24/1960 | | Tori Spelling | 5/16/1973 |
| Antonio Banderas | 8/10/1960 | | Mister Magoo | 7/12/1973 |
| Rick Savage | 12/2/1960 | | Monica Seles | 12/2/1973 |
| Boy George | 6/14/1961 | | Drew Barrymore | 2/22/1975 |
| Ralph Macchio | 11/4/1961 | | Melissa Joan Hart | 4/18/1976 |
| Steve Irwin | 2/22/1962 | | Jennifer Robinson | 12/2/1976 |
| Dan Murphy | 7/12/1962 | | Topher Grace | 7/12/1978 |
| Tracy Austin | 12/2/1962 | | Nelly Furtado | 12/2/1978 |
| Jane Leeves | 4/18/1963 | | Daisy Eagan | 11/4/1979 |
| Eric McCormack | 4/18/1963 | | Jonathan Taylor Thomas | 9/8/1981 |
| Conan O'Brien | 4/18/1963 | | Britney Spears | 12/2/1981 |
| Eilsabeth Shue | 10/6/1963 | | Eric Van Halen | 10/6/1989 |
| Nenah Cherry | 8/10/1964 | | Erik Per Sullivan | 7/12/1991 |
| Matthew Sweet | 10/6/1964 | | | |

# Three of Spades

You are the Three of Spades! This is the most powerful and successful of the artist cards. If you are not a working artist, then you approach your work or your life in an extremely artistic manner, always discovering ways to improve or change things to make them better. It is good to know that you can be a successful artist, if you ever want to explore that area. It is a given. Being a 3♠ means that you are the most creative and most divided of all the Threes. 3♠ often lead double lives, and if you examine any of their lives carefully, you will see that split there somewhere. They can be a little neurotic at times because of the abundance of this creative mental energy, which can turn to doubt and uncertainty at times.

You have a unique karma—if you work for it, success will always be yours. You have a natural gift for sales and promotion, too. Have you used that yet? This is one reason 3♠ make such successful artists. Not only can they create great art, but they know how to sell it as well.

Your mind often gets overworked about your health. Many 3♠ end up with mystery illnesses, hard to diagnose or

# Three of Spades

pinpoint. You should know that your mind is your greatest enemy in this area. The more you think about it, the worse it gets. Most of your problems are caused by your fixation on them more than the problems themselves. Relax, use your creative mind artistically instead of neurotically, and your health will clear up on its own.

People of your card do get married—all the time, in fact. However, there is a strong sexual and romantic drive in this card that often makes commitment a challenge. Many people with this card choose to have lovers rather than partners.

You are here to make a huge contribution to the world through the use and implementation of your creative gifts.

**Some of the best 3♠ marriages happen with:**
4♠, 2♠, K♣, 4♥, 9♥, 3♣, 7♦, and 5♦

**The hottest sex happens with:**
6♠, K♦, 5♦, 5♣, 4♣, 2♠, 3♣, 2♥, 7♥, and J♥

**Your marriageability is:**
Questionable.

**Affirmation for you:**
I am the artist of artists. In whatever I do my creativity leads the way and shines brilliantly.

| Famous 3♠ Birth Card people | |
|---|---|
| Pete Seeger | 5/3/1919 |
| Arthur Hailey | 4/5/1920 |
| Sugar Ray Robinson | 5/3/1920 |
| Brendan Behan | 2/9/1923 |
| Grant Tinker | 1/11/1925 |
| Andy Griffith | 6/1/1926 |
| Marilyn Monroe | 6/1/1926 |
| James Brown | 5/3/1928 |
| Anthony Armstrong Jones | 3/7/1930 |
| Jean Chrétien | 1/11/1934 |
| Willard Scott | 3/7/1934 |
| Pat Boone | 6/1/1934 |
| Englelbert Humperdinck | 5/3/1936 |
| Colin Powell | 4/5/1937 |
| Morgan Freeman | 6/1/1937 |
| Superman | 6/1/1938 |
| Daniel J. Travanti | 3/7/1940 |
| Bobby Goldsboro | 1/11/1941 |
| Carole King | 2/9/1942 |
| Tammy Faye Baker | 3/7/1942 |
| Michael Eisner | 3/7/1942 |
| Joe Pesci | 2/9/1943 |
| Alice Walker | 2/9/1944 |
| Mia Farrow | 2/9/1945 |
| Naomi Judd | 1/11/1946 |
| David Gilmour | 3/7/1946 |
| Jane Asher | 4/5/1946 |

# *Three of Spades*

| | |
|---|---|
| Wendy O. Williams | 6/1/1946 |
| Doug Henning | 5/3/1947 |
| Judith Light | 2/9/1949 |
| Franco Harris | 3/7/1950 |
| Mary Hopkin | 5/3/1950 |
| Lynn Swann | 3/7/1952 |
| David Berkowitz | 6/1/1953 |
| Lisa Hartman | 6/1/1956 |
| Alan Wilder | 6/1/1959 |
| Ivan Lendl | 3/7/1960 |
| Jason Connery | 1/11/1963 |
| Travis Tritt | 2/9/1963 |
| Mike McCready | 4/5/1966 |
| Randy Guss | 3/7/1967 |
| Tabitha Stevens | 3/7/1967 |
| Mary J. Blige | 1/11/1971 |
| Tom Rowlands | 1/11/1971 |
| Amanda Peet | 1/11/1972 |
| Heidi Klum | 6/1/1973 |
| Alanis Morissette | 6/1/1974 |
| Irina Slutskaya | 2/9/1979 |
| Mena Suvari | 2/9/1979 |
| Zhang Ziyi | 2/9/1980 |
| John Walker Lindh | 2/9/1981 |

# The Fours

Home, family, stability, security, contentment, foundation, a good supply of things needed for life—these are the keywords of the number Four and the people who bear this number on their Birth Card. Four people often look rounded or squarish in physical appearance—they both look and act like solid, grounded people. People get a sense of safety and security when they are with a Four person. It is no accident that the fourth house in astrology represents many of the same things. The sign of Cancer, which rules the fourth house, represents nurturing and security. All Fours, but certainly some more than others, are interested in security and stability. In whatever they are doing, we can see them creating this order and stability in their lives and in the lives of those they have chosen to protect.

Protection is another keyword for the number Four. And protection is their birthright. However, this protection only manifests itself to the Four person who is willing to work for things in their life. Through work, all of their dreams can be realized. Avoidance or ignorance of this single principle is probably the biggest cause of unhappiness in the life of a Four. Without this willingness to put in the effort, everything turns against them to varying degrees. With the application of commitment and effort, they can accomplish most anything they desire. The unhappy Four person is invariably the one who either avoids or resents how much work they must do.

Many Fours are also overly security conscious. The Four person who is not living up to their own inner requirements of work and commitment runs the risk of becoming the controller who tries to keep everyone from doing anything that might upset the perfect little box of a world they have created. A good example of this is the mother or father who controls their children and keeps them sheltered at home, not allowing them to develop any responsibility of their own. They will tell their friends and themselves that they are doing it to help their children, but in truth, it is stunting their children's development. They usually don't realize that their true motivation is the fear of losing their children, who represent a large part of their security system.

The boss who micromanages his or her business may also be a Four. He may get so overly concerned with organization and details that he fails to see the big picture and actually does things that are counterproductive to the company's goals of serving its customers. He also may be blind to the possibilities that present themselves for expansion and growth. To a Four, too much growth can represent a threat to their security system. And no one can fight harder to keep things the way they are than a Four. In their eyes, if things are working well enough the way they are, why change them?

This does not mean that Fours dislike change for change's sake. No, they only fight against it if it seems to threaten their security system. As a matter of fact, the 4♠ and 4♣ are fairly progressive in many ways. They also like to travel a lot. The 4♦ and 4♣ seem to have the most conflict between the happiness their work brings and the desire to just take off and leave it all behind.

A Four person is someone who is good at organization, setting boundaries, establishing foundations, managing, and working. They are usually not found in positions of leadership, but instead they tend to gravitate toward finding a suitable job where they can make their contribution without too much hassle from others. They are usually not the most creative people, nor are they the most far-sighted or broad-minded. But they personify an important and necessary element in our lives—the importance of security, stability, and hard work.

They will have to work hard during the course of their lives, but as they get into their later years, they find themselves with more money and freedom to travel and enjoy their lives without so much hard work. If they can let go of their "struggle mentality," they will see that sometimes good things just flow to us without so much effort.

In relationships, their fate is mixed overall. They tend to want to settle down, but some of them, especially the 4♦, have difficult relationship issues to deal with, and there can be no escaping the challenges in their romantic life.

Many 4♦ are able to master certain skills and techniques in a way that is truly amazing. They rise to the top of their professions through the application of their organization and hard work. We can truly admire them for their accomplishments and we can trust them to deliver good products, ideas, and services to us when we employ or hire them. "Good" is a Four word and describes the qualities that they put forth most of the time in everything that they do.

# Four of Hearts

You are the Four of Hearts! Though your card's number may seem low, being only a four, you are actually a person of great power and significance. This power is expressed through your relationships and through your work. You generally get your way in both areas, and 4♥ people have accomplished some truly grand things in their lives. But most of all, you are a relationship person and you highly value those you hold dear. Yours is the card of family and marriage. Though not all 4♥ marry, the vast majority of them do. They are good at it and well-suited for it. Therefore, you make a great husband, wife, mother, or father. You also make a great friend! Anyone who you take in is protected by you and included in your family.

But relationships are not your only area of expertise. You have a great mind and solid sense of values that could benefit you and others in the business arena. You could also be a good business consultant or advisor. You are one of the two most stable cards in the deck. You know what you want out of life and you take whatever steps are necessary to create it. Overall, your life path is a fortunate one.

In relationships, you tend to be idealistic. You want a partner who is a friend,

# Four of Hearts

but also someone with whom you share a great romantic connection. Of course you are very marriageable. You are the marriage card itself! 4♥ also often end up working with their partners. It just seems to fit them.

You have to be careful in the area of your health. Usually the 4♥ constitution is such that they cannot afford to be disrespectful to their bodies by any excesses or bad habits. Alcohol is something to avoid, but primarily, diet and exercise are important for you. A little prevention goes a long way with your Birth Card.

Many 4♥ are destined for greatness. You certainly have the capacity to make an unforgettable mark on the world. By your example we see the beauty and rightfulness of love, family, and friendship.

**Some of the best 4♥ marriages happen with:**
5♥, 4♦, 5♣, 3♥, Q♣, 5♠, J♦, and 3♠

**The hottest sex happens with:**
7♥, A♥, A♣, 3♥, 2♦, A♦, 9♣, 6♦, 8♥, 2♣, 10♦, and Q♣

**Your marriageability is:**
Excellent. It doesn't get much better than you!

# Four of Hearts

**Affirmation for you:**

I create family and friendship wherever I go.

| Famous 4♥ Birth Card people | |
|---|---|
| Marlene Dietrich | 12/27/1901 |
| Dale Evans | 10/31/1912 |
| William Masters | 12/27/1915 |
| Lee Salk | 12/27/1926 |
| Lee Grant | 10/31/1927 |
| Dan Rather | 10/31/1931 |
| Jacques Chirac | 11/29/1932 |
| Diane Ladd | 11/29/1932 |
| John Mayall | 11/29/1933 |
| Michael Landon | 10/31/1936 |
| Tom Paxton | 10/31/1937 |
| John Amos | 12/27/1939 |
| Chuck Mangione | 11/29/1940 |
| Cokie Roberts | 12/27/1943 |
| Petra Kelly | 11/29/1947 |
| Gerard Depardieu | 12/27/1948 |
| Tovah Feldsluh | 12/27/1948 |
| Jerry Lawler | 11/29/1949 |
| Garry Shandling | 11/29/1949 |
| John Candy | 10/31/1950 |
| Jane Pauley | 10/31/1950 |
| David Knopfler | 12/27/1952 |
| Arthrur Kent | 12/27/1953 |
| Joel Coen | 11/29/1954 |
| Howie Mandel | 11/29/1955 |
| Jeff Fahey | 11/29/1957 |
| Cathy Moriarty | 11/29/1960 |
| Peter Jackson | 10/31/1961 |
| Andrew McCarthy | 11/29/1962 |
| Johnny Marr | 10/31/1963 |
| Dermont Mulroney | 10/31/1963 |

| | |
|---|---|
| Kim Delaney | 11/29/1964 |
| Ellen Cleghorne | 11/29/1965 |
| Adam Horovitz | 10/31/1966 |
| Martin Carr | 11/29/1968 |
| Howard K. Stern | 11/29/1968 |
| Heather O'Rourke | 12/27/1975 |
| Piper Perabo | 10/31/1977 |

# Four of Clubs

You are the Four of Clubs! How fortunate for you! This is one of the more fortunate cards in the deck, and no matter how you view your life, you are protected by some unseen force and given more success and opportunity than most. All in all, you have much to be grateful for. You have an incredibly organized mind, one that is also progressive and open to new ideas. However, once you learn how something works, you will never abandon that knowledge—others call you stubborn at times because of your tenacity about the routines and methods on which you base your life. You are a card of security and foundation, and your own security is based more upon what you have learned than any other card in the deck. You have high intelligence and usually good looks to go with it. You are a grounded person who is both marriageable and enjoyable to be with.

No one should ever compete with you in a legal battle. You will win 90 percent of the time. You know that there is no substitute for hard work, and you are willing to pay the price to have the life you want. You are not lazy, and you can see that your success is assured. You are here to serve, and in service you find great contentment.

# Four of Clubs

Your biggest challenge, and especially if you are the female 4♣, is relationships. Though you are strongly family- and security-based, you have an unusual attraction to partners who are not. How you manage to consistently find partners who are freedom-based, erratic, dishonest, and generally just operating with a low value scale is a mystery. You would be like the young girl who grows up going to church in a family of high moral values who suddenly meets and runs away with a guy from a biker gang. And often, if money is involved, your partner may be out to get it from you. If you can recognize your own strange attraction for these types, you can avoid many unpleasant episodes in your life and get on with what you really want— true love and the stability of a true partner. However, both sexes must also be aware of how analytical they are in the area of love. The mind can perhaps help us not make bad decisions. But we need the heart there, too, to tell us we have found what we truly love and want.

All in all, your life is blessed and charmed. Appreciating your many blessings can help you realize just how fortunate you are and keep a smile on your face.

**Some of the best 4♣ marriages happen with:**
2♦, 6♣, K♦, 3♣, 5♣, and 6♥

**The hottest sex happens with:**
7♣, 8♦, J♠, Q♦, 8♣, K♥, 7♠, and A♣

**Your marriageability is:**
Excellent! See how lucky you are?

**Affirmation for you:**
No matter what, I am always protected and blessed. I am aware of just how fortunate I am and have always been.

| Famous 4♣ Birth Card people | |
|---|---|
| Nostradamus | 12/14/1503 |
| Ian Fleming | 5/28/1908 |
| Morey Amsterdam | 12/14/1908 |
| Tom Parker | 6/26/1909 |
| Al Lewis | 4/30/1910 |
| Eve Arden | 4/30/1912 |
| John D. MacDonald | 7/24/1912 |
| Papa John Creach | 5/28/1917 |
| John Lee Hooker | 8/22/1917 |
| Red Auerbach | 9/20/1917 |
| Peg Phillips | 9/20/1918 |
| Pierre Trudeau | 10/18/1919 |
| Ray Bradbury | 8/22/1920 |
| Don Hewitt | 12/14/1922 |
| Melina Mercouri | 10/18/1923 |

# Four of Clubs

| | |
|---|---|
| Cloris Leachman | 4/30/1926 |
| Chuck Berry | 10/18/1926 |
| George C. Scott | 10/18/1927 |
| Jack Kevorkian | 5/28/1928 |
| Charlie Rich | 12/14/1932 |
| Willie Nelson | 4/30/1933 |
| Dionne Quintuplets | 5/28/1934 |
| Diana Sands | 8/22/1934 |
| Sophia Loren | 9/20/1934 |
| Inger Stevens | 10/18/1934 |
| Lee Remick | 12/14/1935 |
| Carl Yastrzemski | 8/22/1939 |
| Mike Ditka | 10/18/1939 |
| Lee Harvey Oswald | 10/18/1939 |
| Valerie Harper | 8/22/1940 |
| Donna McKechnie | 11/16/1940 |
| Chris Sarandon | 7/24/1942 |
| Jill Clayburgh | 4/30/1944 |
| Rudy Giuliani | 5/28/1944 |
| Gladys Knight | 5/28/1944 |
| Annie Dillard | 4/30/1945 |
| John Fogerty | 5/28/1945 |
| Ron Dante | 8/22/1945 |
| Patty Duke | 12/14/1946 |
| Michael Ovitz | 12/14/1946 |
| Sondra Locke | 5/28/1947 |
| Cindy Williams | 8/22/1947 |
| Laura Nyro | 10/18/1947 |
| Michael Richards | 7/24/1949 |
| Anthony John Denison | 9/20/1950 |
| David Leisure | 11/16/1950 |
| Peter Bailey | 9/20/1952 |
| Mick Jones | 6/26/1955 |
| Chris Isaak | 6/26/1956 |
| Martina Navratilova | 10/18/1956 |
| Gary Cole | 9/20/1957 |
| Ethan Coen | 9/21/1957 |

# Four of Clubs

| | | | |
|---|---|---|---|
| Marg Helgenberger | 11/16/1958 | Matthew Nelson | 9/20/1967 |
| Jean-Claude | | Lisa Bonet | 11/16/1967 |
|    Van Damme | 10/18/1960 | Noelle Beck | 12/14/1967 |
| John Easdale | 9/20/1961 | Laura Leighton | 7/24/1968 |
| Wynton Marsalis | 10/18/1961 | Kristen Johnson | 9/20/1968 |
| Erin Moran | 10/18/1961 | Ben Shepherd | 9/20/1968 |
| Brandon Cruz | 5/28/1962 | Chris O'Donnell | 6/26/1970 |
| Francois Henri Pinault | 5/28/1962 | Jennifer Lopez | 7/24/1970 |
| Vincent Spano | 10/18/1962 | Martha Plimpton | 11/16/1970 |
| Tori Amos | 8/22/1963 | Thuy Trang | 12/14/1973 |
| Zina Garrison | 11/16/1963 | Johnny Galecki | 4/30/1975 |
| Veronica Zenner | 11/16/1963 | Elisabeth Hasselbeck | 5/28/1977 |
| Cynthia Gibb | 12/14/1963 | Oksana Baiul | 11/16/1977 |
| Christa Miller | 5/28/1964 | Michael Faustino | 11/16/1979 |
| Barry Bonds | 7/24/1964 | Monica Keena | 5/28/1980 |
| Dwight Gooden | 11/16/1964 | Kirsten Dunst | 4/30/1982 |
| Nuno Bettencourt | 9/20/1966 | Anna Paquin | 7/24/1982 |
| Layne Staley | 8/22/1967 | Nathaniel Houseman | |
| Gunnar Nelson | 9/20/1967 |    Davis | 10/18/1995 |

# *Four of Diamonds*

You are the Four of Diamonds! Solid values are something you possess naturally. You know what you want and what everything is worth to you. You are a great money manager and could even explore that as a profession. You are an organizer of business and finances. Though this number makes you somewhat security oriented, as all Fours are, you are the most restless of the Fours. You long to travel, to see the world. Unfortunately you probably will not get the full opportunity to do so until later in life. The reason—work Karma! It is your Karma to work, and to work hard. I know that you probably wish that wasn't the case. You dream of a life that is easier. But some would call you lazy. And whenever you try to find an easy way out, it always backfires. For example, some 4♦ women think that marrying a rich guy will solve all their problems, only to discover that they become sort of a hired hand to their husbands.

There is no easy way out, but there is a solution—hard work. The more a 4♦ works, the better their life will get. And of course, they can achieve great wealth and notoriety. If you notice, many of the celebrity 4♦ achieved their success through determination and hard work.

# Four of Diamonds

Marriage and romance is a hard spot for many 4♦. Look at Whitney Houston and Roseanne Arnold. Again, it comes down to their perspective. 4♦ dream of an ideal love match, and their qualifications are very high in that department. But in their quest for perfection, they are prone to overlook the faults of their suitors and end up in a relationship of struggle or abuse. Just as in your careers, you must approach love with the willingness to work on it. No relationship will solve your problems, but you can find a relationship that will help you build the perfect dream life you desire. This card has one of the unusual matches rarely found among the cards. J♣ love 4♦ and when they mate, it is often for life, and a good match to boot. Jennifer Garner (4♦) and Ben Affleck (J♣) are an example of this pairing. But you will find many great marriages are made from this pairing.

The last years of life for the 4♦ are the reward years. They are free to travel, have plenty of money, and are popular among their peer group. Having put in the prerequisite hard work, they now enjoy the fruits of their labor.

Many 4♦ show us just how rewarding a life of determination can be.

**Some of the best 4♦ marriages happen with:**
J♣, 3♦, 5♦, 2♠, 4♥, 8♥, and 5♥

**The hottest sex happens with:**
A♦, 7♦, 6♣, K♣, 8♠, Q♥, 9♣, and 9♥

**Your marriageability is:**
Very good. This is something you were made for.

**Affirmation for you:**
My life is productive and fulfilling because I choose to make it that way through my own efforts.

| Famous 4♦ Birth Card people | |
| --- | --- |
| Yul Brynner | 7/11/1920 |
| Charles Bronson | 11/3/1921 |
| Harry Reasoner | 4/17/1923 |
| Richard Avedon | 5/15/1923 |
| Sam Peckinpah | 2/21/1925 |
| Anthony Shaffer | 5/15/1926 |
| Peter Shaffer | 5/15/1926 |
| Paul Lynde | 6/13/1926 |
| Erma Bobeck | 2/21/1927 |
| Robert Shaw | 8/9/1927 |
| Jasper Johns | 5/15/1930 |
| Tab Hunter | 7/11/1931 |
| Chita Rivera | 1/23/1933 |
| Philip Roth | 3/19/1933 |
| Ken Berry | 11/3/1933 |
| Michael Dukakis | 11/3/1933 |

# Four of Diamonds

| | |
|---|---|
| Rue McClanahan | 2/21/1934 |
| Don Kirshner | 4/17/1934 |
| Giorgio Armani | 7/11/1934 |
| Angelo Buono | 10/5/1934 |
| Renee Taylor | 3/19/1935 |
| Woody Allen | 12/1/1935 |
| Barbara Jordan | 2/21/1936 |
| Ursula Andress | 3/19/1936 |
| Anna Maria Alberghetti | 5/15/1936 |
| Buddy Holly | 9/7/1936 |
| Lou Rawls | 12/1/1936 |
| Daffy Duck | 4/17/1937 |
| Madeleine Albright | 5/15/1937 |
| Trini Lopez | 5/15/1937 |
| John Phillip Law | 9/7/1937 |
| Barry Switzer | 10/5/1937 |
| Lee Trevino | 12/1/1939 |
| Richard Pryor | 12/1/1940 |
| David Steinberg | 8/9/1942 |
| David Geffen | 2/21/1943 |
| Malcolm McDowell | 6/13/1943 |
| Steve Miller | 10/5/1943 |
| Rutger Hauer | 1/23/1944 |
| Tyne Daly | 2/21/1944 |
| Sam Elliot | 8/9/1944 |
| Bette Midler | 12/1/1945 |
| Tricia Nixon-Cox | 2/21/1946 |
| Alan Rickman | 2/21/1946 |
| Ruth Pointer | 3/19/1946 |
| Shadoe Stevens | 11/3/1946 |
| Glenn Close | 3/19/1947 |
| Jonathan Katz | 12/1/1947 |
| Anita Pointer | 1/23/1948 |
| Brian Eno | 5/15/1948 |
| Lulu | 11/3/1948 |
| Jerry Harrison | 2/21/1949 |
| Gloria Gaynor | 9/7/1949 |
| Mike Evans | 11/3/1949 |

# Four of Diamonds

| | | | | |
|---|---|---|---|---|
| Larry Holmes | 11/3/1949 | | Ally Sheedy | 6/13/1962 |
| Richard Dean Anderson | 1/23/1950 | | Gail O'Grady | 1/23/1963 |
| Olivia Hussey | 4/17/1951 | | William Baldwin | 2/21/1963 |
| Chazz Palminteri | 5/15/1951 | | Whitney Houston | 8/9/1963 |
| Richard Thomas | 6/13/1951 | | Eazy-E | 9/7/1963 |
| Chrissie Hynde | 9/7/1951 | | Mariska Hargitay | 1/23/1964 |
| Julie Kavner | 9/7/1951 | | Brett Hull | 8/9/1964 |
| Treat Williams | 12/1/1951 | | Debbe Dunning | 7/11/1966 |
| Laura Proctor | 9/7/1952 | | Liz Phair | 4/17/1967 |
| Roseanne Arnold/Barr | 11/3/1952 | | Andy Ashby | 7/11/1967 |
| Christine Ebersole | 2/21/1953 | | Deion Sanders | 8/9/1967 |
| Ricky Wilson | 3/19/1953 | | Guy Pearce | 10/5/1967 |
| George Brett | 5/15/1953 | | Gillian Anderson | 8/9/1968 |
| Tim Allen | 6/13/1953 | | Eric Bana | 8/9/1968 |
| Leon Spinks | 7/11/1953 | | Emmitt Smith | 5/15/1969 |
| Kate Capshaw | 11/3/1953 | | Angie Everhart | 9/7/1969 |
| Kathy Kinney | 11/3/1953 | | Gert Bettens | 3/19/1970 |
| Dennis Miller | 11/3/1953 | | Rivers Cuomo | 6/13/1970 |
| Corbin Bernsen | 9/7/1954 | | Josie Bissett | 10/5/1970 |
| Bob Geldof | 10/5/1954 | | Jennifer Garner | 4/17/1972 |
| Adam Ant | 11/3/1954 | | Tiffani-Amber Thiessen | 1/23/1974 |
| Bruce Willis | 3/19/1955 | | Victoria Beckham | 4/17/1974 |
| Sela Ward | 7/11/1956 | | Lil' Kim | 7/11/1975 |
| Princess Caroline | 1/23/1957 | | Kate Winslet | 10/5/1975 |
| Peter Murphy | 7/11/1957 | | Rachel Blanchard | 3/19/1976 |
| Melanie Griffith | 8/9/1957 | | Devon Sawa | 9/7/1978 |
| Mary Chapin Carpenter | 2/21/1958 | | Jennifer Love Hewitt | 2/21/1979 |
| Amanda Bearse | 8/9/1958 | | Michelle Williams | 12/1/1980 |
| Richie Sambora | 7/11/1959 | | Jamie-Lynn Sigler | 5/15/1981 |
| Suzanne Vega | 7/11/1959 | | Geoffrey Wigdor | 1/23/1982 |
| Kurtis Blow | 8/9/1959 | | Ashley Olsen | 6/13/1986 |
| Daniel Baldwin | 10/5/1960 | | Mary-Kate Olsen | 6/13/1986 |
| Carol Alt | 12/1/1960 | | Destry Allyn Spielberg | 12/1/19961 |
| Kari Michaelsen | 11/3/1961 | | | |

# Four of Spades

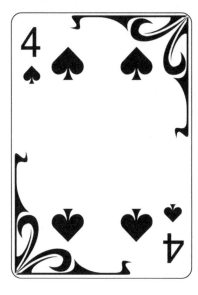

You are the Four of Spades! You are one of the more serious "worker cards." Indeed, your work will always encompass a large part of your life energy. You are organized, highly intelligent, and of course, a hard worker. You may be a workaholic! Learning to balance work and other areas of life harmoniously is important for you. The main thing about you is why you may be working as hard as you do. And you must ask yourself, are you working hard or working smart? You certainly have the intelligence to make smart choices, but there is the possibility with this card that much of your decision-making regarding your livelihood stems from an inner sense of lack. This is probably your biggest challenge in life, to first realize the inner sense of poverty that you may have and then to correct it. Other than that one thing, your life path is one of the more fortunate in the deck, and most things should come to you without too much struggle and effort. Many 4♠ do not ever acknowledge their many gifts because they get mired in the day-to-day struggles of life.

You are also a homemaker and care about the stability and security of your life more than most. You would love to

# Four of Spades

build your life like a solid brick house, one brick at a time, and develop it into your personal castle and refuge. In addition to financial security, you enjoy the security of the people who are closest to you. You might just be the focal point of a large family; you are certainly a person who values family and home the most. And you will do whatever it takes to keep that going. You also enjoy your circle of friends and acquaintances and are considered popular.

You are very marriageable and would prefer to marry someone who is financially successful. You enjoy being friends with people of means, as well. You prefer a mate who is intelligent so that the two of you can have deeper discussions.

Though you are often found working a traditional job, there is an artist hidden within you, a person who is creative and not so encumbered by routine and responsibility. At some point in your life, you will face this other side of yourself and make the transformation to a more free and creative life.

There are only a few birthdays for your Birth Card, so there are fewer

people than with other cards. 4♠ are found in all walks of life and always make a valuable contribution to their family, friends, and society in general.

**Some of the best 4♠ marriages happen with:**
10♥, J♣, 6♦, 9♣, 5♠, 4♦, 3♠, and J♦

**The hottest sex happens with:**
7♠, 8♥, A♠, 2♣, Q♣, 10♦, 9♣, 6♦, 8♠, K♣, J♠, and 7♣

**Your marriageability is:**
As good as it gets. You are the poster child for marriage.

**Affirmation for you:**
I am the worker and organizer. I use my brilliant mind to create structure and stability and peace around me.

| Famous 4♠ Birth Card people | |
|---|---|
| Ed Mc Mahon | 3/6/1923 |
| Audrey Meadows | 2/8/1924 |
| Jack Lemmon | 2/8/1925 |
| Alan Greenspan | 3/6/1926 |
| Maya Angelou | 4/4/1928 |
| James Dean | 2/8/1931 |
| Anthony Perkins | 4/4/1932 |
| Willie McCovey | 1/10/1938 |
| A. Bartlett Giamatti | 4/4/1938 |
| David Horowitz | 1/10/1939 |
| Sal Mineo | 1/10/1939 |

# *Four of Spades*

| | |
|---|---|
| Ted Koppel | 2/8/1940 |
| Nick Nolte | 2/8/1940 |
| Willie Stargell | 3/6/1940 |
| Kitty Kelley | 4/4/1942 |
| Jim Croce | 1/10/1943 |
| Frank Sinatra Jr. | 1/10/1944 |
| Rod Stewart | 1/10/1945 |
| Caroline McWilliams | 4/4/1945 |
| Bianca Jagger | 5/2/1945 |
| Craig T. Nelson | 4/4/1946 |
| Lesley Gore | 5/2/1946 |
| Rob Reiner | 3/6/1947 |
| Jo Ann Pflug | 5/2/1947 |
| Larry Gatlin | 5/2/1948 |
| George Foreman | 1/10/1949 |
| Linda Lovelace | 1/10/1949 |
| Christine Lahti | 4/4/1950 |
| Stedman Graham | 3/6/1951 |
| Christine Baranski | 5/2/1952 |
| Pat Benetar | 1/10/1953 |
| Mary Steenburgen | 2/8/1953 |
| David E. Kelley | 4/4/1956 |
| Tom Arnold | 3/6/1959 |
| Elizabeth Berridge | 5/2/1962 |
| Graham Norton | 4/4/1963 |
| Robert Downey Jr. | 4/4/1965 |
| Lyle Menendez | 1/10/1968 |
| Nancy McKeon | 4/4/1968 |
| Shaquille O'Neal | 3/6/1972 |
| Dwayne Johnson | 5/2/1972 |
| Seth Green | 2/8/1974 |
| David Beckham | 5/2/1975 |
| Heath Ledger | 4/4/1979 |
| Sarah Hughes | 5/2/1985 |

# The Fives

Five is one of the most important of all the numbers because it is what many call "the number of man." Five, more than any other number, symbolizes our race and the characteristics of those of us living here on Earth. It is no accident that we have five fingers on each hand and that there are five visible (to the naked eye) planets in our sky at night. Even the Great Pyramid of Giza, which to this day is the only man-made object that is discernable to those orbiting our planet, has five points. Perhaps its creators intended it to be a sign to any galactic travelers that those living on this particular planet are a Five-like race.

Five is the number of adventure and of seeking new experiences in the realm of duality. The Five constantly seeks to expand itself and to discover what else lies beyond the security of home. We, as a race of beings, have a dominant theme of constantly exploring different experiences and forms of personal expression. We are constantly in motion. Each generation seeks to improve on their parents' generation. Improvement and progress are words dear to the heart of our planet, but especially to Five people. It is interesting to conceive of a planet of beings with a different number as their base. What about a planet of Fours, whose main concern was security? Though your Birth Card may be a Four or a Two, you exhibit many Five characteristics just by the virtue of being human.

Since we are all Fives on one level already, what happens when you are also a Five Birth Card? Fives have a more or less exaggerated version of the Five energy. In many cases, Five Birth Cards exhibit such an extreme example of the quest for new experiences that it is difficult for those around them to understand their motives. Fives will often take great risks and endure hardships, all in the name of adventure. Whatever they are doing in their lives, regardless of what their motivations may seem to be, their true motivation is that of gathering new experiences, ideas, relationships, and value systems. They are explorers with an insatiable thirst to find out what lies beyond the horizon.

In general, Fives do better with occupations that afford travel and variety. Travel brings opportunities to meet new people and be exposed to entirely new situations and customs, which all Fives love and appreciate. Even if they are in one job for a while, they will be progressive and try to take it into new directions.

Sales in one form or another seems to be a common Five occupation. There is something about their desire to understand and experience everything that makes them great salespeople. They seem to be able to relate to almost everyone on their own level, making them feel at ease and understood. These are some of the most important ingredients of a successful sales-person. Sales also fits them because it usually affords them the freedom to create their own schedules.

Being a Five means a great deal of discontentedness and restlessness. Unlike other cards, even the odd-numbered ones, these people will often just get up and leave or move to a new location when a restless urge overtakes them. Though they vary from person to person, many of them are wanderers and often feel as though they have no real home. Home is the domain of the Four, remember, and the Five is the number which evolved out of the Four. For Fives, to seek security would be like going backwards in their evolution. The Five is always seeking to leave the comfort and security of the known. To a Five, settling down into a normal home life can seem like a prison. Freedom is the most important word in their vocabulary. If anything seems to hamper their freedom, they will usually rebel or simply leave. Commitments in personal relationships may also seem to hamper their freedom, and this is why Fives as a group are some of the least marriageable of all the cards. They may actually live with a person for a number of years without any formal commitments or contracts. Some of them do get married, of course, but the usual expression of the Five always leaves some options open. The people they are most attracted to are usually the other cards that dislike commitments as well, such as Threes, the Q♣ and Q♦, for example. The question for a Five in relationship may be, "Can one person truly satisfy my need for a well-rounded experience in the love department?" More often than not the answer is no.

For a Five to be happy, they must fully accept who they are. To go from one job, relationship, or living situation to another, over and over again, is not what our society considers especially honorable. It often leaves the person feeling insecure as well, because no one thing was pursued long enough to make a success of it. This can create an inner conflict with the Five person, many of whom also have urges for financial or romantic security. These urges conflict directly with Five energy and thus we find that many Fives are constantly in conflict within. The happiest Fives are those who claim their birthright and understand that this world is nothing more than something for them to explore. Nothing is as important as what they are learning and getting from their experiences. Five in its highest expression is the number of wisdom. Wisdom only comes through direct experience, and if we talk to a Five, we are talking to someone who has "been there, done that."

# *Five of Hearts*

You are the Five of Hearts! Yours is a restless card that makes you someone who loves to travel and who seeks new adventures whenever possible. This card could also change home locations frequently. Some 5♥ take this restlessness to extremes—they could be called "Calamity Janes" due to the many frequent adventures and misadventures they have. But there are others whose restlessness shows up simply as an ongoing dissatisfaction with their location and circle of friends but who choose not to act on it as impetuously as others.

Regardless of what kind of restlessness you possess, you are clearly here to gain experiences in life. And that urge to gather new experiences is so great that others may not understand your choices, your life, your relationships, or the things you choose to do. There is certainly a fair amount of uncertainty in your card and a changeableness that keeps you moving forward from one experience to the next, and sometimes from one relationship to the next.

You have a gift for sales and promotions, and any work that involves travel will make you very happy. You

# Five of Hearts

have a very creative mind and really could excel in many creative and artistic fields, such as writing. If you are not being creative and self-expressive to some extent, you will probably be bored or miserable. Try not to let your worries about money cause you to take jobs that go against your grain. Instead, use your creative gifts to create wonderful avenues for you to share those gifts with others.

As much as you might be concerned about money sometimes, you are very generous and often just give things away. Your card is surrounded by spiritual energies, and the more in touch you become with those parts of yourself, the happier you will be.

You are restless in love. Many 5♥ will not marry or just try it once. The freedom implied in your number is expressed mostly through relationships. 5♥ will marry, but this is just so they can experience what it is like. Their nature is to be moving forward all the time, often to the detriment of long-term commitments. You like creative people and you are creative in love and sex yourself.

Through your travels and relationships, you gain a broad understanding of the world and of life. Then, you share that with others, and we benefit from the wisdom you have gained. You are a friend of humanity.

**Some of the best 5♥ marriages happen with:**
6♥, 3♦, 4♥, 10♠, 3♣, 5♦, and Q♦

**The hottest sex happens with:**
8♥, 7♥, 2♥, A♣, 9♥, A♥, A♦, 7♦, 10♣, and A♠

**Your marriageability is:**
Questionable. You will probably do it to see what it is like. And maybe more than once! But are you really suited for it?

**Affirmation for you:**
I am an emotional traveler. I broaden my views on life by the many people I meet and get to know. I am a friend of humanity.

# *Five of Hearts*

| Famous 5♥ Birth Card people | |
|---|---|
| Steve Allen | 12/26/1921 |
| Alan King | 12/26/1927 |
| Louis Malle | 10/30/1932 |
| Grace Slick | 10/30/1939 |
| Phil Spector | 12/26/1940 |
| Paul Warfield | 11/28/1942 |
| Randy Newman | 11/28/1943 |
| Henry Winkler | 10/30/1945 |
| Carlton Fisk | 12/26/1947 |
| Paul Shaffer | 11/28/1949 |
| Harry Hamlin | 10/30/1951 |
| Susan Butcher | 12/26/1954 |
| Judd Nelson | 11/28/1959 |
| Tahnee Welch | 12/26/1961 |
| Jon Stewart | 11/28/1962 |
| Jerry De Borg | 10/30/1963 |
| Matt Williams | 11/28/1965 |
| Gavin Rossdale | 10/30/1967 |
| Anna Nicole Smith | 11/28/1967 |
| Dawn Robinson | 11/28/1968 |
| Nia Long | 10/30/1970 |
| Jared Leto | 12/26/1971 |
| Kassidy Osborn | 10/30/1976 |
| Ivanka Trump | 10/30/1981 |
| Truman Theodore Hanks | 12/26/1995 |

# Five of Clubs

You are the Five of Clubs! I like to call you "the most restless card in the deck." Typically you would be both mentally restless and emotionally or romantically restless. Five is the number of freedom and the number of the adventurer and explorer. You either go on great adventures in your mind, or you travel and meet tons of new people along the way. Travel is always something you enjoy, and Fives will often make up excuses to just hit the road. You have a tendency towards dissatisfaction, but this eternal sense of wanting to leave where you are will propel you on many life adventures. However, it can make all things that resemble being tied down a problem for you. Freedom and commitment are often seen as polar opposites. And Fives usually have some difficulty putting themselves in situations that will limit or restrict their freedom. There is often a resistance to structure and a resistance to authority figures and institutions as well, all of which would seem to limit the freedom of expression that Fives prize so highly.

This freedom urge makes relationships a bit of a challenge, as I'm sure you can imagine. You may want to keep your options open. You could find some incredible loves in your life, but that urge

# Five of Clubs

to keep moving may not allow you to stay too long with one person. This is especially true of the male 5♣, of which Woody Harrelson is a good example, since he is also a Leo. But there is more to the story! 5♣ also have an unusual attraction towards secretive relationships, which often manifests itself as affairs with married people. Even when a 5♣ is happily married or in a long-term relationship, there is a secret love somewhere in the back of their mind. Monica Lewinski is a classic example of a 5♣ and the secret affair syndrome, and if we knew all the secrets of the celebrities below, I believe we would find that most of them fit into this pattern. Many 5♣ espouse a philosophy of love and marriage that is progressive and does not involve monogamy. Some of them will settle down in their lives after a period of rampant romantic exploration. But many will become confirmed bachelors and bachelorettes for their entire lifetime.

You can excel at any work, as long as it involves information and communications. You enjoy talking and sharing your thoughts and stories from your many adventures. Financially, you are one of the more blessed cards in the

# Five of Clubs

deck, even though you worry about it sometimes. The 5♣ has what we call "the Millionaire's Spread." In practical terms, this means that usually a lot of money comes their way without them having to work really hard for it. This can come through inheritance, but usually it comes from their own efforts, but with a huge touch of good luck thrown in. In other words, you are lucky when it comes to money.

Ultimately your life purpose is more about exploration and experience than anything else. You are here to experience all that life has to offer. With such a broad range of experience, you are fairly easy to get along with, as you can relate to most everyone—you have been there, remember?

**Some of the best 5♣ marriages happen, if they happen at all, with:**
3♦, 10♠, 4♣, 6♣, Q♦, 6♥, 4♥, and 2♦

**The hottest sex happens with:**
8♣, Q♠, 8♦, K♦, 2♣, 7♥, 8♥, 10♦, 3♠, and 4♠

**Your marriageability is:**
Not so good. You might try it once. And maybe after you have had your years of exploration you could settle down.

**Affirmation for you:**
I am an unlimited being here to find out what life is really all about through my own personal experiences. I am not afraid to try things I have never done.

## Famous 5♣ Birth Card people

| | |
|---|---|
| Rita Hayworth | 10/17/1918 |
| Joseph Wapner | 11/15/1919 |
| Montgomery Clift | 10/17/1920 |
| Calvert DeForest | 7/23/1921 |
| Christopher Lee | 5/27/1922 |
| Henry Kissinger | 5/27/1923 |
| Sidney Lumet | 6/25/1924 |
| Leo Buscaglia | 3/31/1925 |
| June Lockhart | 6/25/1925 |
| Dick Van Dyke | 12/13/1925 |
| Duke Snider | 9/19/1926 |
| William Daniels | 3/31/1927 |
| Christopher Plummer | 12/13/1927 |
| Gordie Howe | 3/31/1928 |
| Adam West | 9/19/1928 |
| Ed Asner | 11/15/1929 |
| Robert Prosky | 12/13/1930 |
| Lonnie Donegan | 4/29/1931 |
| Petula Clark | 11/15/1932 |
| David McCallum | 9/19/1933 |
| Clyde McPhatter | 11/15/1933 |
| Shirley Jones | 3/31/1934 |
| Brian Epstein | 9/19/1934 |

# Five of Clubs

| | |
|---|---|
| Richard Zanuck | 12/13/1934 |
| Herb Alpert | 3/31/1935 |
| Richard Chamberlain | 3/31/1935 |
| Zubin Mehta | 4/29/1936 |

| | |
|---|---|
| Don Drysdale | 7/23/1936 |
| Wilt Chamberlain | 8/21/1936 |
| Jimmy Johnson | 3/31/1938 |
| Kenny Rogers | 8/21/1938 |
| Evel Knievel | 10/17/1938 |
| Don Imus | 7/23/1940 |
| Sam Waterston | 11/15/1940 |
| Cass Elliot | 9/19/1941 |
| Christopher Walken | 3/31/1943 |
| Cilla Black | 5/27/1943 |
| Joe Morgan | 9/19/1943 |
| Jackie Deshannon | 8/21/1944 |
| Peter Weir | 8/21/1944 |
| Al Nichol | 3/31/1945 |
| Carly Simon | 6/25/1945 |
| Patty McCormack | 8/21/1945 |
| Allen Lanier | 6/25/1946 |
| Michael McKean | 10/17/1947 |
| Al Gore | 3/31/1948 |
| Rhea Perlman | 3/31/1948 |
| Jeremy Irons | 9/19/1948 |
| Margot Kidder | 10/17/1948 |
| George Wendt | 10/17/1948 |
| Ted Nugent | 12/13/1948 |
| Jimmie Walker | 6/25/1949 |
| Twiggy | 9/19/1949 |
| Bill Hudson | 10/17/1949 |
| Joan Lunden | 9/19/1950 |
| Wendie Malick | 12/13/1950 |
| Dale Earnhardt | 4/29/1951 |
| Beverly D'Angelo | 11/15/1951 |
| Joe Strummer | 8/21/1952 |
| Sean Hopper | 3/31/1953 |
| James Widdoes | 11/15/1953 |
| Jerry Seinfeld | 4/29/1954 |
| Angus Young | 3/31/1955 |
| Michael Sabatino | 6/25/1955 |

# Five of Clubs

| | | | | |
|---|---|---|---|---|
| Kim Cattrall | 8/21/1956 | Andre Agassi | 4/29/1970 |
| Mae Jemison | 10/17/1956 | Uma Thurman | 4/29/1970 |
| Kim Sledge | 8/21/1957 | Glenn Quinn | 5/27/1970 |
| Kevin Eubanks | 11/15/1957 | Lucy Benjamin | 6/25/1970 |
| Daniel Day Lewis | 4/29/1958 | Sean Hayes | 6/25/1970 |
| Michelle Pfeiffer | 4/29/1958 | Charisma Carpenter | 7/23/1970 |
| Eve Plumb | 4/29/1958 | Left-Eye | 5/27/1971 |
| Linnea Quigley | 5/27/1958 | Monica Lewinsky | 7/23/1973 |
| Johnny Whitaker | 12/13/1959 | Amy Fisher | 8/21/1974 |
| Martin Gore | 7/23/1961 | Eminem | 10/17/1974 |
| Woody Harrelson | 7/23/1961 | John Rocker | 10/17/1974 |
| Mike Judge | 10/17/1962 | Jamie Oliver | 5/27/1975 |
| George Michael | 6/25/1963 | Alicia Witt | 8/21/1975 |
| Norm MacDonald | 10/17/1963 | Tom DeLonge | 12/13/1975 |
| Trisha Yearwood | 9/19/1964 | Alison Sweeney | 9/19/1976 |
| Sean Kinney | 5/27/1966 | Virginie Ledoyen | 11/15/1976 |
| Carrie-Anne Moss | 8/21/1967 | Linda Cardellini | 6/25/1978 |
| Jamie Foxx | 12/13/1967 | Rose Kennedy-Schlossberg | 6/25/1988 |
| Stephanie Seymour | 7/23/1968 | Katherine Eunice Schwarzenegger | 12/13/1989 |
| Ziggy Marley | 10/17/1968 | | |
| Master P | 4/29/1970 | | |

# Five of Diamonds

You are the Five of Diamonds! People who are Fives are those who have evolved from a long time of being a Four. Since Fours represent security, the Five is the one who has had enough of that and just wants to get out of the "box." Five is also the number of freedom and adventure. Putting this all together makes you a very restless person who probably has problems with things that might hamper your freedom or tie you down. You love to travel and are very sociable, and you enjoy going new places and meeting new people. Some 5♦ will travel for any reason. They will make up an excuse just to go somewhere, somewhere else! This is one of the salesman cards. People of this card can sell or promote things very successfully. Sales work is often ideal because it gives them freedom to set their own schedules and to travel. But 5♦ also have a soft spot for helping those in need, so we find some of them in social service or other helping professions.

Some 5♦ come into a great deal of money without having to work much for it. This is especially true of the Aquarius birthday (January 22nd). Others find great financial success once they settle into a job they truly can commit to. This card is extremely creative as well.

# Five of Diamonds

The natural restlessness and aversion to commitment causes problems for the 5♦ relationships. Either they cannot take the relationship very far or they attract others who cannot commit for one reason or the other. They can, and do, marry. But for many of them, marriage never lasts very long and once tried, they rarely want to do it again. One might say that it is just "not in the cards" for some 5♦ to marry at all. They do have significant loves, however, and they are attracted to highly intelligent partners. This is one of their lifetime challenges, and any 5♦ can overcome this if it is important to them. To find stability—and with it, security—is something they will be working toward, off and on, their entire life.

5♦ are the friends to all. Through their many travels and adventures they come to know how to relate to all people at their level, and always in a friendly and supportive manner.

**Some of the best 5♦ marriages happen with:**
J♣, 3♦, 4♦, 6♦, 7♣, 8♦, Q♠, 10♦, and 7♦

**The hottest sex happens with:**
8♦, 2♦, K♥, 10♥, 5♠, 9♦, 2♥, and J♥

**Your marriageability is:**
On the low side. You can have it if you really want it. Do you?

**Affirmation for you:**
I am a traveler of life. Through my many adventures I come to encompass humanity. I am the friend to all.

## Famous 5♦ Birth Card people

| | |
|---|---|
| David Brinkley | 7/10/1920 |
| Peter Ustinov | 4/16/1921 |
| Esther Williams | 8/8/1921 |
| Sidney Poitier | 2/20/1924 |
| Gloria Vanderbilt | 2/20/1924 |
| Henry Mancini | 4/16/1924 |
| George Bush | 6/12/1924 |
| Charlton Heston | 10/4/1924 |
| Robert Altman | 2/20/1925 |
| Peter Graves | 3/18/1926 |
| Joe Perry | 1/22/1927 |
| George Plimpton | 3/18/1927 |
| Robert Pirsig | 9/6/1928 |
| Anne Frank | 6/12/1929 |
| Piper Laurie | 1/22/1932 |
| John Updike | 3/18/1932 |
| Jim Nabors | 6/12/1932 |
| Mel Tillis | 8/8/1932 |
| Felicia Farr | 10/4/1932 |
| Bill Bixby | 1/22/1934 |
| Jackie Collins | 10/4/1934 |
| Sam Cooke | 1/22/1935 |
| Bobby Darin | 5/14/1936 |
| Frank Howard | 8/8/1936 |

# *Five of Diamonds*

| | |
|---|---|
| Joseph Wambaugh | 1/22/1937 |
| Dustin Hoffman | 8/8/1937 |
| Jo Anne Worley | 9/6/1937 |
| Connie Stevens | 8/8/1938 |
| Pat Buchanan | 11/2/1938 |
| Dusty Springfield | 4/16/1939 |
| John Hurt | 1/22/1940 |
| Wilson Pickett | 3/18/1941 |
| Marv Albert | 6/12/1941 |
| Chick Corea | 6/12/1941 |
| Anne Rice | 10/4/1941 |
| Tornado | 6/12/1942 |
| Carol Wayne | 9/6/1942 |
| Shere Hite | 11/2/1942 |
| Stefanie Powers | 11/2/1942 |
| Graham Kerr | 1/22/1943 |
| Jack Bruce | 5/14/1943 |
| Reg Presley | 6/12/1943 |
| Reb Anderson | 7/10/1943 |
| Arthur Ashe | 7/10/1943 |
| George Lucas | 5/14/1944 |
| Swoosie Kurtz | 9/6/1944 |
| Roger Waters | /6/1944 |
| Tony La Russa | 10/4/1944 |
| Keith Emerson | 11/2/1944 |
| Brenda Blethyn | 2/20/1946 |
| Sandy Duncan | 2/20/1946 |
| Susan Sarandon | 10/4/1946 |
| Hazel Dixon-Cooper | 3/18/1947 |
| Kareem Abdul-Jabbar | 4/16/1947 |
| Arlo Guthrie | 7/10/1947 |
| Jane Curtin | 9/6/1947 |
| Ivana Trump | 2/20/1949 |
| Keith Carradine | 8/8/1949 |
| Snoopy | 10/4/1950 |
| Bun Carlos | 6/12/1951 |
| Will Durst | 3/18/1952 |
| David Byrne | 5/14/1952 |
| Robert Zemeckis | 5/14/1952 |

# Five of Diamonds

| | | | | |
|---|---|---|---|---|
| Robin Quivers | 8/8/1952 | | Olivia D'Abo | 1/22/1967 |
| Poison Ivy Rorschach | 2/20/1953 | | Kurt Cobain | 2/20/1967 |
| Donny Most | 8/8/1953 | | Andrew Shue | 2/20/1967 |
| Alfre Woodard | 11/2/1953 | | Lili Taylor | 2/20/1967 |
| Chris Lemmon | 1/22/1954 | | Cate Blanchette | 5/14/1969 |
| Patty Hearst | 2/20/1954 | | Danny Wood | 5/14/1969 |
| Patrick O'Hearn | 9/6/1954 | | Divine Brown | 8/8/1969 |
| Kelsey Grammer | 2/20/1955 | | Fieldy | 11/2/1969 |
| Timothy Busfield | 6/12/1957 | | Queen Latifah | 3/18/1970 |
| Nancy Glass | 8/8/1957 | | Trina McGee-Davis | 9/6/1970 |
| Deborah Norville | 8/8/1958 | | Selena | 4/16/1971 |
| Jeff Foxworthy | 9/6/1958 | | Freaky Tah | 5/14/1971 |
| Linda Blair | 1/22/1959 | | Dolores O'Riordan | 9/6/1971 |
| Irene Cara | 3/18/1959 | | Shanice | 5/14/1973 |
| Rikki Rocket | 8/8/1959 | | Nelly | 11/2/1973 |
| Michael Hutchence | 1/22/1960 | | Stuart Zender | 3/18/1974 |
| Roger Craig | 7/10/1960 | | Michael Ruggles | 8/8/1974 |
| Perry Bamonte | 9/6/1960 | | Nina Persson | 9/6/1974 |
| k.d. lang | 11/2/1961 | | Justin Whalin | 9/6/1974 |
| Diane Lane | 1/22/1963 | | Brian Littrell | 2/20/1975 |
| Charles Barkley | 2/20/1963 | | Lukas Haas | 4/16/1976 |
| Vanessa Williams | 3/18/1963 | | Alicia Silverstone | 10/4/1976 |
| French Stewart | 2/20/1964 | | Foxy Brown | 9/6/1979 |
| Bonnie Blair | 3/18/1964 | | Jessica Simpson | 7/10/1980 |
| Dave Pirner | 4/16/1964 | | Majandre Delfino | 2/20/1981 |
| Rosie Perez | 9/6/1964 | | Princess Beatrice | 8/8/1988 |
| John Melendez | 10/4/1965 | | Dakota Johnson | 10/4/1989 |
| Cindy Crawford | 2/20/1966 | | Lorraine Broussard- | |
| Jerry Cantrell | 3/18/1966 | | Nicholson | 4/16/1990 |
| Mike Inez | 5/14/1966 | | Sasha Spielberg | 5/14/1990 |

# Five of Spades

You are the Five of Spades! Yours is the card of the adventurer and nomad. You may not actually wander around like a nomad, but in some significant ways you express your urge for adventure, change, travel, freedom, and progress. You are naturally sociable and likable. This also makes you good at any work that involves interacting with people, such as sales, which all Fives are known to be good at. It would not surprise me if you are a traveling salesperson of one form or the other. Just be careful that you do not overextend yourself socially, which is something you are prone to do. But even so, your career choice may reflect this urge to have lots of people around you. You will notice there are quite a few celebrity performers in the 5♠ list.

You are a good financial organizer and have good business sense, which helps you and those you might work for. Not that you would want to be confined to some office job, at least not for long. But you do have the skills when they are needed. You are very giving and understanding of others. You have compassion and are on the soft-hearted side for the most part. Your restlessness plays a big part in

# Five of Spades

everything you do in life. If it is not some kind of adventure, it is probably not worth doing.

This same restlessness can make relationships tricky. Most 5♠ do get married—there are many whose urge for freedom precludes such a binding commitment. Even when a 5♠ is married, the reason might just be that they wanted to see what it was like. Once they get a taste of it, they may move on to other adventures and experiences. You might discover, if you take the time to get to know a 5♠ person, that whatever they are doing in life is really just to see what it is like. Yes, their urge for adventure really runs that deep!

Romantic love is a balm for the soul of the 5♠. They benefit from it in many ways and should never be without a lover.

**Some of the best 5♠ marriages happen with:**
6♠, 4♠, 2♠, 4♥, J♥, 7♦, and 9♥

**The hottest sex happens with:**
8♠, 6♣, 2♠, K♣, 9♠, K♥, A♠, 7♥, 7♣, and 8♦

**Your marriageability is:**
Definitely possible, but it depends on how you look at it.

**Affirmation for you:**
I am the adventurer and traveler. I seek out experiences to deepen my understanding of humanity and life.

| Famous 5♠ Birth Card people | |
|---|---|
| Richard Nixon | 1/9/1913 |
| Jack Paar | 5/1/1918 |
| Louis Nye | 5/1/1922 |
| Joseph Heller | 5/1/1923 |
| Marlon Brando | 4/3/1924 |
| Doris Day | 4/3/1924 |
| Terry Southern | 5/1/1924 |
| Scott Carpenter | 5/1/1925 |
| Gus Grissom | 4/3/1926 |
| Jack Cassidy | 3/5/1927 |
| Judith Krantz | 1/9/1928 |
| Helmut Kohl | 4/3/1930 |
| Gay Talese | 2/7/1932 |
| James Sikking | 3/5/1933 |
| Bart Starr | 1/9/1934 |
| Bob Denver | 1/9/1935 |
| Samantha Eggar | 3/5/1938 |
| Judy Collins | 5/1/1939 |
| Joan Baez | 1/9/1941 |
| Wayne Newton | 4/3/1942 |
| Jimmy Page | 1/9/1944 |
| Rita Coolidge | 5/1/1945 |
| Joanna Lumley | 5/1/1946 |
| John Woo | 5/1/1946 |
| Ottis Toole | 3/5/1947 |
| Dann Florek | 5/1/1950 |

# Five of Spades

| Crystal Gayle | 1/9/1951 |
| Marsha Warfield | 3/5/1954 |
| Penn | 3/5/1955 |
| Nick Feldman | 5/1/1955 |
| Andy Gibb | 3/5/1958 |
| Alec Baldwin | 4/3/1958 |
| David Hyde Pierce | 4/3/1959 |
| James Spader | 2/7/1960 |
| Eddie Murphy | 4/3/1961 |
| Garth Brooks | 2/7/1962 |
| Eric Erlandson | 1/9/1963 |
| Chris Rock | 2/7/1966 |
| Michael Irvin | 3/5/1966 |
| Johnny Colt | 5/1/1966 |
| Dave Matthews | 1/9/1967 |
| Tim McGraw | 5/1/1967 |
| Sully | 2/7/1968 |
| D'Arcy Wretsky-Brown | 5/1/1968 |
| Marilyn Manson | 1/9/1969 |
| Javier Bardem | 5/1/1969 |
| John Frusciante | 3/5/1971 |
| Picabo Street | 4/3/1971 |
| Niki Taylor | 3/5/1975 |
| Darius McCrary | 5/1/1976 |
| A. J. McLean | 1/9/1978 |
| Ashton Kutcher | 2/7/1978 |
| Jake Lloyd | 3/5/1989 |
| Paris Jackson | 4/3/1998 |

# The Sixes

One of the symbols for the sign of Libra is the Scales of Justice, symbolizing that all things must ultimately be brought into balance. This symbol is another way of representing the ageless Law of Karma, the law of cause and effect that governs everything that happens in this world that we know. All Sixes are very familiar with karma and the law. They are all aware of this law on some level and find various ways to integrate it within the fabric of their lives. Some are excessively aware of it, being overly cautious never to do or say anything that will upset the karmic balance in their lives. Many of them are concerned about ever having any debts to anyone that must later be repaid. They will go out of their way to avoid incurring any debts for just this reason. Others are aware of the law, but they feel hampered and constricted by it to the point that they try and slip through life without having to pay their way. These Sixes are irresponsible and continually meet up with problems when they try to get something for nothing, or when they expect others to take care of them. But in both extremes, and in all the various stages in between, all Six people are conscious on some level of the Law of Karma. That is their birth number, and it will remain with them until they pass from this life to the next.

Sixes know about destiny and fate. Theirs is the number of fate. They sense that much of their life is destined because of their actions from past lives. They often wonder about what sorts of things, both good and bad, will come to them through the inevitable Law of Karma. They can be guilty of just waiting around for things to happen, and it is known that all of them get into a rut every now and again. Some of them sense that terrible things may be in store for them in the future, and they dread the prospect. Others sense that something good is coming, such as a windfall of money, for some good deeds they performed in past lives. It is surprising how many 6♦ play the lottery, for example. Fate does come to the Six, but often after long periods of waiting. Their lives seem to go a certain way for a long time and then finally change to a new condition. This long time can see good times and bad financially, relationship-wise, or otherwise. In many cases, they must prod themselves out of their complacency to get themselves motivated to make the next step.

Attempts to change them usually meet with failure. A Six person will budge only when they are ready.

Even though Libra represents the seventh house Astrologically, it is the sign most closely associated with the number Six. Six is symbolized by the Star of David, the two interlocking triangles, one pointing up, the other down. This symbolizes balance and peace. Like Librans, Sixes are definitely peacemakers of a sort. They love peace and harmony and will go out of their way to promote it. But also like Librans, Sixes can be guilty of not accepting the aggressiveness and other emotional qualities that life often contains. They may try to avoid their own feelings and situations of conflict because that would upset their peace and balance. When this drive for peace becomes an escape from reality, it inevitably backfires, and their own naturally aggressive side comes out for all to see. The Six person can be the one who ignores their own anger until it builds up and explodes like a volcano.

At heart, Sixes are fairly competitive, which seems like a paradox because of how much they like peace. It is interesting to note how many successful athletes are Sixes. Because of their balanced nature, when their competitors press on them, they press back with equal force. This is a key to their success in sports and in business, where they often excel. They have a sense of fairness and competition that can bring them success in the eyes of the world. It is interesting that the 6♥ card falls in the Mars row and column of the Life Spread, giving it a double Mars connotation. Though we may think of the Sixes as being the most docile and quiet, they can be the most aggressive and competitive when they are stirred up.

Sixes are known to be some of the most psychic cards in the deck. Perhaps this is because they do achieve enough peace in their life that they are in a better position to hear the voice within. Many Six people become professional psychics, and all will admit to receiving impressions from time to time. Many people who are Sixes have come to fulfill a special and unique purpose during the course of their lives that will involve becoming a signpost to others of a better way of life. John the Baptist is a classic example. Though he himself was not Jesus, the son of God, he cleared the way for the coming of Jesus and led people to him. So it is with many of the Sixes. Some will become famous spiritual leaders and teachers, while others will practice their uplifting of souls among the members of their family or co-workers. It is those Sixes who listen to their inner voice who realize that they are here to bring others to the light. They find that their life has much more meaning than just getting by day to day and fulfilling their personal desires and ambitions.

# Six of Hearts

You are the Six of Hearts! Your card is often called the 'peacemaker card.' You definitely appreciate peace, but on the other hand you are very competitive and believe that everyone should play fair. You see, Sixes are all about responsibility—who's responsible for what, who owes who, and what is fair and equitable in matters of love and relationships. But 6♥ often excel in sports because of their inherent competitive edge. Anyone born a Six will be wrestling with the concept of fairness and responsibility their whole lives, or at least until they gain a complete understanding that will guide their way.

Though very relationship oriented, you are also highly intelligent and creative. Your work will always involve people but you have many gifts, which means that you have many avenues open to you as far as work is concerned. You could be anything from an artist to a research scientist to a counselor or healer. And yours is a fairly easy life path, though no life path is perfect. But much of what you want in life will be handed to you.

In relationships, you are marriageable and tend to stay with one person for a long time, even if it is not working out that well. You can get into a form of relationship rut

# Six of Hearts

at times—some part of you just resists change in that area. You are bound to have one or more destined relationships as well. Your card literally means "love karma" and so you will have karmic loves; that is, you will get involved with those you have known before to settle old debts and scores. Your intuition is quite high, and you always know when you have met such a person. You recognize them immediately.

Part of your destiny is to step out from behind the shadows and put yourself in a place where others will get to see you, recognize you, and applaud you. Let it be okay to become the center of attention. There is really nothing that you cannot do. Your life will be a balance between work and love and will sometimes combine the two. But your highest purpose is to love.

**Some of the best 6♥ marriages happen with:**
7♥, 5♥, A♠, 5♣, 4♣, K♦, and 3♣

**The hottest sex happens with:**
9♥, 3♥, 7♦, Q♣, J♣, 10♥, 8♦, 7♣, J♠, 7♣, 2♥, and A♣

**Your marriageability is:**

Very good. This is not one of your issues.

**Affirmation for you:**
I am the peacemaker and show others the path of love.

| Famous 6♥ Birth Card people | |
|---|---|
| Anwar Sadat | 12/25/1918 |
| Rod Serling | 12/25/1924 |
| Leon Redbone | 10/29/1929 |
| Bruce Lee | 11/27/1940 |
| Jimi Hendrix | 11/27/1942 |
| Melba Moore | 10/29/1945 |
| Jimmy Buffett | 12/25/1946 |
| Larry Csonka | 12/25/1946 |
| Richard Dreyfuss | 10/29/1947 |
| Kate Jackson | 10/29/1948 |
| James Avery | 11/27/1948 |
| Barbara Mandrell | 12/25/1948 |
| Sissy Spacek | 12/25/1949 |
| Karl Rove | 12/25/1950 |
| Annie Lennox | 12/25/1954 |
| Bill Nye | 11/27/1955 |
| Rick Rockwell | 11/27/1956 |
| Caroline Kennedy | 11/27/1957 |
| Finola Hughes | 10/29/1959 |
| Charlie Burchill | 11/27/1959 |
| Charlie Benante | 11/27/1962 |
| Mike Bordin | 11/27/1962 |
| Fisher Stevens | 11/27/1963 |
| Robin Givens | 11/27/1964 |
| Joely Fisher | 10/29/1967 |
| Sean Kenniff | 11/27/1969 |
| Doug Matinez | 10/29/1970 |
| Brooke Langton | 11/27/1970 |
| Winona Ryder | 10/29/1971 |
| Erik Menendez | 11/27/1971 |
| Jaleel White | 11/27/1976 |

# Six of Clubs

You are the Six of Clubs! Did you know that you are considered the most fortunate card in the deck? That's right, the most fortunate card in the deck. What that means is that there is no reason you will not have everything you want in life. That includes love, marriage, a great career, and lots of recognition. You are blessed with everything you need to have whatever you truly desire. You are naturally intuitive, and some of you are extremely psychic. You are guided by an inner voice, if you only take the time to listen. This is important because you might be a 6♣ who is destined to do something very big and very important for mankind. Many 6♣ have become spiritual leaders and other kinds of leaders, and all 6♣ think big when they think about their careers and occupations. It is the purpose behind what you do that is most important, and your purpose will usually include helping the world around you by connecting them with information that can make a difference. You are the card of the light-bringer. If you look down the list of celebrities with your card, you may notice just how many of them there are! This tells you that you, more than any other card in the deck, have

# Six of Clubs

the greatest possibility of achieving success and fame in your lifetime.

Love is also important to you. And no matter what you may think, you are very partnership oriented. The good news is that you have good luck in this area. You may not be experiencing the relationship of your dreams right now, but it is always within your power. Once you are really clear on what kind of partner fits you best, he or she will seem to magically appear, due to your inherited good fortune in this area. You are very marriageable and usually the most satisfied when you are in a committed relationship. As a matter of fact, female 6♣ are prone to an early marriage, sometime even before age twenty. Since both sexes are very career-oriented, your ideal partner will allow you to have that career and will support you in it.

Your biggest challenge is not with your life as it relates to your accomplishments and work but to your relationship with yourself. 6♣ are usually their own greatest critics. This often stems from a challenging relationship with a mother or father or both. Since 6♣ are often so hard

on themselves, they can fight with others who appear to be criticizing them as well. And 6♣ are great fighters! They are naturally competitive and usually win whatever conflict they get into. Others would be wise not to start a legal battle with you. But for your own peace of mind, learn to lighten up and give yourself a break. Life can be fun and easy if you let it.

Though your life will seem to be in a rut at times, like you are waiting for something to happen, your gift of intuition will always lead you in the right direction. Just tune in and all your answers are there for the taking.

**Some of the best 6♣ marriages happen with:**
2♦, 7♣, 8♣, 5♦, J♣, Q♣, K♣, and 2♠

**The hottest sex happens with:**
9♣, 10♣, 3♣, and 4♦

**Your marriageability is:**
Great!

**Affirmation for you:**
I am guided by my destiny and intuition to do great things in my life for the benefit of mankind.

# Six of Clubs

| Famous 6 Birth Card people | | D.B. Sweeney | 11/14/1961 |
|---|---|---|---|
| Pope John Paul II | 8/20/1933 | MC Hammer | 3/30/1962 |
| Jeff Beck | 6/24/1944 | Bobcat Goldthwait | 5/26/1962 |
| Richard Davies | 7/22/1944 | Joanne Catherall | 9/18/1962 |
| Eric Clapton | 3/30/1945 | Flea | 10/16/1962 |
| Connie Chung | 8/20/1946 | Eric Schenkman | 12/12/1962 |
| Suzanne Somers | 10/16/1946 | Rob Estes | 7/22/1963 |
| Albert Brooks | 7/22/1947 | Emily Saliers | 7/22/1963 |
| Danny Glover | 7/22/1947 | Tracy Chapman | 3/30/1964 |
| Bob Weir | 10/16/1947 | Ian Ziering | 3/30/1964 |
| David Zucker | 10/16/1947 | Lenny Kravitz | 5/26/1964 |
| P.J. O'Rourke | 11/14/1947 | David Spade | 7/22/1964 |
| Stevie Nicks | 5/26/1948 | Helena Bonham Carter | 5/26/1966 |
| Robert Plant | 8/20/1948 | Curt Schilling | 11/14/1966 |
| Michael Tylo | 10/16/1948 | Sherry Stringfield | 6/24/1967 |
| Prince Charles | 11/14/1948 | Donna D'Errico | 3/30/1968 |
| Paul Rodgers | 12/12/1948 | Celine Dion | 3/30/1968 |
| Bruno Kirby | 4/28/1949 | Howard Donald | 4/28/1968 |
| Jay Leno | 4/28/1950 | Scott Putesky | 4/28/1968 |
| Sally Ride | 5/26/1951 | Sheri Margrave | 6/24/1970 |
| Sandahl Bergman | 11/14/1951 | Jennifer Connelly | 12/12/1970 |
| Doug Fieger | 8/20/1952 | Matt Stone | 5/26/1971 |
| Dee Dee Ramone | 9/18/1952 | Fred Durst | 8/20/1971 |
| Martha Smith | 10/16/1953 | Lance Armstrong | 9/18/1971 |
| Theresa Saldana | 8/20/1954 | Jada Pinkett-Smith | 9/18/1971 |
| Gavin de Becker | 10/16/1954 | Violent J | 4/28/1972 |
| Yanni | 11/14/1954 | Alicia Goranson | 6/24/1973 |
| Willem Dafoe | 7/22/1955 | Daniel Jones | 7/22/1973 |
| Joan Allen | 8/20/1956 | Penelope Cruz | 4/28/1974 |
| Debbi Fields | 9/18/1956 | Kellie Martin | 10/16/1975 |
| Sheila E. | 12/12/1956 | Kelly Wiglesworth | 6/24/1977 |
| Paul Reiser | 3/30/1957 | Bridget Hall | 12/12/1977 |
| Tim Robbins | 10/16/1958 | Jessica Alba | 4/28/1981 |
| Victoria Jackson | 8/20/1959 | Vili Fualaau | 6/24/1983 |
| Jon Oliva | 7/22/1960 | Sasha Cohen | 10/16/1984 |
| James Gandolfini | 9/18/1961 | Patrick Arnold | |
| Laura San Giacomo | 11/14/1961 | Schwarzenegger | 9/18/1993 |

# Six of Diamonds

You are the Six of Diamonds! This is an unusual card that has particularly unusual karma when it comes to money. This can be expressed in many different ways. I have found that most 6♦ sense, deep inside, that a large sum of money is meant to come to them somehow. And thus, they search for it. And many do find it. In this card, there are long periods of great financial prosperity and some of financial limitation. In the Tarot deck, this is the Six of Pentacles. And if you look at the picture on this card, in the Ryder Waite deck, you see a person holding a scale, dispensing money to the poor, giving each his or her proper due. As a 6♦ your life involves, on some level, the redistribution of wealth. You are fair with money and keenly aware of what is owed to whom. You are also naturally competitive, and some of our greatest sports heroes share your card. 6♦ can be so aware of their financial obligations that they will pay their bills ahead of time. No other card in the deck has this particular trait.

The 6♦ is very marriageable. There are the rare exceptions, but most of them are attracted to marriage and are settled down from an early age. However, this card is sensitive emotionally, and sometimes

# Six of Diamonds

marriage and relationships involve fighting. No one would ever know about their inner sensitivity because they do not show it. 6♦ women often seek and marry a man of means. Like it or not, most of them are highly attracted to men of financial power. They often have good careers themselves, but once they marry the rich guy, they go about putting his money to work. There are some 6♦ men and women who seem to expect their mates to take care of them financially. This often creates problems. They need to be responsible for their expenses and watch their expectations. As you can probably tell, money is often a factor in their romantic life, for better or worse. I was just reading about Patti Boyd, a 6♦ woman who was married to both George Harrison and Eric Clapton. She might be a classic example of all that I have mentioned here. Her new book is just out about her life with these famous men, and she was given over a million dollars up front to write it. She's back in the money again, which is how life goes for many 6♦.

6♦ is another one of the cards in the deck that has an unusually common pairing, this time with the 9♣. These two are Karma Cards, who usually do not marry, but in this case, often do.

The highest expression of the 6♦ is to find their mission in life. This is one of the cards in the deck who has a higher purpose, one that is given to them at birth. If they tune in, they can discover this and from then on, their life is guided.

**Some of the best 6♦ marriages happen with:**
7♦, 5♦, 4♠, 8♣, 4♦, 10♥, 9♦, and 7♥

**The hottest sex happens with:**
9♦, 3♦, A♣, 8♥, 7♥, 10♠, and 10♦

**Your marriageability is:**
Great!

**Affirmation for you:**
I am on a mission to help others by the redistribution of wealth so that all may benefit.

# Six of Diamonds

| Famous 6♦ Birth Card people | |
|---|---|
| Nat King Cole | 3/17/1919 |
| Jack Valenti | 9/5/1921 |
| Paul Scofield | 1/21/1922 |
| Harold Washington | 4/15/1922 |
| Bea Arthur | 5/13/1923 |
| Benny Hill | 1/21/1924 |
| Telly Savalas | 1/21/1924 |
| Lee Marvin | 2/19/1924 |
| Gore Vidal | 10/3/1925 |
| Babe Ruth | 4/15/1927 |
| James Randi | 8/7/1928 |
| Bob Newhart | 9/5/1929 |
| Jim Jones | 5/13/1931 |
| Donald Rumsfeld | 7/9/1932 |
| Roy Clark | 4/15/1933 |
| Elizabeth Montgomery | 4/15/1933 |
| Carol Lawrence | 9/5/1934 |
| Gene Wilder | 6/11/1935 |
| Gary Player | 11/1/1935 |
| David Hockney | 7/9/1937 |
| William Devane | 9/5/1937 |
| Bill Anderson | 11/1/1937 |
| Michael Wincott | 1/21/1938 |
| Rudolph Nureyev | 3/17/1938 |
| Brian Dennehy | 7/9/1938 |
| Eddie Cochran | 10/3/1938 |
| Wolfman Jack | 1/21/1939 |
| Claudia Cardinale | 4/15/1939 |
| Harvey Keitel | 5/13/1939 |
| Christina Crawford | 6/11/1939 |
| Jackie Stewart | 6/11/1939 |
| George Lazenby | 9/5/1939 |
| Jack Nicklaus | 1/21/1940 |
| Smokey Robinson | 2/19/1940 |
| Jeffrey Archer | 4/15/1940 |
| Raquel Welch | 9/5/1940 |

| | |
|---|---|
| Placido Domingo | 1/21/1941 |
| Richie Havens | 1/21/1941 |
| Ritchie Valens | 5/13/1941 |
| Chubby Checker | 10/3/1941 |
| Kenneth Lay | 4/15/1942 |
| Garrison Keillor | 8/7/1942 |
| B.J. Thomas | 8/7/1942 |
| Larry Flynt | 11/1/1942 |
| Pattie Boyd | 3/17/1944 |
| John Sebastian | 3/17/1944 |
| John Glover | 8/7/1944 |
| Karen Silkwood | 2/19/1946 |
| Freddie Mercury | 9/5/1946 |
| Loudon Wainwright III | 9/5/1946 |
| O.J. Simpson | 7/9/1947 |
| Lindsey Buckingham | 10/3/1947 |
| Patrick Duffy | 3/17/1949 |
| Stevie Wonder | 5/13/1950 |
| Cathy Guisewite | 9/5/1950 |
| Kurt Russell | 3/17/1951 |
| Sam McMurray | 4/15/1952 |
| John Tesh | 7/9/1952 |
| Lesley-Anne Down | 3/17/1954 |
| Debbie Sledge | 7/9/1954 |
| Dennis Eckersley | 10/3/1954 |
| Stevie Ray Vaughan | 10/3/1954 |
| Jeff Daniels | 2/19/1955 |
| Margaux Hemingway | 2/19/1955 |
| Gary Sinise | 3/17/1955 |
| Ellen Barkin | 4/15/1955 |
| Fred Norris | 7/9/1955 |
| Diane Downs | 8/7/1955 |
| Joe Montana | 6/11/1956 |
| Tom Hanks | 7/9/1956 |
| Geena Davis | 1/21/1957 |
| Kelly McGillis | 7/9/1957 |
| Lyle Lovett | 11/1/1957 |

# Six of Diamonds

| | | | |
|---|---|---|---|
| Steve Miller | 11/1/1957 | Darius Rucker | 5/13/1966 |
| Jimmy Smits | 7/9/1958 | Terry Ellis | 9/5/1966 |
| Bruce Dickinson | 8/7/1958 | Benicio Del Toro | 2/19/1967 |
| Emma Thompson | 4/15/1959 | Billy Corgan | 3/17/1967 |
| Fred Couples | 10/3/1959 | Charlotte Ross | 1/21/1968 |
| Prince Andrew | 2/19/1960 | Ed O'Brien | 4/15/1968 |
| Julianne Phillips | 5/13/1960 | Brad Wilk | 9/5/1968 |
| David Duchovny | 8/7/1960 | Ennis Cosby | 4/15/1969 |
| Dennis Rodman | 5/13/1961 | Dweezil Zappa | 9/5/1969 |
| Anne Donovan | 11/1/1961 | Gwen Stefani | 10/3/1969 |
| Tommy Lee | 10/3/1962 | Mia Hamm | 3/17/1972 |
| Anthony Kiedis | 11/1/1962 | Jenny McCarthy | 11/1/1972 |
| Rick Allen | 11/1/1963 | Seal | 2/19/1973 |
| Rob Lowe | 3/17/1964 | Neve Campbell | 10/3/1973 |
| Courtney Love | 7/9/1964 | Charlize Theron | 8/7/1975 |
| Kristian Alfonso | 9/5/1964 | Rose McGowan | 9/5/1975 |
| Jon Fishman | 2/19/1965 | Emma Bunton | 1/21/1976 |
| Justine Bateman | 2/19/1966 | Fred Savage | 7/9/1976 |
| Samantha Fox | 4/15/1966 | Emma Watson | 4/15/1990 |

# Six of Spades

You are the Six of Spades! Yours is the card of Destiny and Fate, as well as the card of Karma. Many people of your Birth Card are destined for greatness in some form. Your own potential for success is enormous. You can have huge success, recognition, and even fame in your lifetime. Many 6♠ are called by destiny to achieve great ends. If you are willing to listen to the voice within you, you can find your own destiny. All 6♠ are psychic. They have access to the inner frequencies of transmission and reception. And really, being a 6♠, it is nearly imperative that you do listen. Otherwise you can spend a great deal of valuable time waiting for something to happen in your life. All Sixes can get into a rut at times. They have difficulty initiating new ideas and plans, as if they are waiting to be called into action by some unseen force. If you are to avoid this tendency, it can only come by tuning in to your inner guidance.

You have a naturally competitive nature, which contributes to your success in your occupation. You also think in bigger terms than most people. Why not shoot for the stars? At least you will hit the moon!

# Six of Spades

Relationships are some of your biggest challenges. There is an inner fear in most 6♠, a fear of not getting enough love, and an often-chronic uncertainty about their love life in general. This makes it hard for them to trust others and to really have an intimate relationship on the emotional level. The question is, can anyone really get close to the 6♠? They are actually quite marriageable, but any relationship is bound to have some difficulties. The 6♠s can, however, apply themselves to healing this inner wound and find the fulfillment they seek in love and marriage.

As a 6♠, you may be someone who will make an enormous contribution to the world. Looking down the list of 6♠ celebrities we see names like Elvis Presley and Billy Graham, people who have a place in history.

**Some of the best 6♠ marriages happen with:**
7♠, 8♥, 5♠, 4♦, Q♥, 10♠, 6♣, and 8♠

**The hottest sex happens with:**
9♠, 3♠, J♦, A♦, A♥, J♣, 10♥, 8♦, 10♥, and J♣

**Your marriageability is:**
Good to very good. It's what you do once you are married that tells the real story.

**Affirmation for you:**
I am destined for greatness. I must listen to the voice within to find out my true soul's purpose and unlock the keys to my special destiny.

| Famous 6♠ Birth Card people | |
| --- | --- |
| Babe Ruth | 2/6/1895 |
| Buddy Ebsen | 4/2/1908 |
| Harry Helmsly | 3/4/1909 |
| Ronald Reagan | 2/6/1911 |
| Jose Ferrer | 1/8/1912 |
| Eva Braun | 2/6/1912 |
| Alec Guinness | 4/2/1914 |
| Zsa Zsa Gabor | 2/6/1917 |
| Jack Webb | 4/2/1920 |
| Larry Storch | 1/8/1923 |
| Soupy Sales | 1/8/1926 |
| Billy Graham | 1/8/1931 |
| Francois Truffaut | 2/6/1932 |
| Charles Osgood | 1/8/1933 |
| Jane Goodall | 3/4/1934 |
| Elvis Presley | 1/8/1935 |
| Shirley Bassey | 1/8/1937 |
| Bob Eubanks | 1/8/1938 |
| Yvette Mimieux | 1/8/1939 |
| Paula Prentiss | 3/4/1939 |
| Marvin Gaye | 4/2/1939 |
| Graham Chapman | 1/8/1941 |
| Dr. Demento | 4/2/1941 |

# Six of Spades

| | |
|---|---|
| Stephen Hawking | 1/8/1942 |
| Fabian | 2/6/1943 |
| Mary Wilson | 3/4/1944 |
| Bob Marley | 2/6/1945 |
| Linda Hunt | 4/2/1945 |
| Don Sutton | 4/2/1945 |
| David Bowie | 1/8/1947 |
| Emmylou Harris | 4/2/1947 |
| Camille Paglia | 4/2/1947 |
| Wolfgang Puck | 1/8/1949 |
| Pamela Reed | 4/2/1949 |
| Natalie Cole | 2/6/1950 |
| Kay Lenz | 3/4/1953 |
| Debralee Scott | 4/2/1953 |
| Gary Strobel | 1/8/1954 |
| Catherine O'Hara | 3/4/1954 |
| Patricia Heaton | 3/4/1958 |
| Axl Rose | 2/6/1962 |
| Jason Newsted | 3/4/1963 |
| Rodney King | 4/2/1965 |
| Paul Hester | 1/8/1969 |
| Chastity Bono | 3/4/1969 |
| Kathlyn Bening-Beatty | 1/8/1992 |

# The Sevens

Seven is the first of what I call the spiritual numbers; Nine is the other. Seven in some ways is the most significant. If we take all the cards from one suit of the deck and lay them out left to right from the Ace to the King, the Seven will fall in the exact center. There are seven visible planets, seven days of the week, seven chakras in the body, and seven seals mentioned in the Book of Revelations in the Bible. The number Seven has great significance in the calculations used to create the Yearly Spreads and in other calculations involving esoteric mathematics and geometry. It has always been regarded as an important spiritual symbol and is used in many religions and cultures.

As another of the odd numbers, Seven represents a state of imbalance and a movement away from stasis and balance. In this case, the movement is away from the stability of the Six. Because the Six can represent that state of receiving instructions and directions from a higher source, the Seven represents a stepping off from that place into what could be a scary place, where nothing is known for sure. In the Seven, we step away from the security that comes from organization and harmony in the external world and are asked to find peace and contentment within ourselves in spite of external circumstances. To do this represents a high spiritual state of being, and one that is not easily obtained. Even Jesus said that it is more difficult for a man to enter into the Kingdom of Heaven than it is for a camel to pass through the eye of a needle. The Seven is the gateway to the Kingdom of Heaven. At its very essence, the Seven represents faith.

People with Seven Birth Cards walk the line between the mundane and the spiritual, and they get the chance to experience both during the course of their lives. However, being a Seven, they are not truly content and happy unless they are in the spiritual side of life. When they are carefree and full of appreciation for the wonder and splendor of their lives, they are happy and content. They are carefree because they live knowing that all of their needs are being provided for. They have a direct connection to a higher source that guarantees that they will be taken care of. They have no worries in the world and are actually experiencing higher states of consciousness: spiritual consciousness.

When the Seven person falls back into the material world, they meet with untold problems and concerns. They are afraid of not having enough. They feel insecure and unloved. They worry, and this worry tortures them. They try to manipulate others and their environment to protect themselves, but it just makes matters worse. They can become morose and depressed and, in some cases, develop very negative attitudes about life that seem to perpetuate their misery. Miserable or miserly is a good description of the Seven person who is operating on the mundane side of their personality. They live in a world where there just isn't enough.

Having been born a Seven actually means that this life will be sort of a do-or-die crash course in spiritual lifestyle. The Seven person, probably more than any other card in the deck, will not be able to get away with any behavior that is less than "living in the truth." The ultimate truth is that we are all loved and cared for by God, the Universe, or whatever you want to call it. The Seven person will have to walk and live in this truth or suffer greatly as a consequence. As a result, we find that Sevens often come in two varieties—those who are very happy and unattached about things in their lives, and those who are unhappy and worried all the time. The ones who are unattached seem to live magical lives, where things just come to them when they need them. They are giving and understanding and, for the most part, carefree about their needs being met. They are often engaged in service to others and are capable of great deeds for the cause of humanity. The other Sevens are living in a world of lack and poverty, trickery and manipulation. They are rarely happy with their lives.

So, the Seven is constantly challenged, and for the most part it is not an easy path. But also present are the possibilities for experiencing higher states of consciousness and being. Many Sevens accomplish what no other card in the deck can—spiritual enlightenment and freedom from the cares of the world.

# Seven of Hearts

You are the Seven of Hearts! Yours is the card of unconditional love. Not that you can always live in that reality, but you do often enough to know that this is your destiny. When you are not on the high side of your card, you are afraid that others will use you, betray you, or abandon you. Every 7♥ is a mixture of both these qualities, and the most important dramas of your life are played out in your relationships. It is those who are closest to you that play the crucial roles in your life.

And 7♥ usually choose powerful partners. You have a subconscious memory of having been very powerful in some past existence. At that time, you had much power over people and were able to get your way nearly all the time. But you have evolved beyond that stage and now are learning how to tune in to a higher frequency of love that does not need to control or manipulate others. This is a card of spiritual, unattached love—you radiate the power of love wherever you go. People feel it and are attracted to you.

You have a great mind when it comes to money and business. Most 7♥, like Bill Gates, do well in business and the world of finance. Some become financial advisors. It is a field that should be explored as a possible career. But your gifts make for success in most any field, as long as it has people for you to work with.

# Seven of Hearts

You enjoy travel, especially with a loved one. You are marriageable and faithful. You can have the partner and love of your dreams, as long as you are not too demanding or forceful with them.

Your destiny includes finding a higher purpose for all you do. It involves bringing love to the world in some tangible way.

**Some of the best 7♥ marriages happen with:**
8♥, 6♥, 3♦, 7♦, 9♥, A♠, 6♣, and 2♠

**The hottest sex happens with:**
10♥, 5♠, 4♥, 10♠, Q♣, 10♦, J♥, 5♣, 5♥, 3♠, and 6♦

**Your marriageability is:**
Very good. It will likely be the stage where you play your most important role in life.

**Affirmation for you:**
I am here to express unconditional love to all. I am the vessel for this conduit to divine love.

| Famous 7♥ Birth Card people | |
|---|---|
| Jonas Salk | 10/28/1914 |
| Buddy Rich | 9/30/1917 |
| Deborah Kerr | 9/30/1921 |
| Charles Schultz | 11/26/1922 |
| Ava Gardner | 12/24/1922 |
| Truman Capote | 9/30/1924 |

| | |
|---|---|
| Cleo Laine | 10/28/1927 |
| Robert Joffrey | 12/24/1930 |
| Angie Dickinson | 9/30/1931 |
| Robert Goulet | 11/26/1933 |
| Johnny Mathis | 9/30/1935 |
| Tina Turner | 11/26/1938 |
| Dean Corll | 12/24/1939 |
| John Levene | 12/24/1941 |
| Dewey Martin | 9/30/1942 |
| Roy Horn | 9/30/1944 |
| Dennis Franz | 10/28/1944 |
| Lemmy Kilmister | 12/24/1945 |
| Art Shell | 11/26/1946 |
| Marc Bolan | 9/30/1947 |
| Bruce Jenner | 10/28/1949 |
| Frank Zincavage | 9/30/1952 |
| Annie Potts | 10/28/1952 |
| Bill Gates | 10/28/1955 |
| Vondie Curtis-Hall | 9/30/1956 |
| Stephanie Hodge | 12/24/1956 |
| Fran Drescher | 9/30/1957 |
| Kim Rogers-Gallagher | 11/26/1957 |
| Crystal Bernard | 9/30/1961 |
| Eric Stoltz | 9/30/1961 |
| Charles Ng | 12/24/1961 |
| Marley Marl | 9/30/1962 |
| Lauren Holly | 10/28/1963 |
| Mary Ramsey | 12/24/1963 |
| Trey Anatasio | 9/30/1964 |
| Robby Takac | 9/30/1964 |
| Julia Roberts | 10/28/1967 |
| Diedrich Bader | 12/24/1968 |
| Jenna Elfman | 9/30/1971 |
| Ricky Martin | 12/24/1971 |
| Joaquin Phoenix | 10/28/1974 |
| Martina Hingis | 9/30/1980 |
| Lacey Chabert | 9/30/1982 |
| Kieran Culkin | 9/30/1982 |

# *Seven of Clubs*

You are the Seven of Clubs! The amazing thing about being a Seven, besides the fact that it is considered to be the "lucky number," is that a Seven sits at the center of its suit, exactly halfway between the Ace and the King. What this signifies is that you have one foot in the mundane world and one foot in a place where everything is possible. Most Seven people visit both extremes of those two spectrums. For the 7♣, this means going from carefree, inspired, and illuminated mentally, riding on a cloud, to being unhappy, skeptical, worried, and mentally negative overall. You will experience both many times in your life, and it is one of your duties to develop the enlightened side more. The highs and lows you experience mentally are really the main issue that affects all other departments of your life. Every effort made there will reap huge benefits.

It is very likely that you have a mental gift of significance. It may be the gift of comedy, such as Robin Williams or Mike Myers. Or that mental brilliance can be expressed in different areas, as demonstrated by Bill Clinton, Gene Roddenberry, and Ernest Hemingway. You also have the gift of creativity, and

# Seven of Clubs

this gift is one that is found in great abundance. One challenge some 7♣ face is to control their creativity and keep it from being expressed in dishonesty. It is interesting that the only two people who had any success in prosecuting ex-president Bill Clinton were also 7♣ themselves (Paula Jones and Kenneth Starr). I was reminded of how brilliant 7♣ people are when I watched Robin Williams in the movie *Man of the Year*. He is simply a creative genius.

Everyone who is a 7♣ has a secret relationship with the desire for recognition and prominence. All desire it in some manner and many achieve it. They want—and enjoy—the benefits of fame and money. 7♣ like to spend money and should take some care in their finances to make sure they don't spend themselves into great debt.

7♣ has pretty good marriage karma. They do enjoy marriage and relationships and make great partners.

**Some of the best 7♣ marriages happen with:**
5♦, 9♥, 8♣, 6♣, Q♠, 3♣, 6♦, and 4♥

# Seven of Clubs

**The hottest sex happens with:**
10♣, 4♣, J♣, 3♣, 5♠, Q♦, and 2♠

**Your marriageability is:**
Very good. Certain male 7♣ will want to play the field, but they are the minority.

**Affirmation for you:**
Through gratitude and seeing the glass half full, I embrace a life of great abundance and share my mental gifts with the world.

| Famous 7♣ Birth Card people | |
|---|---|
| Mario Puzo | 10/15/1920 |
| Gene Roddenberry | 8/19/1921 |
| Jack Klugman | 4/27/1922 |
| Hank Williams Sr. | 9/17/1923 |
| Don Knotts | 7/21/1924 |
| Lee Iacocca | 10/15/1924 |
| Mark Lenard | 10/15/1924 |
| Norman Jewison | 7/21/1926 |
| Bob Fosse | 6/23/1927 |
| George Blanda | 9/17/1927 |
| Michel Gauquelin | 11/13/1928 |
| Beverly Sills | 5/25/1929 |
| June Carter Cash | 6/23/1929 |
| Anne Bancroft | 9/17/1931 |
| Rita Moreno | 12/11/1931 |
| Anouk Aimee | 4/27/1932 |
| Casey Kasem | 4/27/1932 |
| Richard Mulligan | 11/13/1932 |
| Garry Marshall | 11/13/1934 |
| Ken Kesey | 9/17/1935 |

| | |
|---|---|
| Billy Carter | 3/29/1937 |
| Sandy Dennis | 4/27/1937 |
| Orlando Cepeda | 9/17/1937 |
| Linda Lavin | 10/15/1937 |
| Janet Reno | 7/21/1938 |
| Ian McKellen | 5/25/1939 |
| David Souter | 9/17/1939 |
| Wilma Rudolph | 6/23/1940 |
| Stuart Sutcliffe | 6/23/1940 |
| Ginger Baker | 8/19/1940 |
| Jill St. John | 8/19/1940 |
| Robert Hunter | 6/23/1941 |
| Penny Marshall | 10/15/1942 |
| Eric Idle | 3/29/1943 |
| Brenda Lee | 12/11/1943 |
| Tony Scott | 7/21/1944 |
| August Wilson | 4/27/1945 |
| Ted Shackelford | 6/23/1946 |
| Kenneth Starr | 7/21/1946 |
| Bill Clinton | 8/19/1946 |
| Richard Carpenter | 10/15/1946 |
| Joe Mantegna | 11/13/1947 |
| Kate Pierson | 4/27/1948 |
| Clarence Thomas | 6/23/1948 |
| Cat Stevens | 7/21/1948 |
| Garry Trudeau | 7/21/1948 |
| Tipper Gore | 8/19/1948 |
| Gerald McRaney | 8/19/1948 |
| John Ritter | 9/17/1948 |
| Christina Onassis | 12/11/1950 |
| John Deacon | 8/19/1951 |
| Elvira | 9/17/1951 |
| Robin Williams | 7/21/1952 |
| Jonathan Frakes | 8/19/1952 |
| Andy Partridge | 12/11/1952 |
| Alison Stern | 5/25/1954 |
| Jere Burns | 10/15/1954 |
| Christopher Noth | 11/13/1954 |
| Jermaine Jackson | 12/11/1954 |

## Seven of Clubs

| | | | | |
|---|---|---|---|---|
| Earl Campbell | 3/29/1955 | | Mike Myers | 5/25/1963 |
| Connie Sellecca | 5/25/1955 | | John Stamos | 8/19/1963 |
| Peter Gallagher | 8/19/1955 | | Elle Macpherson | 3/29/1964 |
| Rita Rudner | 9/17/1955 | | Kevin Dillon | 8/19/1965 |
| Tanya Roberts | 10/15/1955 | | Kyra Sedgwick | 8/19/1965 |
| Whoopi Goldberg | 11/13/1955 | | Paula Jones | 9/17/1966 |
| Adam Arkin | 8/19/1956 | | John Major | 3/29/1967 |
| Mike Mesaros | 12/11/1956 | | Tabitha Soren | 8/19/1967 |
| Frances McDormand | 6/23/1957 | | Jimmy Kimmel | 11/13/1967 |
| Jon Lovitz | 7/21/1957 | | Lucy Lawless | 3/29/1968 |
| Paul Weller | 5/25/1958 | | Anne Heche | 5/25/1969 |
| Anthony Munoz | 8/19/1958 | | Matthew Perry | 8/19/1969 |
| Nikki Sixx | 12/11/1958 | | Zen Gesner | 6/23/1970 |
| Clint Easton | 4/27/1959 | | Ginuwine | 10/15/1970 |
| Sarah Ferguson | 10/15/1959 | | Selma Blair | 6/23/1972 |
| Emeril Lagasse | 10/15/1959 | | Lauryn Hill | 5/25/1975 |
| Lance Guest | 7/21/1960 | | Jennifer Capriati | 3/29/1976 |
| Jim Martin | 7/21/1961 | | Josh Hartnett | 7/21/1978 |
| Chuck Billy | 6/23/1962 | | Devon Gummersall | 10/15/1978 |
| Steve Shelley | 6/23/1962 | | Max Madrus | 7/21/1986 |

# Seven of Diamonds

You are the Seven of Diamonds! This is often called the lucky money card. But the truth is, it is the spiritual money card. It is true that being a 7♦ can make you extremely wealthy. But it can also make you desperately poor. The reason for this is that the number Seven is one of the two spiritual numbers. Success with this card cannot come in the normal way dictated by society. It must come from an inner perspective. In other words, the abundance must be on the inside first before it will manifest in the life of the 7♦. Whether you are always worrying about money or are fabulously wealthy is all in your hands. You can have it either way.

People of your card have extremely gifted and creative minds when it comes to money, business, promoting, advertising, and so forth. It is as if you really know how to sell things. There is no doubt of your capability in this area, and it is usually something that you find fun and enjoyable. There is a part of you that knows that money is actually an unlimited resource. And the ways and means to move it around and make it are also limitless. In this regard, you can be effective in many kinds of work. You are always able to sell yourself or your ideas for a profit. Many 7♦ are truly financial geniuses.

# Seven of Diamonds

The area of relationships is, as with many other cards, probably your biggest challenge. You have a fixed love nature, one that says "family and marriage are sacred" and should never be broken. Indeed, those you love are held dear to you and you will do most anything for them. But your own proclivities in terms of sex and romance are often averse to the same things you espouse. 7♦ will do anything to keep a family together, but often they, themselves, are not really marriage material. It is one of the paradoxes of this card system. Yes, you really want family and home. But are you really a homebody and family person? That is the question you must ask yourself. 7♦ are often very progressive and unusual in the romantic and sexual department, or they attract others who are.

Once you sort that out, you are actually very marriageable and will stay married for a long time.

If 7♦ are role models of anything, it would be that of unlimited resources and the power of faith. They can show the rest of us that there is always more than enough money and love, for everyone, and that the

# Seven of Diamonds

true nature of the universe is unlimited in all respects.

**Some of the best 7♦ marriages happen with:**
J♥, 5♠, 7♥, 8♦, 6♦, 3♠, and 8♣

**The hottest sex happens with:**
10♦, 4♦, 9♣, 5♥, J♣, 9♥, and 3♦

**Your marriageability is:**
Pretty good overall, once you know who you are and who you are not.

**Affirmation for you:**
I am on a mission to help others by the redistribution of wealth so that all may benefit.

| Famous 7♦ Birth Card people | |
|---|---|
| Robert Mitchum | 8/6/1917 |
| Henry Ford II | 9/4/1917 |
| Julius Rosenberg | 5/12/1918 |
| Paul Harvey | 9/4/1918 |
| Federico Fellini | 1/20/1920 |
| Jack Palance | 2/18/1920 |
| Prince Philip | 6/10/1921 |
| Helen Gurley Brown | 2/18/1922 |
| Judy Garland | 6/10/1922 |
| Freddie Laker | 8/6/1922 |
| Rod Steiger | 4/14/1925 |
| Yogi Berra | 5/12/1925 |
| Jerry Lewis | 3/16/1926 |
| John Warner | 2/18/1927 |
| Rudy Boesch | 1/20/1928 |
| Andy Warhol | 8/6/1928 |
| Dick York | 9/4/1928 |

| | |
|---|---|
| Burt Bacharach | 5/12/1929 |
| Buzz Aldrin | 1/20/1930 |
| Gahan Wilson | 2/18/1930 |
| Mitzi Gaynor | 9/4/1930 |
| Johnny Hart | 2/18/1931 |
| Toni Morrison | 2/18/1931 |
| Roone Arledge | 7/8/1931 |
| Milos Forman | 2/18/1932 |
| Yoko Ono | 2/18/1933 |
| F. Lee Bailey | 6/10/1933 |
| Loretta Lynn | 4/14/1935 |
| Frank Stella | 5/12/1936 |
| Johnnie Cochran | 10/2/1936 |
| George Carlin | 5/12/1937 |
| Susan Hampshire | 5/12/1938 |
| Bernardo Bertolucci | 3/16/1940 |
| Chuck Woolery | 3/16/1940 |
| Julie Christie | 4/14/1941 |
| Alan Price | 4/14/1941 |
| Pete Rose | 4/14/1941 |
| Jennifer Salt | 9/4/1944 |
| David Lynch | 1/20/1946 |
| Cynthia Gregory | 7/8/1946 |
| Alan Greisman | 9/4/1947 |
| Steve Winwood | 5/12/1948 |
| Michael Peters | 8/6/1948 |
| Donna Karan | 10/2/1948 |
| Cybill Shepherd | 2/18/1949 |
| Erik Estrada | 3/16/1949 |
| Bruce Boxleitner | 5/12/1950 |
| Gabirel Bryne | 5/12/1950 |
| Ian Hill | 1/20/1951 |
| Kate Nelligan | 3/16/1951 |
| Dan Fouts | 6/10/1951 |
| Angelica Huston | 7/8/1951 |
| Catherine Hicks | 8/6/1951 |
| Judith Ivey | 9/4/1951 |
| Sting | 10/2/1951 |

# Seven of Diamonds

| | | | |
|---|---|---|---|
| Paul Stanley | 1/20/1952 | Dr. Dre | 2/18/1965 |
| Juice Newton | 2/18/1952 | Elizabeth Hurley | 6/10/1965 |
| Marianne Williamson | 7/8/1952 | Stacey Dash | 1/20/1966 |
| Brian Levant | 8/6/1952 | David Justice | 4/14/1966 |
| John Travolta | 2/18/1954 | Greg Maddux | 4/14/1966 |
| Nancy Wilson | 3/16/1954 | Stephen Baldwin | 5/12/1966 |
| Gilbert Gottfried | 2/18/1955 | Gina Gershon | 6/10/1966 |
| Isabelle Huppert | 3/16/1955 | George Palermo | 3/16/1967 |
| Lorraine Bracco | 10/2/1955 | Melissa Rivers | 1/20/1968 |
| Bill Mayer | 1/20/1956 | Molly Ringwald | 2/18/1968 |
| Ozzie Newsome | 3/16/1956 | Anthony Michael Hall | 4/14/1968 |
| Stepfanie Kramer | 8/6/1956 | Billy Crudup | 7/8/1968 |
| Vanna White | 2/18/1957 | Mike Piazza | 9/4/1968 |
| Khandi Alexander | 9/4/1957 | Skeet Ulrich | 1/20/1969 |
| Pat Tallman | 9/4/1957 | Beck | 7/8/1970 |
| Christian Brando | 5/12/1958 | Ione Skye | 9/4/1970 |
| Kevin Bacon | 7/8/1958 | Kelly Ripa | 10/2/1970 |
| Flavor Flav | 3/16/1959 | Geri Halliwell | 8/6/1972 |
| William Kennedy Smith | 9/4/1959 | Faith Evans | 6/10/1973 |
| Greta Scacchi | 2/18/1960 | Jason Frank | 9/4/1973 |
| Kim Thayil | 9/4/1960 | Sarah Michelle Gellar | 4/14/1977 |
| Damon Wayans | 9/4/1960 | Jason Biggs | 5/12/1978 |
| Andy Fletcher | 7/8/1961 | Wes Bentley | 9/4/1978 |
| Emilio Estevez | 5/12/1962 | Da Brat | 4/14/1980 |
| Joan Osborne | 7/8/1962 | Beyonce Knowles | 9/4/1981 |
| Michelle Yeoh | 8/6/1962 | Tara Lipinski | 6/10/1982 |
| Kimberley Conrad | 8/6/1963 | Leelee Sobieski | 6/10/1982 |
| Matt Dillon | 2/18/1964 | John Lee Malvo | 2/18/1985 |
| Jimmy Chamberlin | 6/10/1964 | JonBenet Ramsey | 8/6/1990 |
| Lisa Boyle | 8/6/1964 | Maya Ray Thurman- | |
| Sophie Rhys-Jones | 1/20/1965 | Hawke | 7/8/1998 |

# Seven of Spades

You are the Seven of Spades! You are the card of faith. This one word, faith, has so many meanings for you, and I am not talking about religious meanings, though that could be one expression. Yours is a blessed card in many ways, but your blessings can only manifest if you are living a life of true appreciation for all that you have. You will be presented with challenges and obstacles, and some of them may seem very difficult to deal with. But in fact, all your dreams can come true. For example, look at Alexander Graham Bell. He was a 7♠ who believed he could create a light bulb. After thousands of failures, he did not give up. His faith brought him, and us, electric light! In a similar way, you must have faith in the vision you have for your life, and not allow the obstacles put before you to sway your determination.

Many 7♠ will have some sort of physical affliction. These are no different from the challenges faced by all 7♠. If one leg is damaged, for example, be grateful for the other leg that is working fine. It will all come down to one thing: you must be grateful and happy in the face of conditions that might depress other people. That is really all that you have to do.

# Seven of Spades

You are very marriageable and are naturally attracted to highly intelligent mates. You have a natural understanding of business and finance. But you must watch a tendency to be ruthless or dominating with those around you, lest you push away the very people who can be your greatest assets, both personally and professionally.

For you to discover your inner purpose and pursue it is your greatest accomplishment. The actual nature of the work that you do is not as important as whether or not it is your true calling. Once you are on your path, and accessing the power of faith, nothing can stand in your way.

**Some of the best 7♠ marriages happen with:**
8♠, 6♣, 2♣, A♠, 6♠, 2♠, K♣, 9♦, and Q♦

**The hottest sex happens with:**
10♣, 4♠, Q♥, 4♥, J♦, 3♠, Q♠, 8♣, 2♦, 9♣, and 10♦

**Your marriageability is:**
Very good. You are lucky in this area.

**Affirmation for you:**
By the practice of positive thinking my life is magical beyond description.

# Seven of Spades

| Famous 7♠ Birth Card people | |
|---|---|
| William S. Burroughs | 2/5/1914 |
| Red Buttons | 2/5/1919 |
| Vincent Gardenia | 1/7/1922 |
| William Peter Blatty | 1/7/1928 |
| Gordon Jump | 4/1/1932 |
| Debbie Reynolds | 4/1/1932 |
| Hank Aaron | 2/5/1934 |
| Paul Revere | 1/7/1937 |
| Ali McGraw | 4/1/1938 |
| Phil Niekro | 4/1/1939 |
| Roger Staubach | 2/5/1942 |
| Nolan Bushnell | 2/5/1943 |
| Charlotte Rampling | 2/5/1946 |
| Ronnie Lane | 4/1/1946 |
| Jann Wenner | 1/7/1947 |
| David Eisenhower | 4/1/1947 |
| Kenny Loggins | 1/7/1948 |
| Christopher Guest | 2/5/1948 |
| Barbara Hershey | 2/5/1948 |
| Ed Marinaro | 3/3/1950 |

| | |
|---|---|
| Billy Currie | 4/1/1952 |
| Annette O'Toole | 4/1/1952 |
| AdZe MiXXe | 3/3/1953 |
| Katie Couric | 1/7/1957 |
| Miranda Richardson | 3/3/1958 |
| Kathy Valentine | 1/7/1959 |
| Mary Page Keller | 3/3/1961 |
| Jennifer Jason Leigh | 2/5/1962 |
| Jackie Joyner-Kersee | 3/3/1962 |
| Herschel Walker | 3/3/1962 |
| Nicolas Cage | 1/7/1964 |
| Laura Linney | 2/5/1964 |
| Scott E. Anderson | 4/1/1964 |
| Carolyn Bessette Kennedy | 1/7/1966 |
| Chris Barron | 2/5/1968 |
| Bobby Brown | 2/5/1969 |
| John Hargrave | 4/1/1969 |
| Method Man | 4/1/1971 |
| David Faustino | 3/3/1974 |
| Bijou Phillips | 4/1/1980 |
| Jessica Biel | 3/3/1983 |

# The Eights

"Power corrupts, absolute power corrupts absolutely."
—Adlai Stevenson

Having passed through the challenge imposed by the Seven, the Eight represents a multiplication of energy, twice that of the Four. Where the Four represents good supply, security, and foundation, the Eight symbolizes all that plus more. This translates as power—the ability to effect change in whatever direction they choose by focusing their energies. The number eight, in the cycle from one to ten, represents the point of fullness and the time of harvest. With Eights we see one of the strongest manifestations of their suit, shining examples of what that suit can produce or create. Most Eights are producers and hard workers. They enjoy watching their power manifest things so well and so quickly. But like any of the other gifts represented by our Birth Card, power can be used or abused. Eights are faced with this choice throughout their lives. Power can be used to help others and to create more goodwill and prosperity, or it can become an addiction and a means to escape from inner fears and insecurities.

All power stems from the highest power, and the highest power is that of God or the Creator. If it is true that all things happen only by the will of God, then when we are given some power to play with, we tend to feel as though we have a divine right to its use. However, just because we have been given the commission of power doesn't mean that we have become perfect and incapable of making mistakes. This is the misconception that people in positions of power sometimes have. Instead of seeing themselves as vessels of God's will, they begin to see themselves in distorted ways. They begin to think that they are perfect and infallible. They begin to imagine they are God-like or, in some cases, immortal. This is when power becomes dangerous, like giving a real gun to a child. If an Eight person is not aware enough to realize that they are only vessels of God's power, they will make the mistakes associated with the misuse of power.

All Eights will behave a little like Scorpios, regardless of their sun sign. Pluto is the overall ruler of this element. He is the planet of death and destruction, and this Pluto influence has profound meanings to the Eight person. The essential meaning of Pluto and Scorpio is self-transformation. When the Pluto or Scorpio influence is strong within a person's makeup, as it is with Eights, there will inevitably be some major changes in the person's life from time to time. These changes can range from the way they approach relationships to the way they think or deal with money. We might say that all Eights will pass through several "personal deaths" during the course of their lives. Some part of their personality will die, making way for the new. Like the Phoenix, the Eight person will arise from the ashes of their own burial to fly again with new wings. The eagle is the symbol for Scorpio, but it only represents the Scorpio that has undergone this essential transformation. This will be the same for the Eight.

Eights usually attract powerful people into their lives, people whose power matches their own. There will be some degree of power struggles or attempts to control or manipulate until the Eight person learns that the change that is really needed is within themselves. When the Eight turns their tremendous power back onto themselves in an effort to make internal changes, they access some of their highest power. When the "little deaths" occur for the Eight person, they are assisted by these spiritual energies and are reborn with even more power than before. The new person they become often bears little resemblance to the person they were before. Some people may even have difficulty recognizing them. It is much like the snake shedding its skin.

Eights all share this scorpionic legacy to some extent. They are the people that shine forth with all the brilliance of their suit to exemplify the best of what that suit can manifest.

Because the eighth house and Scorpio deal with the goods and possessions of others, by necessity Eights get involved with the finances of others at certain points in their lives, often inheriting the responsibility of handling the estates of their parents and others. As a rule, they do well with this and can be trusted to fairly and honestly manage funds. Whether it involves the care of the family estate or managing the finances of a family-run business, they perform their duty in a way that is to be admired. The enlightened Eight person stands as an example of someone who has passed through the fires of self-transformation. The power that at one time was turned upon the world outside of them has been turned within and has effected a truly inspired change. They become reminders to us of our own divinity.

# Eight of Hearts

You are the Eight of Hearts! We often call your card the "playboy card" such is the abundance of charm and magnetism you possess. Whether you are male or female, the temptation to use this "power of love" that you possess will always be there. Will you use it to help others or to get what you want from them? It's yours, and you can do with it as you see fit. For better or worse, your biggest lessons in life will revolve around this power you were given.

You have one of the most fortunate life paths in the deck. You have success with relationships and your work. What more could anyone ask? And you could easily become very well known or even famous for what you do. You have an incredible mind. Many 8♥ become teachers, lawyers, or scientists.

In the area of relationships, you generally get whatever you want. However, your power must be applied with caution here lest you forget what really makes you happy. To be truly loved for who you are is more important than being able to get whomever you want. Finding true love may take some time. But in the meantime, why not have some fun!

# Eight of Hearts

Your eventual marriage will be a fated one, with someone you were destined to be with. Some 8♥ choose to remain single and enjoy their playboy status. But most will settle down and create a powerful family. Often there will be eight significant people in the immediate circle of an 8♥. I have met several who had eight children, or who had six, which, including them and their spouse, totals eight. 8♥ can mean "eight loves."

What can we say about you in conclusion? You can have anything you want. So, what will you do with this awesome power at your command?

**Some of the best 8♥ marriages happen with:**
9♥, 7♦, A♣, 7♥, 6♣, 8♠, 2♠, and 6♠

**The hottest sex happens with:**
J♥, 5♥, 5♣, 6♦, 3♠, 10♦, Q♣, Q♥, 4♥, 10♠, and 4♠

**Your marriageability is:**
Very good, if that is the path you choose.

**Affirmation for you:**
I am a healer. With the power of love on my side I can help others regain their self-love, and in turn, achieve my highest goals.

| Famous 8♥ Birth Card people | |
| --- | --- |
| Dylan Thomas | 10/27/1914 |
| Joe DiMaggio | 11/25/1914 |
| Nanette Fabray | 10/27/1920 |
| Ricardo Montalban | 11/25/1920 |
| Roy Lictenstein | 10/27/1923 |
| Buddy Hackett | 8/31/1924 |
| James Coburn | 8/31/1928 |
| Sylvia Plath | 10/27/1932 |
| Eldridge Cleaver | 8/31/1935 |
| Frank Robinson | 8/31/1935 |
| Jerry Lee Lewis | 9/29/1935 |
| Paul Hornung | 12/23/1935 |
| Frederic Forrest | 12/23/1936 |
| Willie Wood | 12/23/1936 |
| John Cleese | 10/27/1939 |
| John Gotti | 10/27/1940 |
| Joe Gibbs | 11/25/1940 |
| Tim Hardin | 12/23/1941 |
| Madeline Kahn | 9/29/1942 |
| Lech Walesa | 9/29/1943 |
| Harry Shearer | 12/23/1943 |
| Ben Stein | 11/25/1944 |
| Van Morrison | 8/31/1945 |
| Itzhak Perlman | 8/31/1945 |
| Carrie Snodgress | 10/27/1946 |
| Susan Lucci | 12/23/1946 |
| John Larroquette | 11/25/1947 |
| Bryant Gumbel | 9/29/1948 |
| Richard Gere | 8/31/1949 |

# Eight of Hearts

| | |
|---|---|
| Roberto Benigni | 10/27/1952 |
| Marcia Clark | 8/31/1953 |
| Suzzy Roche | 9/29/1956 |
| Andrew Dice Clay | 9/29/1957 |
| Julie Brown | 8/31/1958 |
| Simon Le Bon | 10/27/1958 |
| Amy Grant | 11/25/1960 |
| John F. Kennedy Jr. | 11/25/1960 |
| Marla Maples | 10/27/1963 |
| Paul Bernardo | 10/27/1964 |
| Matt Drudge | 10/27/1966 |
| Eddie Vedder | 12/23/1966 |
| Scott Weiland | 10/27/1967 |
| Debbie Gibson | 8/31/1970 |
| Emily Lloyd | 9/29/1970 |
| Natasha Wagner | 9/29/1970 |
| Catriona Le May Doan | 12/23/1970 |
| Christina Applegate | 11/25/1971 |
| Corey Haim | 12/23/1971 |
| Barbara Bush | 11/25/1981 |
| Jenna Bush | 11/25/1981 |
| Kelly Osbourne | 10/27/1984 |

# Eight of Clubs

You are the Eight of Clubs! Yours is one of three special cards in the deck that we call "Fixed." But among these three you are the only one who is of the Clubs suit. So, your fixed quality applies to your mind and your thinking. Essentially, you were born with a set of fixed principles by which you have chosen to live your life. And you are the only card in the deck that has this unique purpose in mind. These life principles of yours were not learned in childhood, though one or more of your parents may have reflected them. They are yours and yours alone; rules that you live by and no one, not even you, has the power to change them. This fixed nature of yours gives you an almost magical power. You can fix your mind on a goal and make it happen. Once your mind is made up, you rarely change it. And for the most part, 8♣ are fixed upon a goal and by principles that are lofty and of a higher ideal. There are instances of 8♣, such as Charles Manson, whose fixed mind is set but without the bigger picture in mind. And even for you, you must be watchful that the blinders you wear that help you move ahead so steadily do not blind you to other aspects of life or factors in life that you need to see and recognize.

# Eight of Clubs

This is especially true in the romantic area. Many 8 , and especially the women, become set in a pattern of sameness in their marriage, only to be awakened at some point to other dimensions of love that they had never perceived before. This nearly always happens because of the influence of a Diamond man or individual. It is one of the mysteries of the cards that we still do not fully understand. A♦ and Q♦ especially are common cards for the catalyst that inevitably appears in their lives to broaden their views on love, sex, and romance.

The same fixed nature makes it difficult when life presents changes to you, as it will often do. Even you must change and grow in new directions at times. And as strong as your will is, it is nothing compared to the will of the Creator, something you will learn, be it the easy way or the hard way.

The 8♣ who is directed in a positive way is an inspiration to those around them. Look at Robert Redford as a good example of this. He almost always plays the good guy, the man who is working his life philosophy against all odds. And many 8♣ have this same aura about them. They are super workers,

# Eight of Clubs

dependable and honest. They are what they say they are and do what they say they will do. They get the job done, period, always making a contribution in their chosen field or occupation. They are living examples of people whose lives are dedicated to a higher purpose and as such role models, we own them much.

**Some of the best 8♣ marriages happen with:**
2♦, 6♣, 6♦, 4♠, 9♠, Q♥, 7♣, and 8♦

**The hottest sex happens with:**
A♦, J♣, 10♥, Q♥, Q♦, K♦, 8♦, and 7♠

**Your marriageability is:**
Great!

**Affirmation for you:**
I am a person of purpose and principle. I live a model life, one guided by important principles designed to make me a person who makes a great contribution to society.

| Famous 8♣ Birth Card people | |
|---|---|
| Chet Huntley | 12/10/1911 |
| Allen Funt | 9/16/1914 |
| Dorothy Lamour | 12/10/1914 |
| I.M. Pei | 4/26/1917 |
| Edmund Hillary | 7/20/1919 |
| Dirk Bogarde | 3/28/1920 |
| Shelley Winters | 8/18/1920 |
| Joseph Papp | 6/22/1921 |
| Bill Blass | 6/22/1922 |
| Kim Hunter | 11/12/1922 |
| Lauren Bacall | 9/16/1924 |
| Brian Aldiss | 8/18/1925 |
| B.B. King | 9/16/1925 |
| Peter Falk | 9/16/1927 |
| Roger Moore | 10/14/1927 |
| Grace Kelly | 11/12/1929 |
| Dan Rooney | 7/20/1932 |
| Dan Blocker | 12/10/1932 |
| Carol Burnett | 4/26/1933 |
| Dianne Feinstein | 6/22/1933 |
| Roman Polanski | 8/18/1933 |
| Charles Manson | 11/12/1934 |
| Kris Kristofferson | 6/22/1936 |
| Robert Redford | 8/18/1936 |
| Duane Eddy | 4/26/1938 |
| Diana Rigg | 7/20/1938 |
| Natalie Wood | 7/20/1938 |
| Ralph Lauren | 10/14/1939 |
| Cliff Richard | 10/14/1940 |
| Brenda Schwarzkopf | 3/28/1941 |
| Bob Dylan | 5/24/1941 |
| Christopher Jones | 8/18/1941 |
| Fionnula Flanagan | 12/10/1941 |
| Tommy Kirk | 12/10/1941 |
| Conchata Ferrell | 3/28/1943 |
| Martin Mull | 8/18/1943 |
| Patti LaBelle | 5/24/1944 |

# *Eight of Clubs*

| | | | |
|---|---|---|---|
| Peter Asher | 6/22/1944 | Jet Li | 4/26/1963 |
| Udo Kier | 10/14/1944 | Amy Brenneman | 6/22/1964 |
| Al Michaels | 11/12/1944 | Chirs Cornell | 7/20/1964 |
| Priscilla Presley | 5/24/1945 | Molly Shannon | 9/16/1964 |
| Neil Young | 11/12/1945 | Stone Gossard | 7/20/1966 |
| Justin Hayward | 10/14/1946 | David Schwimmer | 11/12/1966 |
| Dan McCafferty | 10/14/1946 | Heavy D | 5/24/1967 |
| Dianne Wiest | 3/28/1948 | Tracey Needham | 3/28/1968 |
| Todd Rundgren | 6/22/1948 | Max Perlich | 3/28/1968 |
| Meryl Streep | 6/22/1949 | Marc Anthony | 9/16/1968 |
| Lindsay Wagner | 6/22/1949 | Sammy Sosa | 11/12/1968 |
| Ed Begley Jr. | 9/16/1949 | Salt | 3/28/1969 |
| Susan Ruttan | 9/16/1950 | Rich Robinson | 5/24/1969 |
| Patrick Swayze | 8/18/1952 | Edward Norton | 8/18/1969 |
| Harry Anderson | 10/14/1952 | Erik Schrody | 8/18/1969 |
| Susan Dey | 12/10/1952 | Christian Slater | 8/18/1969 |
| Mickey Rourke | 9/16/1953 | Vince Vaughn | 3/28/1970 |
| Freddie Prinze | 6/22/1954 | T-Boz | 4/26/1970 |
| Reba Mc Entire | 3/28/1955 | Melania Knauss | 4/26/1970 |
| Roseanne Cash | 5/24/1955 | Malcolm-Jamal Warner | 8/18/1970 |
| Paul Cook | 7/20/1956 | Jon Seda | 10/14/1970 |
| David Copperfield | 9/16/1956 | Tonya Harding | 11/12/1970 |
| Giancarlo Esposito | 4/26/1958 | Shawntel Smith | 9/16/1971 |
| Madeleine Stowe | 8/18/1958 | Carson Daly | 6/22/1973 |
| Orel Hershiser | 9/16/1958 | Natalie Maines | 10/14/1974 |
| Thomas Dolby | 10/14/1958 | Shaznay Lewis | 10/14/1975 |
| Megan Mullally | 11/12/1958 | Usher | 10/14/1978 |
| Roger Taylor | 4/26/1960 | Jordana Brewster | 4/26/1980 |
| Kristin Scott Thomas | 5/24/1960 | Sarah Chang | 12/10/1980 |
| Tracy Pollan | 6/22/1960 | Julia Stiles | 3/28/1981 |
| Kenneth Branagh | 12/10/1960 | Jessica Lynch | 4/26/1983 |
| Joan Chen | 4/26/1961 | Jennifer Katherine Gates | 4/26/1996 |
| Isaac Mizrahi | 10/14/1961 | Lourdes Ciccone-Leon | 10/14/1996 |
| Nadia Comaneci | 11/12/1961 | Charles Foster | 7/20/1998 |
| Nia Peeples | 12/10/1961 | | |

# Eight of Diamonds

You are the Eight of Diamonds, commonly known as the Sun Card! And yes, you are special! Your card sits at the very top center of all the cards in what we call the Grand Solar Spread. And this makes you special in a number of ways. First of all, you are born to shine and as I like to say, 'When an 8♦ smiles, the Sun comes out.' There is always something beaming about your countenance. This also means that you are meant to be in front of people, play a leadership role in some way, or to become rich and famous. There, I said it, rich and famous. Paris Hilton is one of your card, along with hundreds of other famous people. Not that all 8♦ become rich and famous, but all definitely want some piece of that for themselves. You are also somewhat independent due to your crownly position. You would not want anyone telling you what to do. Last but not least, you love to spend money. You are the main power-shopper of the deck. Spending large sums of money gives you that feeling of power that you enjoy, but you must be careful not to spend yourself into great debt. Money management could be very helpful.

You are powerful, and you are attracted to others of power. You will

# Eight of Diamonds

have power struggles with them—this is part of your life karma. It's all part of the lessons you learn. But indeed you are responsible, especially about money. Invariably, parents will chose their 8♦ child to manage their estates. They instinctively know that they alone can be trusted with such a responsibility.

Romantically, 8♦ can be somewhat reckless. Though marriageable, 8♦ also have a flirtatious side and a side that can become bored with the same-old, same-old. Many 8♦ are serial monogamists—they have five or more marriages. One that I met recently told me, "I am looking for my next future ex-wife." We laughed, of course, but there was some truth in that. Your life could easily become a series of lovers or marriages, or you could choose a long term relationship. It is up to you.

8♦ are hard workers and demand their due. And, they are worth what they ask. We are enlivened by their presence and inspired to reach our own dreams.

**Some of the best 8♦ marriages happen with:**
J♥, 7♦, 9♦, Q♦, 10♣, K♣, 6♦, and A♣

# Eight of Diamonds

**The hottest sex happens with:**
J♦, 5♦, 10♥, 5♠, 4♣, K♥, 8♣, and 3♠

**Your marriageability is:**
Okay to below average. It really depends upon how important it is to you.

**Affirmation for you:**
I am a person of power and significance. I inspire others and am a role model of financial self-worth.

## Famous 8♦ Birth Card people

| | |
|---|---|
| Walter Matthau | 10/1/1920 |
| Pierre Cardin | 7/7/1922 |
| Jean Stapleton | 1/19/1923 |
| Jimmy Carter | 10/1/1924 |
| Hal Holbrook | 2/17/1925 |
| Norm Van Brocklin | 3/15/1926 |
| Mort Sahl | 5/11/1927 |
| Doc Severinsen | 7/7/1927 |
| George Peppard | 10/1/1928 |
| Johnny Ace | 6/9/1929 |
| Jackie Mason | 6/9/1930 |
| Neil Armstrong | 8/5/1930 |
| Albert DeSalvo | 9/3/1931 |
| Ruth Bader Ginsburg | 3/15/1933 |
| Louis Farrakhan | 5/11/1933 |
| Alan Bates | 2/17/1934 |
| Barry Humphries | 2/17/1934 |
| Donald Duck | 6/9/1934 |
| Cammie King | 8/5/1934 |
| Jimmy Swaggart | 3/15/1935 |
| Lyle Waggoner | 4/13/1935 |
| Eileen Brennan | 9/3/1935 |

| | |
|---|---|
| Julie Andrews | 10/1/1935 |
| Jim Brown | 2/17/1936 |
| Paul Sorvino | 4/13/1939 |
| Christina Pickles | 2/17/1940 |
| Phil Lesh | 3/15/1940 |
| Ringo Starr | 7/7/1940 |
| Gene Pitney | 2/17/1941 |
| Mike Love | 3/15/1941 |
| Al Jardine | 9/3/1942 |
| Janis Joplin | 1/19/1943 |
| Faith Popcorn | 5/11/1943 |
| Valerie Perrine | 9/3/1943 |
| Sylvester Stone | 3/15/1944 |
| Ty Warner | 9/3/1944 |
| Brenda Fricker | 2/17/1945 |
| Tony Dow | 4/13/1945 |
| Rod Carew | 10/1/1945 |
| Dolly Parton | 1/19/1946 |
| Loni Anderson | 8/5/1946 |
| Ry Cooder | 3/15/1947 |
| Robert Palmer | 1/19/1949 |
| Shelley Duvall | 7/7/1949 |
| Annie Leibovitz | 10/1/1949 |
| Ron Perlman | 4/13/1950 |
| David Hodo | 7/7/1950 |
| Randy Quaid | 10/1/1950 |
| Peabo Bryson | 4/13/1951 |
| Peter Gill | 6/9/1951 |
| Desi Arnaz, Jr. | 1/19/1953 |
| Rene Russo | 2/17/1954 |
| Eddie Ojeda | 8/5/1954 |
| Dee Snider | 3/15/1955 |
| Richard Karn | 2/17/1956 |
| Maureen McCormick | 8/5/1956 |
| Park Overall | 3/15/1957 |
| Renny Harlin | 3/15/1959 |
| Martha Quinn | 5/11/1959 |
| Jessica Hahn | 7/7/1959 |
| Pat Smear | 8/5/1959 |

# Eight of Diamonds

| | | | | |
|---|---|---|---|---|
| Fabio | 3/15/1961 | | Mark McGrath | 3/15/1970 |
| Michael J. Fox | 6/9/1961 | | Rick Schroder | 4/13/1970 |
| Tawny Kitaen | 8/5/1961 | | John Wozniak | 1/19/1971 |
| Lou Diamond Phillips | 2/17/1962 | | Billie Joe Armstrong | 2/17/1972 |
| Patrick Ewing | 8/5/1962 | | Denise Richards | 2/17/1972 |
| Michael Jordan | 2/17/1963 | | Mark Hoppus | 3/15/1972 |
| Bret Michaels | 3/15/1963 | | Bryan White | 2/17/1974 |
| Garry Kasparov | 4/13/1963 | | Eva Longoria | 3/15/1975 |
| Natasha Richardson | 5/11/1963 | | Jonathan Brandis | 4/13/1976 |
| Johnny Depp | 6/9/1963 | | Anastasia Horne | 8/5/1978 |
| Vonda Shepard | 7/7/1963 | | Michelle Kwan | 7/7/1980 |
| James Wilder | 8/5/1963 | | Joseph Gordon-Levitt | 2/17/1981 |
| Mark McGwire | 10/1/1963 | | Paris Hilton | 2/17/1981 |
| Adam Yauch | 8/5/1964 | | Natalie Portman | 6/9/1981 |
| Paula Devicq | 7/7/1965 | | Owen Bryan | 5/11/1986 |
| Charlie Sheen | 9/3/1965 | | Mae Whitman | 6/9/1988 |
| Melissa Belland | 2/17/1966 | | Dylan Frances Wright- | |
| Jonathan Silverman | 8/5/1966 | | Penn | 4/13/1991 |
| Chante Moore | 2/17/1967 | | Cooper Bradford Hefner | 9/3/1991 |
| Dean Dinning | 6/9/1967 | | Jett Travolta | 4/13/1992 |
| Dean Felber | 6/9/1967 | | John Henry Kelley | 8/5/1994 |
| Cindy Margolis | 10/1/1968 | | | |

# Eight of Spades

You are the Eight of Spades! You are the card of "power through work." But in truth, you express power in most every area of your life. But in the long run, there is nothing that an 8♠ loves to see more than items removed from their to-do list and goals accomplished. You can handle more work than at least two or maybe three regular folks. You know how to focus and apply yourself for success. You are indeed one of the most powerful cards in the deck. You have the passion, the desire, and the means to accomplish most any goal you set your heart upon. And your work will always be your place of refuge and satisfaction.

Along with power comes a responsibility. If you have not learned this yet, you certainly will. Power must be used with wisdom, lest it become destructive in nature. Being powerful and a super worker is no problem, but challenges arise when you begin to apply your forcefulness to others. Being as good as you are could turn to arrogance and a superiority complex, and you might alienate yourself from those who you will have to interact with. No man or woman is an island. No matter how good you are, you will need

# Eight of Spades

others to complete the picture. The Peter Principle may apply to you: This principle essentially states that super-workers eventually get promoted to management, an area that they are often not so good at. The same is likely to happen to you, and you will have to deal with others and learn the techniques that enlist cooperation and mutual reward.

You have fairly good marriage karma. You are definitely marriageable. Your card indicates a tendency to choose a partner based upon financial considerations. This may not produce negative results, but true love would be a better motive. There is no doubt that you will get married, however. Remember that destiny has a date with you, and that date involves your interactions with others.

You have a sense of purpose and destiny about you. You could easily find a great purpose for your life and achieve great goals for the good of mankind or community. It all depends upon how much consciousness your immense power has behind it.

# Eight of Spades

**Some of the best 8♠ marriages happen with:**
A♥, A♦, 6♠, 9♠, 7♠, 8♥, 10♦, and Q♣

**The hottest sex happens with:**
J♠, 5♠, 10♣, 4♦, K♣, 6♣, 10♥, J♣, A♥, and A♦

**Your marriageability is:**
Very good. You are more or less destined to experience it and learn from it.

**Affirmation for you:**
I have the power to accomplish anything. I direct that power onto myself for personal transformation and outwardly to achieve goals that benefit mankind.

| Famous 8♠ Birth Card people | |
|---|---|
| Joan of Arc | 1/6/1412 |
| Sam Houston | 3/2/1793 |
| Sherlock Holmes | 1/6/1854 |
| Charles Lindbergh | 2/4/1902 |
| Dr. Seuss | 3/2/1904 |
| Clyde Tombaugh | 2/4/1906 |
| Mel Ott | 3/2/1909 |
| Loretta Young | 1/6/1913 |
| Danny Thomas | 1/6/1914 |
| Desi Arnaz | 3/2/1917 |
| Jennifer Jones | 3/2/1919 |
| Betty Friedan | 2/4/1921 |

| John Delorean | 1/6/1925 |
|---|---|
| Vic Tayback | 1/6/1929 |
| Mikhail Gorbachev | 3/2/1931 |
| Tom Wolfe | 3/2/1931 |
| John Irving | 3/2/1942 |
| Lou Reed | 3/2/1942 |
| David Brenner | 2/4/1945 |
| Syd Barrett | 1/6/1946 |
| Dan Quayle | 2/4/1947 |
| Alice Cooper | 2/4/1948 |
| Karen Carpenter | 3/2/1950 |
| Malcolm Young | 1/6/1953 |
| Nancy Lopez | 1/6/1957 |
| Kathie Sledge | 1/6/1959 |
| Lawrence Taylor | 2/4/1959 |
| Howie Long | 1/6/1960 |
| Clint Black | 2/4/1962 |
| Jon Bon Jovi | 3/2/1962 |
| Jon Bon Jovi | 3/2/1962 |
| Jazzie B | 1/6/1963 |
| Noodles | 2/4/1963 |
| Charles Haley | 1/6/1964 |
| John Singleton | 1/6/1968 |
| Gabrielle Reece | 1/6/1970 |
| Natalie Imbruglia | 2/4/1975 |
| Danny Pintauro | 1/6/1976 |

# The Nines

"All good things must to come to an end."

In the natural course of the cycle of all things, both living and inanimate, there comes the time of dissolution, of ending. In the course of a lifetime, we will pass through many such cycles with things such as relationships, ideas, jobs, living locations, and personal possessions. In all these things will be a beginning, represented by an Ace, and an ending, represented by the Nine. Nine represents that stage of experience where that which was is now ending. It is much like our graduation year in high school. During that year, we are still in school, but there is a knowledge that everything that has been will be gone after that year is up. It is as much a year of farewells as it is a year to celebrate our accomplishments. Graduation can be cause for celebration or for sadness and concern for our future. As with all things, our personal attitude determines how each of us will experience it—it can also be a time of great excitement.

Being born a Nine is like having an entire lifetime that is like your senior year in high school. The lifetime of a Nine marks the ending of a great cycle in the person's evolution, one in which much was learned and gained by the individual, but also one which is now complete and must be allowed to fade out in preparation for a new cycle to begin. During their lifetime, Nines will inevitably have to say goodbye to people, things, ideas, lifestyles and ways of communicating that have reached the end of their usefulness in their lives. But whether this lifetime is looked upon with joy and celebration, or with sadness and feelings of loss and trepidation about the future, will again depend upon the individual.

Nine follows the eight numerologically. Eight represents the point of fullness, the harvest season in the cycle from one to nine. Once we have tasted the fullness of the eight and harvested it for all its value to us, we enter the nine stage of death and decay. Being a Nine is sort of like the field of wheat that has already been harvested. There is nothing there but the remains of a bountiful crop.

The suit of the Nine person will give us insight into the area in which they have reached a point of fulfillment. For the 9♥, there is completion with key relationships and ways of loving others. The 9♣ will let go of beliefs, ideas about life and themselves, and ways of communicating with others. The 9♦ will find that things and people they value will be taken away, or at least need to be released. The 9♠ in many ways has the strongest burden. They need to sublimate their will to the will of God. They will have to let go of power struggles with others, as well as things related to their lifestyle, health, and occupation.

Like a person who is moving to a new house and holding a garage or yard sale where they sell their possessions at a fraction of what they are worth, the Nine person will be seen giving away things throughout their life. Indeed, a Nine is never truly fulfilled unless they find ways to give of themselves to others. Many of them take this to the highest level and become saviors of humanity. Many great spiritual leaders and teachers have Nines as their Birth Cards. Often it is the utter frustration with all the disappointments in their personal lives that motivates Nines to take on such cosmic or universal work. In many ways, the Nine is the opposite of the Ace. Whereas the Ace actually needs to be selfish and self-centered, the Nine cannot. Each time the Nine tries to do things just for themselves, they reap untold misery and pain. It simply goes against the grain of their soul's essence. Nine is the second and last of the spiritual numbers, Seven being the first. Like the Seven, the Nine must follow a higher path to be completely fulfilled. And often this path is the exact opposite of what is believed and taught in our society. Thus, early life can be very confusing for the Nine person, who tries to approach life in the traditional manner and meets up with repeated failure. The conscious ones catch on quickly and realize that they are different and need different motivations in order to have a successful life.

Nines can develop strong victim-savior complexes and all of them exhibit this to some degree. Nine represents the letting go of our personal desires and identity and merging ourselves into the universal consciousness. In this regard, the Nine person often identifies themselves with a great purpose—that of saving the world in some way. Instead of just thinking of themselves and their own personal needs, the Nine person now identifies with the world at large. In their "nine-ness," Piscean manner, they go about trying to save people in their world. They are softhearted and gentle and are there for you if you need a shoulder to cry on or someone to sympathize with your problems. They will nurse you back to health and will accept you when no one else will.

However, there are two big problems with the savior complex that many Nines exhibit. First of all, it represents a complete denial of our personal power. If a Nine person is out to save you, they are, in effect, telling you that you are incapable of taking care of yourself. Whether those words are actually used or not, that is the underlying message of saviors of all kinds. Secondly, in most cases, the Nine person has not yet resolved their internal conflict about their own personal needs and the needs of the world that they feel compelled to resolve as part of their life's work. A lot of confusion can occur for the Nine person because they have a hard time separating their personal motives from their universal motives. This often creates a scenario where the Nine person professes to be motivated from the purest of intentions, such as saving the world or saving individuals, when in truth they are often selfishly motivated. Just like the rest of us, Nines get afraid, and some of them thirst for power or fame or wealth. Ultimately their true motivations are revealed, or the person they are trying to save resents being labeled a failure and rebels against them. There have been some Nines who genuinely make a selfless contribution to the lives of others, and all of them experience truly selfless acts at times during their life. It is the Nine's personal challenge to make the clear distinction between their selfish and selfless actions, thoughts and words.

Nines who are accessing the power of letting go that is inherent in their Birth Card are happy and somewhat carefree. They are giving and less attached to people and things in their life. They have a look of wisdom on their face. They understand life as no others can because they can see well beyond their personal identity to the broad picture of the universe. The compassion they exude is real and comes from having consciously passed through many endings. Their happiness is real because it is not based on the acquisition of any thing or person. It is based on the knowledge that they are in tune with the will of God and the cosmic flow.

# Nine of Hearts

You are the Nine of Hearts! Your card is all about universal love—about loving humanity, about giving instead of receiving, and about surrender to the higher will of love for all. Many people of your card find a way to express this in their work. They are counselors, teachers, or caregivers. But others will take it to a much larger arena and create things that will benefit millions. Think of Hillary Clinton, who is so committed to having a working health care system in our country! It is this desire to help the world that brings the greatest inspiration to any 9♥. So, how will you express that?

You certainly have fine equipment to do most any kind of work you choose. You have an inspired mind and a good work ethic. You are also creative and blessed with many incredible ideas. With those elements, you can go in almost any direction. Whatever you do, it has an element of what has been mentioned before—helping others.

Yours is considered one of the more challenging cards when it comes to personal and intimate relationships. Since you have to give away love most of your life, you may feel like you rarely get your gifts returned to you in kind.

# Nine of Hearts

You can tend to be co-dependent and pick partners whom you would like to save—but of course this rarely works. And you are very fixed in your love habits, in the ways you approach love and relationships. There is something very important for you to learn in this lifetime about love, something that will utterly change your life once you get that clear. Don't give up—seek and you shall find.

Once any 9♥ aligns themselves with their higher purpose and finds the avenue that helps them best love the world, there is little that can stop them. 9♥s make significant contributions to our world, all in the name of love.

**Some of the best 9♥ marriages happen with:**
10♥, J♣, 5♠, 8♥, 7♥, 7♣, 8♦, 3♠, and 6♦

**The hottest sex happens with:**
Q♥, 9♣, 6♥, 3♦, 7♦, J♦, J♣, Q♠, 10♦, 5♥, and 4♦

**Your marriageability is:**
Good. It may not be easy to do, but you are marriageable.

# Nine of Hearts

**Affirmation for you:**

I am here to give love to the world. The more I give and the more people I give to, the more fulfilled I am.

| Famous 9♥ Birth Card people | |
|---|---|
| Scott Joplin | 11/24/1868 |
| Dale Carnegie | 11/24/1888 |
| Huey P. Long | 8/30/1893 |
| Shirley Booth | 8/30/1898 |
| Judy Johnson | 10/26/1899 |
| Ed Sullivan | 9/28/1901 |
| Joan Blondell | 8/30/1906 |
| Fred MacMurray | 8/30/1908 |
| Al Capp | 9/28/1909 |
| Mahalia Jackson | 10/26/1911 |
| Geraldine Fitzgerald | 11/24/1912 |
| Garson Kanin | 11/24/1912 |
| Lady Bird Johnson | 12/22/1912 |
| Ethel Rosenberg | 9/28/1915 |
| Peter Finch | 9/28/1916 |
| Ted Williams | 8/30/1918 |
| Barbara Billingsley | 12/22/1922 |
| Marcello Mastroianni | 9/28/1924 |
| Seymour Cray | 9/28/1925 |
| William F. Buckley | 11/24/1925 |
| Geoffrey Beene | 8/30/1927 |
| Brigitte Bardot | 9/28/1934 |
| Hector Elizondo | 12/22/1936 |
| Jim Yester | 11/24/1939 |
| Paul Tagliabue | 11/24/1940 |
| Pete Best | 11/24/1941 |
| Bob Hoskins | 10/26/1942 |
| Diane Sawyer | 12/22/1945 |
| Pamela Courson | 12/22/1946 |
| Peggy Lipton | 8/30/1947 |
| Hillary Clinton | 10/26/1947 |
| Jaclyn Smith | 10/26/1947 |
| Steve Garvey | 12/22/1948 |
| Linda Tripp | 11/24/1949 |
| Maurice Gibb | 12/22/1949 |
| Robin Gibb | 12/22/1949 |
| John Sayles | 9/28/1950 |
| Timothy Bottoms | 8/30/1951 |
| Maggie Roche | 10/26/1951 |
| Thierry Lhermitte | 11/24/1952 |
| Keith Strickland | 10/26/1953 |
| David Paymer | 8/30/1954 |
| Steve Largent | 9/28/1954 |
| Clem Burke | 11/24/1955 |
| Susan Powter | 12/22/1957 |
| Lynne Thigpen | 12/22/1957 |
| Luther Campbell | 12/22/1959 |
| John Squire | 11/24/1962 |
| Ralph Fiennes | 12/22/1962 |
| Michael Chiklis | 8/30/1963 |
| Natalie Merchant | 10/26/1963 |
| Shae D'Lyn | 11/24/1963 |
| Janeane Garofalo | 9/28/1964 |
| Brad Sherwood | 11/24/1964 |
| Moon Unit Zappa | 9/28/1967 |
| Keith Urban | 10/26/1967 |
| Carre Otis | 9/28/1968 |
| Mira Sorvino | 9/28/1970 |
| Chad Taylor | 11/24/1970 |
| Cameron Diaz | 8/30/1972 |
| Lisa Ling | 8/30/1973 |
| Heather Donahue | 12/22/1974 |
| Colin Hanks | 11/24/1977 |
| Katherine Heigl | 11/24/1978 |

# Nine of Clubs

You are the Nine of Clubs! Some call you the sexiest card in the deck—many of the sexy men in Hollywood are 9♣ (Robert De Niro, John Malkovich, Leonardo DiCaprio, Tommy Lee Jones, Sean Penn, and Al Pacino, just to mention a few). And most of them are confirmed bachelors. Like it or not, sex and romance do play an especially important role in your life. They are part of your lifetime plan and can be played out in several different ways. Your card has the highest potential for love fulfillment. But the love we are talking about here is not the marriage kind, it is the sexual and romantic kind. Essentially, you are a lover looking for the love of a lifetime, or to be more accurate, a love that spans many lifetimes. You are drawn to those with whom you feel a special connection, as if you had known them before. People of your card do get married, but marriage was never the goal—they just want to be with their beloved. 9♣ who marry the wrong person will continue to seek that perfect union outside of their marriage.

But that is where the karma comes in. And Love Karma is another thing that your card is all about. This varies from one 9♣ to the other, but sexual/romantic

# Nine of Clubs

liaisons will ultimately take their toll. One common thing that happens is children. Yes, sex makes children! And for many 9♣, the love of their children will compete with their love of their lover in some form. Some may give up their lover or lovers for the sake of their children, and others will do just the opposite. But either way, it is a difficult choice. Others will have magical relationships that just do not work out. There seems to always be something that causes a conflict.

The main essence of your card is one of completion. This is of significance to you throughout your lifetime. You are here to give knowledge and information to the world and also to let go of any beliefs, concepts, ideals, or ideas that may not serve you. 9♣ often have a troubled childhood, with one or more significant deaths connected to them or their family. This often colors their outlook on life and one of their missions is to uplift their mental outlook to higher levels. Others will confide in you because they can sense that you will understand and have compassion.

By aligning yourself with a purpose involving helping humanity, you will find the greatest fulfillment of all.

**Some of the best 9♣ marriages happen with:**
K♥, 9♠, J♥, 6♦, 10♣, 8♣, 5♠, and K♦

**The hottest sex happens with:**
K♥, Q♦, Q♣, 6♣, 7♦, and 2♦

**Your marriageability is:**
Pretty good if you are female. The men have fewer propensities but are able to if they really want it.

**Affirmation for you:**
I am the giver of knowledge and the giver of love.

| Famous 9♣ Birth Card people | |
|---|---|
| Lenny Bruce | 10/13/1925 |
| Margaret Thatcher | 10/13/1925 |
| Jonathan Winters | 11/11/1925 |
| Rosemary Clooney | 5/23/1928 |
| LaVern Baker | 11/11/1929 |
| Paul Mazursky | 4/25/1930 |
| Buck Henry | 12/9/1930 |
| David Janssen | 3/27/1931 |
| Barbara Barrie | 5/23/1931 |
| Meadowlark Lemon | 4/25/1932 |
| Joan Collins | 5/23/1933 |
| Morton Downey Jr. | 12/9/1933 |
| Robert Moog | 5/23/1934 |
| Judi Dench | 12/9/1934 |

| | |
|---|---|
| Junior Wells | 12/9/1934 |
| Francoise Sagan | 6/21/1935 |
| Alex Rocco | 2/29/1936 |
| Philip Glass | 1/31/1937 |
| Suzanne Pleshette | 1/31/1937 |
| Deacon Jones | 12/9/1938 |
| Al Pacino | 4/25/1940 |
| Joseph Brodsky | 5/23/1940 |
| Merlin Olsen | 9/15/1940 |
| Vikki Carr | 7/19/1941 |
| Paul Simon | 10/13/1941 |
| Michael York | 3/27/1942 |
| Jerry Jones | 10/13/1942 |
| Dick Butkus | 12/9/1942 |
| Gary Burghoff | 5/23/1943 |
| Robert De Niro | 8/17/1943 |
| Ray Davies | 6/21/1944 |
| Lauren Chapin | 5/23/1945 |
| Edwin Schlossberg | 7/19/1945 |
| Jessye Norman | 9/15/1945 |
| Talia Shire | 4/25/1946 |
| Ilie Nastase | 7/19/1946 |
| Tommy Lee Jones | 9/15/1946 |
| Oliver Stone | 9/15/1946 |
| Nolan Ryan | 1/31/1947 |
| Meredith Baxter | 6/21/1947 |
| Sammy Hagar | 10/13/1947 |
| Ken Wilber | 1/31/1949 |
| Linda Kasabian | 6/21/1949 |
| Paul Cowsill | 11/11/1950 |
| Beverly Johnson | 10/13/1951 |
| Maria Schneider | 3/27/1952 |
| Marvin Hagler | 5/23/1952 |
| George Anderson | 8/17/1952 |
| Kelly Keagy | 9/15/1952 |
| Lisabet Sarai | 1/31/1953 |
| Johnny Rotten | 1/31/1956 |
| Chris Carter | 10/13/1956 |
| Donny Osmond | 12/9/1957 |

# *Nine of Clubs*

| | |
|---|---|
| Drew Carey | 5/23/1958 |
| Belinda Carlisle | 8/17/1958 |
| Marie Osmond | 10/13/1959 |
| Sean Penn | 8/17/1960 |
| Karen Duffy | 5/23/1961 |
| Susan Hawk | 8/17/1961 |
| Dan Marino | 9/15/1961 |
| Anthony Edwards | 7/19/1962 |
| Wendie Jo Sperber | 9/15/1962 |
| Kelly Preston | 10/13/1962 |
| Jerry Rice | 10/13/1962 |
| Demi Moore | 11/11/1962 |
| Felicity Huffman | 12/9/1962 |
| Quentin Tarantino | 3/27/1963 |
| Derrick Mckenzie | 3/27/1964 |
| Hank Azaria | 4/25/1964 |
| Calista Flockhart | 11/11/1964 |
| Clea Lewis | 7/19/1965 |
| Steve Gorman | 8/17/1965 |
| David Conrad | 8/17/1967 |

| | |
|---|---|
| Joshua Bell | 12/9/1967 |
| Renée Zellweger | 4/25/1969 |
| Donnie Wahlberg | 8/17/1969 |
| Nancy Kerrigan | 10/13/1969 |
| Jakob Dylan | 12/9/1969 |
| Mariah Carey | 3/27/1970 |
| Brendan Hill | 3/27/1970 |
| Minnie Driver | 1/31/1971 |
| Antonio Sabato Jr. | 2/29/1972 |
| Tre Cool | 12/9/1972 |
| Juliette Lewis | 6/21/1973 |
| Jewel | 5/23/1974 |
| Leonardo DiCaprio | 11/11/1974 |
| Justin Timberlake | 1/31/1981 |
| Prince William | 6/21/1982 |
| Anne Hathaway | 11/11/1982 |
| Prince Harry | 9/15/1984 |
| Tiffany Trump | 10/13/1993 |
| Gabriel Jagger | 12/9/1997 |
| Rory John Gates | 5/23/1999 |

# Nine of Diamonds

Aren't you glad you are the Nine of Diamonds?! In the cycles of life, Nine represents the conclusion of a great cycle. Your being a Nine has this same significance. You have come a long way in your soul's evolution and now you have reached the stage of graduation and completion. It is no wonder that many Nines feel this will be their last lifetime. But the life of a Nine is kind of like a yard sale or garage sale. It seems you must give everything away, for a fraction of what it is worth, and that you can have little or nothing for yourself. And it may seem that you usually get the short end of situations in your life—you end up being the one who did the most giving. Giving is what your card is all about! Not all 9♦ enjoy being such givers in their lives, especially in their personal lives. But still, the pattern is set, and this will be one of the most important themes of your life.

The trouble is that on some level you remember who you were before. Before the Nine was the Eight, and the Eight enjoys power, majesty, fame and adulation by others. The Eight is the one who has all the power to get what they want whenever they want it. You will not consciously remember this as a Nine, but there is a part of you that probably

# Nine of Diamonds

wonders at times, "Why am I not as powerful as I feel I should be?" or, "Why can't I get everything I want, when I want it?" You were powerful before and famous and mighty. But you completed that stage and now you must let it all go. You can choose to cry over or celebrate your graduation!

You can feel this inside. Your naturally psychic nature attunes you to the needs and desires of those around you. You can't help but feel what they feel and know their innermost desires and dreams. You naturally gravitate towards helping those in need, and others sense in you a place where they can unload their burdens. Many 9♦ are successful counselors and healers for just this reason. But from your point of view, these same people seem to take advantage of your kindness and take too much in the bargain, leaving you feeling drained or taken advantage of.

Among your gifts are a high intelligence (Einstein was a 9♦) and incredibly good promotional skills. Any 9♦ can make money by selling or promoting things or people. But you have great intellectual gifts as well that you most likely want to express to feel fulfilled in your work. Family is important and you are definitely marriageable. But family in your case often involves a burden to you. You generally take this on willingly as part of the special role you have to play in this life. The happiest and most fulfilled 9♦ are those who have found their special mission in life, one that puts them in the role of the giver.

You enjoy the company of those of intelligence and beauty and will usually attract a mate with whom you have a great intellectual connection. You like smart people!

**The best 9♦ marriages happen with:**
2♣, 7♠, J♣, K♣, J♦, and Q♠

**The hottest sex happens with:**
Q♦, A♣, J♥, K♣, J♠, and 5♠

**Your marriageability is:**
Very good!

**Affirmation for you:**
The more I give to others and the more people I give to, the more connected I feel to my true source and the more fulfilled is my life.

# Nine of Diamonds

## Famous 9♦ Birth Card people

| | |
|---|---|
| Barbara Bush | 6/8/1925 |
| Merv Griffin | 7/6/1925 |
| Bill Haley | 7/6/1925 |
| John Schlesinger | 2/16/1926 |
| Janet Leigh | 7/6/1927 |
| Pat Paulsen | 7/6/1927 |
| Leonard Katzman | 9/2/1927 |
| Yasser Arafat | 8/4/1929 |
| Della Reese | 7/6/1931 |
| Otis Blackwell | 2/16/1932 |
| John Boorman | 1/18/1933 |
| Ray Dolby | 1/18/1933 |
| Michael Caine | 3/14/1933 |
| Quincy Jones | 3/14/1933 |
| Joan Rivers | 6/8/1933 |
| Sonny Bono | 2/16/1935 |
| Dalai Lama | 7/6/1935 |
| Ned Beatty | 7/6/1937 |
| Nancy Sinatra | 6/8/1940 |
| David Ruffin | 1/18/1941 |
| Robert Shapiro | 9/2/1942 |
| William Calley | 6/8/1943 |
| Burt Ward | 7/6/1945 |
| Donovan | 5/10/1946 |
| Maureen Lipman | 5/10/1946 |
| George Bush Jr. | 7/6/1946 |
| Fred Dryer | 7/6/1946 |
| Sylvester Stallone | 7/6/1946 |
| Jamie Wyeth | 7/6/1946 |
| Maureen Cox | 8/4/1946 |
| David Letterman | 4/12/1947 |
| Billy Crystal | 3/14/1948 |
| Nate Archibald | 9/2/1948 |
| Terry Bradshaw | 9/2/1948 |
| Christa McAuliffe | 9/2/1948 |
| John Riggins | 8/4/1949 |
| David Cassidy | 4/12/1950 |

# Nine of Diamonds

| | | | |
|---|---|---|---|
| Geoffrey Rush | 7/6/1951 | Mick Hucknall | 6/8/1960 |
| Mark Harmon | 9/2/1951 | Eric Dickerson | 9/2/1960 |
| Jimmy Connors | 9/2/1952 | Andy Taylor | 2/16/1961 |
| Kevin Costner | 1/18/1955 | Gary Dell'abate | 3/14/1961 |
| Chris Berman | 5/10/1955 | Kirby Puckett | 3/14/1961 |
| Homer Simpson | 5/10/1955 | Art Alexakis | 4/12/1962 |
| Billy Bob Thornton | 8/4/1955 | Keanu Reeves | 9/2/1964 |
| Linda Purl | 9/2/1955 | Linda Evangelista | 5/10/1965 |
| Tom Bailey | 1/18/1956 | Julianna Margulies | 6/8/1967 |
| Tama Janowitz | 4/12/1956 | Camille Donatacci | 9/2/1968 |
| LeVar Burton | 2/16/1957 | Salma Hayek | 9/2/1968 |
| Vince Gill | 4/12/1957 | Cynthia Watros | 9/2/1968 |
| Sid Vicious | 5/10/1957 | Nick Hexum | 4/12/1970 |
| Scott Adams | 6/8/1957 | Jonathan Davis | 1/18/1971 |
| Lisa Loring | 2/16/1958 | Shannon Doherty | 4/12/1971 |
| Prince Albert | 3/14/1958 | Lindsay Davenport | 6/8/1976 |
| Jennifer Saunders | 7/6/1958 | Tamera Mowry | 7/6/1978 |
| Mary Decker Slaney | 8/4/1958 | Tia Mowry | 7/6/1978 |
| John McEnroe | 2/16/1959 | Chris Klein | 3/14/1979 |
| John Keeble | 7/6/1959 | Claire Danes | 4/12/1979 |
| Bono | 5/10/1960 | Taylor Hanson | 3/14/1983 |

# Nine of Spades

You are the Nine of Spades! You are the "Giver of Givers." You may not really like being a giver all the time, but it is where you find the greatest fulfillment. This is a last lifetime for you in some significant way. You are here to complete a major chapter in your soul's evolution. It is sort of like half of you is here and another half somewhere else. You find it easy to tune in to dimensions outside the physical universe. On some level, you know that you are connected to all beings.

Many 9♠ have an unusual artistic talent or two. They are often really good at one or more of the arts or music. There is a charm with this card as well. You know how to seduce others when you want to and can maintain a high level of popularity with those around you.

This is a universal experience that all Nines enjoy to some extent, but your card, being the strongest of them, will likely experience it the most. This causes compassion and understanding. You can relate to others and feel what they are feeling. Those are some of the perks of being a Nine. But the other side could be that it is hard to turn off

# Nine of Spades

their feelings and that you care too much about them, to the point of your own detriment.

This can be especially problematic in personal relationships. Being there just for our partners and expecting them to return the favor will nearly always cause problems and a lack of fulfillment. You certainly have the power to attract a partner. The trouble would be once you are together, you both need to communicate your needs and wants in a harmonious manner. Many 9♠ are, or have been, happily married. Some 9♠ men realize how much charm they have and just prefer to go the playboy route.

For the highest fulfillment, align yourself with a mission or purpose much larger than yourself. If you dedicate your life to something of this nature, you will not only make a grand contribution, but in the process, you will have every one of your dreams come true.

**Some of the best 9♠ marriages happen with:**
2♥, A♣, 9♣, Q♥, 10♠, 8♠, and 6♣

**The hottest sex happens with:**
Q♠, 8♦, 6♠, 2♠, J♣, 10♥, A♦, A♥, K♦, 3♣, 5♠, and 5♦

**Your marriageability is:**
Very good. There is no reason not to do it, unless that is your real preference.

**Affirmation for you:**
I am here to complete a major chapter in my soul's development. I give whatever is asked of me and in doing so, I connect to the infinite source of all.

| Famous 9♠ Birth Card people | |
|---|---|
| Gertrude Stein | 2/3/1874 |
| Norman Rockwell | 2/3/1894 |
| Glen Miller | 3/1/1904 |
| James Michener | 2/3/1907 |
| David Niven | 3/1/1910 |
| Jean Dixon | 1/5/1918 |
| Joey Bishop | 2/3/1918 |
| Henry Heimlich | 2/3/1920 |
| William Gaines | 3/1/1922 |
| Yitzhak Rabin | 3/1/1922 |
| Shelley Berman | 2/3/1926 |
| Peter Rozelle | 3/1/1926 |
| Harry Belafonte | 3/1/1927 |
| Walter Mondale | 1/5/1928 |
| Robert Duvall | 1/5/1931 |
| Umberto Eco | 1/5/1932 |
| Chuck Noll | 1/5/1932 |

# Nine of Spades

| | |
|---|---|
| Robert Conrad | 3/1/1935 |
| Judith Rossner | 3/1/1935 |
| Jim Otto | 1/5/1938 |
| Michael Cimino | 2/3/1939 |
| Frank Tarkenton | 2/3/1940 |
| Peter Guber | 3/1/1942 |
| Blythe Danner | 2/3/1943 |
| Mike D'Abo | 3/1/1944 |
| Roger Daltry | 3/1/1944 |
| Bob Griese | 2/3/1945 |
| Diane Keaton | 1/5/1946 |
| Lana Wood | 3/1/1946 |
| Brian Johnson | 1/5/1947 |
| Dave Davies | 2/3/1947 |
| Alan Thicke | 3/1/1947 |
| Morgan Fairchild | 2/3/1950 |
| Arthur Kane | 2/3/1951 |
| Pamela Sue Martin | 1/5/1954 |
| Catherine Bach | 3/1/1954 |
| Ron Howard | 3/1/1954 |
| Nathan Lane | 2/3/1956 |
| Timothy Daly | 3/1/1956 |
| Thomas Calabro | 2/3/1959 |
| Bill Leen | 3/1/1962 |
| Elisa Donovan | 2/3/1971 |

# The Tens

To truly understand the Tens, we must also be familiar with the Aces, because these two cards are very much alike and share important qualities. The Ten even has the familiar One at the head of its number. This alone should be a clue to the student of the cards as to the nature of the people of these cards. Like the Aces, Tens possess a lot of drive and ambition. Also like the Aces, Tens can be very self-centered or selfish.

Tens are on a soul search over the course of their lives. They turn their attention upon themselves to find answers and reasons for the value of their lives. To others, this can show up as selfishness. While they are focused upon their own feelings, thoughts, needs, and desires, the Ten may not pay much attention to others in their environment. Indeed, many Tens look upon themselves as selfish, and it is an important personal issue that they must come to terms with during the course of their lifetime. Are they truly selfish? Is being selfish really a bad thing? Is there such a thing as good selfishness? Is there a way to balance out the needs of others with their own needs? These are all questions they must answer for themselves.

The main difference between Tens and Aces is the Zero after the One and what that represents. Just as an Eight is two Fours, the Ten can be looked upon as two Fives. Five being the number of experience, the Ten person has a great deal of experience they can draw upon for success. This Zero represents the experience of completing a major cycle of evolution, going all the way from the Ace through the Nine and now to the Ten, where a new cycle begins. However, in this new cycle, the Ten will carry with it all of the wisdom that was acquired in the previous cycle. This explains why the Tens have such a capacity for success in their lives. All Tens have great success potential, and many rise to prominence if that is what they desire. Their suit will tell us the main area of their wisdom and success in this lifetime. The 10♥ has a command over people or children. The 10♣ arrived here with a head full of knowledge to share with the world. The 10♦ can handle a business with ease, the larger the better, and the 10♠ has the drive to accomplish anything they set their minds to. They are unparalleled workers and achievers. Unlike the Aces, the Tens don't have to learn very much to achieve success. They do like to learn new things, but they already possess a great deal of experience which they discover as they apply themselves to their careers.

The Zero is also the number we associate with the Joker. The Joker is the only card in the deck which has no personal identity of its own. Instead, the Joker borrows identities from other cards and can essentially become that card for whatever length of time he or she chooses. The Ten person also has this capacity to some extent. They have all the numbers from Ace through Nine already under their belt. They understand all the principles and abilities of these numbers and can implement their qualities at will.

The downside of being a Ten is that they can become obsessive with respect to something about their suit. The 10♥ can be obsessed with their families, or with their audiences if they are performers. 10♣ have difficulty sleeping at night because their heads are so full of thoughts and ideas. The 10♦ can make money the most important thing in their life and the 10♠ can be the world's worst workaholic and type A personality. This obsession can become destructive in some cases. Tens can be very "all or nothing" kinds of people. When they pursue something, they go full tilt. Then they crash when they go to the opposite extreme. They can get hooked on harmful things because "all or nothing" is a personality type that's prone to addiction.

We can relate Tens to the tenth house of the Astrological chart. The tenth house is governed by Saturn and is concerned with reputation and career. Many Tens, it will be noted, have either strong tenth house planets or planets in Capricorn, or they are aspected by Saturn in their natal charts. This creates a drive for prominence and achievement, and in some cases an emotional need for attention and recognition. It is part of the Ten's life work to understand this drive and to come to terms with it. Yes, Tens can achieve great things, things that we may applaud them for, but the real question they must answer is whether they did it for the right reasons. Only they know the answer to this. If approached consciously, their work will bring additional happiness to them and those around them. If not, it will cause one problem after another and deprive them of the real goal for which they were working. Tens, like the rest of us, are seeking inner contentment and peace. In their case, this seems to come through the avenue of achievement, success, recognition, and respect. Over the course of their lives, they will learn that even these qualities must come from within.

# Ten of Hearts

You are the Ten of Hearts! Yours is the card of popularity. The world is your audience and wherever you go, you are most attracted to groups. The Ten in Hearts means ten people or large numbers of people. Most 10♥ create a life where there are many people around them most of the time. And most like to be in the center of that group, enjoying the attention they garner there. This is an ideal card for a performer, a teacher, or a public speaker—thus the long list of celebrities. Overall, the life path is very fortunate, and satisfaction is gained through the many groups that you either create or join.

You have an incredible mind. Some 10♥ have photographic memories. And your mind is attuned to money-making opportunities. It is easy for you to run your own business if you choose, because you know how to make it successful. You can combine that good business sense with your performances or whatever group-related activity you choose. This always brings success. You can actually do well in many different areas. Your people skills are well polished and useful for success anywhere you go.

# Ten of Hearts

There is no doubt that your natural ambition will motivate you to accomplish a lot!

There is a freedom issue that must be addressed before relationships are successful. Most 10♥ do marry and they are marriageable. But a few will find the confines of marriage too limiting for their taste. Many 10♥ view marriage as a means to an end. These are the ones that really have difficulty trusting others and being intimate on all levels. But for the most part, 10♥ enjoy the family situation that marriage brings and are happy.

With your popularity and fun-loving nature, you can have most anything you want in life. Remember that even though your mind is capable of creating anything you need, honesty will always bring the best results.

**Some of the best 10♥ marriages happen with:**
J♥, 9♥, 7♦, 10♦, Q♣, 4♠, and 10♣

**The hottest sex happens with:**
7♥, Q♠, K♥, 9♠, 8♦, 7♣, 6♠, 2♠, A♥, A♦, 8♣, and Q♣

**Your marriageability is:**
Pretty good. But the choice is always in your hands.

**Affirmation for you:**
I encourage like-minded people to join together in fun and love.

| Famous 10♥ Birth Card people | |
| --- | --- |
| Pablo Picasso | 10/25/1881 |
| Boris Karloff | 11/23/1887 |
| Gene Autry | 9/27/1907 |
| Ingrid Bergman | 8/29/1915 |
| Isabel Sanford | 8/29/1917 |
| Dinah Washington | 8/29/1924 |
| Jayne Meadows | 9/27/1926 |
| Wilford Brimley | 9/27/1934 |
| Barbara Howard | 9/27/1934 |
| Robert Towne | 11/23/1934 |
| Phil Donahue | 12/21/1935 |
| Jane Fonda | 12/21/1937 |
| Elliott Gould | 8/29/1938 |
| Robert Rubin | 8/29/1938 |
| Susan Anspach | 11/23/1939 |
| Bobby Knight | 10/25/1940 |
| Frank Zappa | 12/21/1940 |
| Robin Leach | 8/29/1941 |
| Helen Reddy | 10/25/1941 |
| Geraldine Chaplin | 7/31/1944 |
| Sherry Lansing | 7/31/1944 |
| James Carville | 10/25/1944 |
| Joe Eszterhas | 11/23/1944 |
| Carl Wilson | 12/21/1946 |
| Karl Green | 7/31/1947 |
| Meat Loaf | 9/27/1947 |
| Cheryl Tiegs | 9/27/1947 |

# Ten of Hearts

| | |
|---|---|
| Samule L. Jackson | 12/21/1948 |
| David Rappaport | 11/23/1951 |
| Chris Evert-Lloyd | 12/21/1954 |
| Jane Kaczmarek | 12/21/1955 |
| Joshua Mostel | 12/21/1956 |
| Daniel Ash | 7/31/1957 |
| Paul Provenza | 7/31/1957 |
| Ray Romano | 12/21/1957 |
| Bill Berry | 7/31/1958 |
| Michael Jackson | 8/29/1958 |
| Shaun Cassidy | 9/27/1958 |
| Nancy Cartwright | 10/25/1959 |
| Maxwell Caulfield | 11/23/1959 |
| Florence Griffith Joyner | 12/21/1959 |
| Wesley Snipes | 7/31/1962 |
| Rebecca De Mornay | 8/29/1962 |
| Chad Smith | 10/25/1962 |
| Norman Cook | 7/31/1963 |
| Stephan Jenkins | 9/27/1964 |
| Michael Boatman | 10/25/1964 |
| J.K. Rowling | 7/31/1965 |
| Andy Dick | 12/21/1965 |
| Perry Saturn | 10/25/1966 |
| Kiefer Sutherland | 12/21/1966 |
| Salli Richardson | 11/23/1967 |
| Gwyneth Paltrow | 9/27/1972 |
| Kurupt | 11/23/1972 |
| Harry Potter | 7/31/1980 |
| Daniel Radcliffe | 7/31/1989 |

# Ten of Clubs

You are the Ten of Clubs! Your card occupies a special place in the deck, a place that is shared by only two other cards (K♠ and 8♦). We call this place the Crown Line and to be there means you are royalty, just as much as any real-world King, Queen, or Jack. Instinctively you know that. You know that you can accomplish anything you set your mind to and that the world is your oyster. The only problem you face is, what is it that you will do? Which occupation shall you invest yourself in? Which role in life should you pursue? Like a kid in a candy shop with a dollar in their pocket, you are surrounded by so many possibilities.

This is the card of the most powerful mind and a mind that wants something BIG to sink its teeth into. Only a really big project or career will truly satisfy. A quick glance down the list of 10♣ should prove to you the immense potential inherent in this card—there are nearly twice as many people in this list as there are for the other cards. There is no better mental equipment to be found in the deck, but it does have its downside. Most 10♣ have difficulty turning off their mind; things such as sleeping at night and relaxing can be a challenge. This can be alleviated by being fully involved in your work. And what sort of work shall you

# Ten of Clubs

engage in? Well, one clue is that your card is often called "The Teacher Card." And if you look at the list of celebrities here, you will see that in their own way, they all teach. Many through their performances, others through books they write, or though other leadership roles they play in life. But for all, their life's mission centers around the dissemination of knowledge to the world, and the bigger the better. Female 10♣ should note just how many successful female 10♣ are out there. Sex is no barrier for this card whatsoever.

The same uncertainty that hampers your career decisions can also affect your romantic life. In some cases, 10♣, and especially the male 10♣, choose to just date people and leave their options open. Also, the large amount of independence found in your card can make commitment difficult. Some 10♣ do find happy marriages, but none will sacrifice their work for it. It would be difficult to find a 10♣ housewife—they are not the woman behind the man. The 10♣ stands behind no one.

With such potential it would be a shame if you did not really accomplish something great in your life. And you will never be truly happy until you do.

# Ten of Clubs

Some of the best 10♣ marriages happen with:

9♣, Q♥, K♠, 8♦, 7♥, and K♦

The hottest sex happens with:

K♣, 3♥, 7♣, 8♦, J♠, 8♠, and 5♥

Your marriageability is:

Average to below average, unless you are female. And even some of the females may not choose to settle down.

Affirmation for you:

Through knowledge and love, I discover my true identity and seek to express the beauty I behold inside.

| Famous 10♣ Birth Card people | |
|---|---|
| Tennessee Williams | 3/26/1911 |
| Hume Cronyn | 7/18/1911 |
| Paul Erdos | 3/26/1913 |
| Red Skelton | 7/18/1913 |
| Menachem Begin | 8/16/1913 |
| Vance Packard | 5/22/1914 |
| Harriet Nelson | 7/18/1914 |
| Clayton Moore | 9/14/1914 |
| Zero Mostel | 2/28/1915 |
| Nelson Mandela | 7/18/1918 |
| John Glenn | 7/18/1921 |
| Dick Martin | 1/30/1922 |
| Charles Durning | 2/28/1923 |
| Chet Atkins | 6/20/1924 |
| Sammy Davis Jr. | 12/8/1925 |
| Lois Rodden | 5/22/1928 |
| Nappy Brown | 10/12/1929 |
| Gene Hackman | 1/30/1930 |

| | |
|---|---|
| Sandra Day O'Connor | 3/26/1930 |
| Frank Gifford | 8/16/1930 |
| Gavin Macleod | 2/28/1931 |
| Leonard Nimoy | 3/26/1931 |
| Dick Gregory | 10/12/1932 |
| Shirley MacLaine | 4/24/1934 |
| Peter Nero | 5/22/1934 |
| Kate Millet | 9/14/1934 |
| Luciano Pavarotti | 10/12/1935 |
| Jill Ireland | 4/24/1936 |
| Vanessa Redgrave | 1/30/1937 |
| Boris Spassky | 1/30/1937 |
| Richard Benjamin | 5/22/1938 |
| Tommy Tune | 2/28/1939 |
| James Caan | 3/26/1939 |
| Dion DiMucci | 7/18/1939 |
| Hunter S. Thompson | 7/18/1939 |
| Mario Andretti | 2/28/1940 |
| James Brolin | 7/18/1940 |
| Dick Cheney | 1/30/1941 |
| Stephen Frears | 6/20/1941 |
| Brian Jones | 2/28/1942 |
| Erica Jong | 3/26/1942 |
| Barbara Streisand | 4/24/1942 |
| Ted Kaczynski | 5/22/1942 |
| Brian Wilson | 6/20/1942 |
| Melvin Franklin | 10/12/1942 |
| Bob Woodward | 3/26/1943 |
| Jeffrey MacDonald | 10/12/1943 |
| Jim Morrison | 12/8/1943 |
| Diana Ross | 3/26/1944 |
| Anne Murray | 6/20/1945 |
| Bob Vila | 6/20/1946 |
| Lesley Ann Warren | 8/16/1946 |
| Stephanie Beacham | 2/28/1947 |
| Sam Neill | 9/14/1947 |
| Chris Wallace | 10/12/1947 |
| Dave Loggins | 11/10/1947 |

# Ten of Clubs

| | | | | |
|---|---|---|---|---|
| Greg Allman | 12/8/1947 | Mackenzie Phillips | 11/10/1959 |
| Bernadette Peters | 2/28/1948 | Richard Ramirez | 2/28/1960 |
| Mercedes Ruehl | 2/28/1948 | Dorothy Stratten | 2/28/1960 |
| Steven Tyler | 3/26/1948 | Paula Yates | 4/24/1960 |
| Vicki Lawrence | 3/26/1949 | Timothy Hutton | 8/16/1960 |
| Lionel Richie | 6/20/1949 | Elmer Sperry | 10/12/1960 |
| Donna Fargo | 11/10/1949 | Elizabeth McGovern | 7/18/1961 |
| Ann Reinking | 11/10/1949 | Melissa Leo | 9/14/1961 |
| Martin Short | 3/26/1950 | Billy Gould | 4/24/1963 |
| Richard Branson | 7/18/1950 | Faith Ford | 9/14/1964 |
| Susan Anton | 10/12/1950 | Teri Hatcher | 12/8/1964 |
| Jack Scalia | 11/10/1950 | Sinead O'Connor | 12/8/1966 |
| Rick Baker | 12/8/1950 | Patty Schemel | 4/24/1967 |
| Phil Collins | 1/30/1951 | Nicole Kidman | 6/20/1967 |
| Kenneth Bianchi | 5/22/1951 | Dan Cortese | 9/14/1967 |
| John Goodman | 6/20/1952 | James Iha | 3/26/1968 |
| Eric Bogosian | 4/24/1953 | Aaron Comess | 4/24/1968 |
| Cyndi Lauper | 6/20/1953 | Hugh Jackman | 10/12/1968 |
| Kathie Lee Gifford | 8/16/1953 | Adam Rich | 10/12/1968 |
| Kim Basinger | 12/8/1953 | Naomi Campbell | 5/22/1970 |
| Sam Kinison | 12/8/1953 | Craig Montoya | 9/14/1970 |
| James Cameron | 8/16/1954 | Kirk Cameron | 10/12/1970 |
| Barry Cowsill | 9/14/1954 | Charlie Ward | 10/12/1970 |
| Michael O'Keefe | 4/24/1955 | Twiggy Ramirez | 6/20/1971 |
| Pat DiNizio | 10/12/1955 | Kimberly Williams | 9/14/1971 |
| Dave Vanian | 10/12/1956 | Chipper Jones | 4/24/1972 |
| Cindy Wilson | 2/28/1957 | Emily Robison | 8/16/1972 |
| Boris Williams | 4/24/1957 | Eric Lindros | 2/28/1973 |
| Tim Farriss | 8/16/1957 | Chino Moreno | 6/20/1973 |
| Butch Vig | 12/8/1957 | Christian Bale | 1/30/1974 |
| Brett Butler | 1/30/1958 | A.J. Langer | 5/22/1974 |
| Madonna | 8/16/1958 | Brittany Murphy | 11/10/1977 |
| Angela Bassett | 8/16/1958 | Tony Fagenson | 7/18/1978 |
| Jody Wateu | 1/30/1959 | Heather Matarazzo | 11/10/1982 |
| Morrissey | 5/22/1959 | Rumer Glenn Willis | 8/16/1988 |
| Laura Innes | 8/16/1959 | Jack Henry Quaid | 4/24/1992 |
| Mary Crosby | 9/14/1959 | Frances Bean Cobain | 8/16/1992 |

# Ten of Diamonds

You are the Ten of Diamonds! Your Birth Card sits in a very unusual and beneficial position where Jupiter influences it in two directions. Since Jupiter is considered the planet of good fortune, we call you the most blessed card in the deck. You are protected by Jupiter whether you realize it or not, and no matter what happens to you, there seems to be this divine intervention that comes in to save you. Actually, your life could be much easier than it is. Abundance surrounds you constantly and your life could be an experience of one blessing after another. There is just one catch, and it is kind of a cosmic joke. Here you are the most blessed card in the deck, but you have one major issue—you refuse to receive. Basically you are a good giver and provider, but you have forgotten that to receive is just as important. Many 10♦ are like beggars at the banquet. They should be enjoying the banquet that life is but instead they act like they there is not enough for them. It is for this reason and this reason only that your life has any sort of limitation in it. You may tell yourself that being successful on your own is a real achievement. But in truth, being successful at letting others give to you would be a much greater accomplishment. You are

# Ten of Diamonds

good at being the Lone Ranger, so good, in fact, that it can hinder you.

You have innate business sense and ability. 10♦ always do well in business and should have their own business because it fulfills them so much. You have passion and ambition, which, combined with this innate business sense, can make you very successful in whatever direction you choose. You have a lot of self-exploration and self-discovery to do in this life, and on one level you are alone. But on the other hand, whenever you find yourself in a group, you love being the center of attention. For this same reason, 10♦ make good teachers and performers.

The area of relationships is both promising and challenging. Being as self-centered as you are, your partner must be really into you too, and open to being a support person to your dreams and goals. It generally will not work for you to be someone else's support person in that way. Your partner must also be someone "of quality" because for you, they are part of the reflection of your own worth. Marriage is definitely possible. 10♦ ladies must learn to trust their man and let him provide for her. So often

# Ten of Diamonds

they feel they have to work for everything, as mentioned, which limits the abundance in their marriage. All 10♦ have the possibility of one difficult divorce. It is a karma brought with them from a past life.

The world is your oyster. But if all the kings and queens were here to offer it to you, would you be able to receive it? Turning inward, you actually possess one of the rarest of gifts, that of intuition. If you access that, your life will be guided to the place of your highest fulfillment.

**Some of the best 10♦ marriages happen with:**
K♣, J♦, Q♦, 9♦, 8♠, J♣, 10♥, and Q♣

**The hottest sex happens with:**
K♦, 7♦, A♦, 6♦, 5♣, 4♥, 3♥, Q♥, and A♠

**Your marriageability is:**
50-50. Like other Diamonds, you can have it if you really want it.

**Affirmation for you:**
Guided by my inner voice, I direct my passion towards meaningful goals that benefit mankind.

| Famous 10♦ Birth Card people | |
| --- | --- |
| Betty White | 1/17/1922 |
| Yvonne De Carlo | 9/1/1922 |
| Rocky Marciano | 9/1/1923 |
| Leon Uris | 8/3/1924 |
| Tony Bennett | 8/3/1926 |
| Eartha Kitt | 1/17/1927 |
| Harvey Korman | 2/15/1927 |
| Vidal Sassoon | 1/17/1928 |
| Ethel Kennedy | 4/11/1928 |
| James Ivory | 6/7/1928 |
| Warren Oates | 7/5/1928 |
| Peter Breck | 3/13/1929 |
| Mary Maxwell Gates | 7/5/1929 |
| James Earl Jones | 1/17/1931 |
| Claire Bloom | 2/15/1931 |
| Barbara Feldon | 3/13/1932 |
| Joel Grey | 4/11/1932 |
| Ann Richards | 9/1/1933 |
| Conway Twitty | 9/1/1933 |
| Katherine Helmond | 7/5/1934 |
| Albert Finney | 5/9/1936 |
| Glenda Jackson | 5/9/1936 |
| Shirley Knight | 7/5/1936 |
| Alan Dershowitz | 9/1/1938 |
| Maury Povich | 1/17/1939 |
| Neil Sedaka | 3/13/1939 |
| Louise Lasser | 4/11/1939 |
| Lily Tomlin | 9/1/1939 |
| James L. Brooks | 5/9/1940 |
| Tom Jones | 6/7/1940 |
| Martin Sheen | 8/3/1940 |
| Martha Stewart | 8/3/1941 |
| Muhammad Ali | 1/17/1942 |
| John Ashcroft | 5/9/1942 |
| Ken Osmond | 6/7/1943 |
| Robbie Robertson | 7/5/1943 |
| Don Stoud | 9/1/1943 |

# Ten of Diamonds

| | | | |
|---|---|---|---|
| Clarence White | 6/7/1944 | Dee Dee Myers | 9/1/1961 |
| Marisa Berenson | 2/15/1945 | Jim Carrey | 1/17/1962 |
| Candice Bergen | 5/9/1946 | John Corbett | 5/9/1962 |
| Jenny Jones | 6/7/1946 | Dave Gahan | 5/9/1962 |
| Barry Gibb | 9/1/1946 | Nigel Pulsford | 4/11/1963 |
| Peter Riegert | 4/11/1947 | Gordon Gano | 6/7/1963 |
| Meshach Taylor | 4/11/1947 | James Hetfield | 8/3/1963 |
| Julie Nixon-Eisenhower | 7/5/1948 | Isaiah Washington | 8/3/1963 |
| Andy Kaufman | 1/17/1949 | Chris Farley | 2/15/1964 |
| Billy Joel | 5/9/1949 | Will Clark | 3/13/1964 |
| William H. Macy | 3/13/1950 | Eric Kretz | 6/7/1966 |
| John Landis | 8/3/1950 | Shirley Manson | 8/3/1966 |
| Jane Seymour | 2/15/1951 | Dylan Keefe | 4/11/1970 |
| Fred Berry | 3/13/1951 | Ghostface Killah | 5/9/1970 |
| Huey Lewis | 7/5/1951 | Stephen Carpenter | 8/3/1970 |
| Larry Fortensky | 1/17/1952 | Kid Rock | 1/17/1971 |
| Liam Neeson | 6/7/1952 | Renee O'Connor | 2/15/1971 |
| Deborah Raffin | 3/13/1953 | Annabeth Gish | 3/13/1971 |
| Matt Groening | 2/15/1954 | Khujo | 3/13/1972 |
| Glenne Headly | 3/13/1955 | Bengt Lagerberg | 7/5/1973 |
| David Caruso | 1/17/1956 | Brandon Boyd | 2/15/1976 |
| Dana Delaney | 3/13/1956 | Danny Masterson | 3/13/1976 |
| Gloria Estefan | 9/1/1957 | Cassidy Rae | 6/7/1976 |
| Prince | 6/7/1958 | Tom Brady | 8/3/1977 |
| Tony Gwynn | 5/9/1960 | Tarmo Tammark | 8/3/1979 |
| Vincent Gallo | 4/11/1961 | Anna Kournikova | 6/7/1981 |
| Lucky Vanous | 4/11/1961 | Larisa Oleynik | 6/7/1981 |

# Ten of Spades

You are the Ten of Spades! Yours is the card of the Super Achiever. There is little you cannot do, and you will certainly accomplish a great deal over the course of your lifetime. You have the drive and ambition, combined with an uncanny knowing, that will serve you time and time again—the bigger the project or goal, the better. And most 10♠ are not satisfied with small goals anyway. But you have an evenly powerful drive to have a home and family. It is your particular karma to be somewhat at conflict between these two extremes. Christy Brinkley, a famous 10♠, was all career for years, then married Billy Joel and was all home and family for a while, only to return to her career again. Your life may have a similar pattern.

You are one of the most marriageable cards in the deck. You are so marriageable that you can even make unmarriageable Birth Cards marriage material. You are the "super-doer" and could easily become a workaholic. The one thing you might want to be sure you are aware of is what's going on inside of you—you are prone to forgetting that because of all you are doing externally. Taking care of your body, being mindful

# Ten of Spades

of your feelings, all these things demand just as much of your attention if you are to live a truly balanced and fulfilling life.

You are here to be a shining example of what a highly motivated and accomplished person can do. Your achievements inspire us all.

**Some of the best 10♠ marriages happen with:**
10♣, J♠, 9♠, 6♠, 5♣, Q♣, J♦, and 3♠

**The hottest sex happens with:**
K♠, 7♠, 8♥, A♠, 3♥, 7♥, A♥, Q♣, 10♦, 6♦, and A♦

**Your marriageability is:**
As good as it gets. No question.

**Affirmation for you:**
I am a creator and a doer. I am here to accomplish many things and inspire others to do the same.

| Liz Smith | 2/2/1923 |
|---|---|
| Floyd Patterson | 1/4/1935 |
| Dyan Cannon | 1/4/1937 |
| Tom Smothers | 2/2/1937 |
| Graham Nash | 2/2/1942 |
| Farrah Fawcett | 2/2/1947 |
| Christie Brinkley | 2/2/1954 |
| Patty Loveless | 1/4/1957 |
| Don Shula | 1/4/1960 |
| Michael Stipe | 1/4/1960 |
| Julia Ormond | 1/4/1965 |
| Robert Deleo | 2/2/1966 |
| Ben Mize | 2/2/1971 |
| Shakira | 2/2/1977 |

| Famous 10♠ Birth Card people | |
|---|---|
| Jacob Grimm | 1/4/1785 |
| Louis Braille | 1/4/1809 |
| Tom Thumb | 1/4/1838 |
| James Joyce | 2/2/1882 |
| George Halas | 2/2/1895 |
| Ayn Rand | 2/2/1905 |
| Jane Wyman | 1/4/1914 |

# The Jacks

"I won't grow up!"

—Peter Pan

The Jack is the youngest member of the royal family. He can be looked upon in several ways, all of them meaningful. First, he can be seen as the Prince who will someday become the King. As the Prince, he is youthful, romantic, creative, witty, and charming. However, he has not yet been given the responsibility and power that comes from being the King. Nor does he want so much responsibility. Jacks just want to have fun and play. At the same time, they want to be treated with respect and some measure of admiration. Someday, perhaps, they will become Kings. The transformation from youthfulness to responsibility is one of the most important life-long themes for the Jack person.

Another way to see a Jack is as the counsel to the King. He has influence with the King, but he has his own interests at heart. He sits in the royal court, but he assumes none of the overall responsibility for what happens. He can be bribed if you want him to act on your behalf in influencing the King in a certain way. Overall, he is somewhat dishonest but very creative and resourceful in keeping all of his affairs in balance without getting caught. He is a master of deception and stealth and can never truly be trusted.

These two pictures sum up the usual qualities of Jack Birth Cards. The youthful creativity is there in overwhelming abundance. Along with that is the temptation to misuse that creative energy for fun or profit, or simply to avoid unpleasant situations that one may have to face as a result

of being 100 percent honest. The J♥ stands out as the only exception to this, but in truth, many of these people also succumb to the misuse of their creative forces. However, overall, the J♥ has such a spiritual connection that they tend to focus more of their energy on being the martyr or savior and don't have much time for the craftiness of the other Jacks. Still, they are Jacks, and every once in awhile even they get that mischievous gleam in their eyes that tells you they are up to something.

But Jacks are also deemed the initiates of the deck. Initiation implies rising to a new, usually higher, level. It is this new beginning that implies ending of some past ways of being. For many Jacks, they are here to show that they can rise above their material nature to one that is more spiritual and less attached to worldly goods and matters. For a Jack to be truly self-realized, they will have to access the higher qualities of their suit in some fashion. This would mean the J♥ becomes a vessel for spiritual love, the J♣ for spiritual knowledge, the J♦ a representative of higher values and the J♠ an example of one whose life is lived on higher, spiritual principles. Many Jacks achieve this and many do not.

In their highest expression, they represent that person who has lifted him or herself up to a higher level of self expression. This also implies letting go of their lower natures, which in many cases are quite strong and difficult to renounce.

Jacks are always tempted to misuse their tremendous gifts, and many of them will never rise up to anything but a thief. They have such a creative mind that they can tell lies that anyone would believe without question. This mind represents a great gift, but it is up to them to put it to a positive use. Those who do can achieve much.

The Jack's naturally mental nature also makes it more difficult for them to know their own feelings. When they have so much success using their minds, their hearts are rarely used in getting what they want. All of these qualities combine in the Jack person to give them their life's biggest challenge—to seek the solutions to their problems by looking within, instead of using their wits and craftiness to get by. This turning within is the initiation that all Jacks represent.

# Jack of Hearts

You are the Jack of Hearts! Your card is one of the most unusual in the deck. We call you the card of sacrifice, or the Christ-card. This is because you are a person who will do literally anything for those you love. Love is the most important thing in your life—not romantic love, but really loving the people in your life. No matter what kind of work you do, your work has in it an element of your giving to those around you. You may be a leader where you work, but even if not, you are there for others when they need you. You are proud and fixed in nature. No one can dissuade you from the way you love the people in your life.

You also have a playful side. No Heart person ever really grows up. They are all children on one level. But the Jack especially loves to play and have fun. This can present problems in the romantic department because some Jacks never want to become responsible. So, we do have some playboys and playgirls among J♥, but the norm is for marriage, children, and family.

Your drive to help the world can be a big part of your chosen occupation. Some J♥ want to save the world and

# Jack of Hearts

others just make it a better and safer place. In most cases, the bigger you set your sights, the better.

In love, there can be challenges, mostly because it is not possible to "save" your partner or to be saved by them. It is hard for a J♥ to make that distinction. It is often hard for them to speak up for their own needs and desires, chiefly because they are so involved in taking care of their partners. Success can come, but usually after some trial and error. There is no doubt that you are marriageable, however. You would make a great partner and husband or wife. Most female J♥ have a good deal of masculine energy, which also plays a role in their partnerships to some extent.

By finding your mission in life you achieve great success. You remind us all of the true nature of love and the power inherent there.

**Some of the best J♥ marriages happen with:**
Q♥, 10♥, 9♣, 5♠, and 8♦

**The hottest sex happens with:**
2♥, A♣, 8♥, 7♥, 9♦, 5♦, Q♦, and 3♦

**Your marriageability is:**
Very good once you decide to settle down.

**Affirmation for you:**
I am the model of true love and friendship. The example I set inspires those around me.

| Famous J♥ Birth Card people | |
|---|---|
| Henry Ford | 7/30/1863 |
| Sybil Thorndike | 10/24/1882 |
| T.S. Eliot | 9/26/1888 |
| Casey Stengal | 7/30/1890 |
| Charles DeGaulle | 11/22/1890 |
| Charles Boyer | 8/28/1897 |
| Paul VI | 9/26/1897 |
| George Gershwin | 9/26/1898 |
| Wiley Post | 11/22/1898 |
| Irene Dunne | 12/20/1898 |
| Moss Hart | 10/24/1904 |
| Nancy Kulp | 8/28/1921 |
| Rodney Dangerfield | 11/22/1921 |
| George Roy Hill | 12/20/1922 |
| Donald O'Connor | 8/28/1925 |
| Y.A. Tittle | 10/24/1926 |
| Ben Gazzara | 8/28/1930 |
| The Big Bopper (J.P. Richardson) | 10/24/1930 |
| Bud Selig | 7/30/1934 |
| Buddy Guy | 7/30/1936 |
| David Nelson | 10/24/1936 |
| Bill Wyman | 10/24/1936 |
| Peter Bogdanovich | 7/30/1939 |
| Eleanor Smeal | 7/30/1939 |
| F. Murray Abraham | 10/24/1939 |

# Jack of Hearts

| | | | | |
|---|---|---|---|---|
| Terry Gilliam | 11/22/1940 | | Kate Bush | 7/30/1958 |
| Tom Conti | 11/22/1941 | | Jamie Lee Curtis | 11/22/1958 |
| Billie Jean King | 11/22/1942 | | Ian Baker-Finch | 10/24/1960 |
| David Soul | 8/28/1943 | | B.D. Wong | 10/24/1960 |
| Anne Robinson | 9/26/1944 | | Laurence Fishburne | 7/30/1961 |
| Mary Beth Hurt | 9/26/1946 | | Mariel Hemingway | 11/22/1961 |
| Uri Geller | 12/20/1946 | | Melissa Sue Anderson | 9/26/1962 |
| John Spencer | 12/20/1946 | | Tracey Thorn | 9/26/1962 |
| Arnold Schwarzenegger | 7/30/1947 | | Lisa Kudrow | 7/30/1963 |
| Harry Reems | 8/28/1947 | | Shania Twain | 8/28/1965 |
| Kevin Kline | 10/24/1947 | | Dean Cain | 7/30/1966 |
| Olivia Newton-John | 9/26/1948 | | Shannon Hoon | 9/26/1967 |
| Paul McGee | 11/22/1948 | | Boris Becker | 11/22/1967 |
| Claudia Jennings | 12/20/1949 | | James Caviezel | 9/26/1968 |
| Tina Weymouth | 11/22/1950 | | Jason Priestley | 8/28/1969 |
| Wayne Osmond | 8/28/1951 | | Tom Green | 7/30/1971 |
| Jenny Agutter | 12/20/1952 | | Susan Smith | 9/26/1971 |
| Delta Burke | 7/30/1956 | | Hilary Swank | 7/30/1974 |
| Anita Hill | 7/30/1956 | | David Pelletier | 11/22/1974 |
| Linda Hamilton | 9/26/1956 | | Max Collins | 8/28/1978 |
| Rat Scabies | 7/30/1957 | | Serena Williams | 9/26/1981 |
| Anita Baker | 12/20/1957 | | LeAnn Rimes | 8/28/1982 |
| Billy Bragg | 12/20/1957 | | Scarlett Johansson | 11/22/1984 |

# Jack of Clubs

You are the Jack of Clubs! You are a member of the royal family, akin to the prince. Someday you will be king— well, you will if you really want to. For now, what's the hurry? It is fun to get all the perks of the royal family without all the responsibility that goes along with being a Queen or King. And Jacks do really like to have fun! In your particular case you are one of the most mentally gifted cards in the deck. Many J♣ have a photographic memory, and all are known for their powerful memories. You are also creative to the extreme. Jacks are the most resourceful cards in the deck. The J♣ can be very fixed mentally as well. You know what you know and no one can dissuade you of that. With such great mental power, you really could excel at any work where detail and high intelligence are prerequisites. So we find J♣ in many professions. Oprah Winfrey is a famous J♣ whose love for information has become her shining career choice.

J♣ love to argue and discuss things. They have an aggressive mind that enjoys the competition. To them, it is sort of like a mental workout to have a good heated discussion with someone else. They usually win.

# Jack of Clubs

The challenges you may face can vary. Some J♣ have more challenges with their mates or family members than themselves—sometimes their loved ones have illnesses or other problems that the J♣ inherits. If the J♣ chooses to operate on the low side of their card, they will be dishonest in a variety of ways. This is one of the thief cards when expressed negatively. It is hard for anyone to catch a J♣ lying because of their great memory and creativity. They always remember what they said to whom and have the ability to generate a plausible excuse for most anything. The danger for some is that they then lose touch with reality and feel lost. If the world really has no boundaries and nothing said is really all that important, what is the meaning of life, anyway?

J♣ are marriageable and many are happily married. They are considered sexually neutral—half man and half woman. The women especially will often have that "ambi-sexual" look about them. The men are generally boyish and good looking. And they have a reputation as being the best lovers in the deck. However, they do have a strange trait. Once a J♣ man marries a woman, he produces an exhaustive list of "shoulds" and "should-nots" that he expects her to follow. As in the case of Jessica Simpson (5♦) and Nick Lachey (J♣), his fixed ideas about how she should be, combined with his dishonesty, guaranteed they would not last. As of this writing, he seems very happy with his new love, Vanessa Minnillo. Amazingly, they have the exact same birthday. He has truly met his match! Also, many J♣ marry 4♦. See Ben Afflect and Jennifer Garner. When they meet a 4♦, they meet the woman, or man, of their dreams.

**Some of the best J♣ marriages happen with:**
9♦, Q♠, Q♣, 10♣, 10♦, 7♠, and K♦

**The hottest sex happens with:**
A♦, 8♣, 2♣, 7♣, 2♦, K♦, 9♠, and 6♥

**Your marriageability is:**
Great!

**Affirmation for you:**
I enjoy the God-given mental gifts that I was born with. I use my creative brilliance to generate ideas for the benefit of others and to communicate higher knowledge.

# Jack of Clubs

| Famous J♣ Birth Card people | |
|---|---|
| Shirley Temple | 4/23/1928 |
| Nancy Marchand | 6/19/1928 |
| Noam Chomsky | 12/7/1928 |
| Joanne Woodward | 2/27/1930 |
| Elizabeth Taylor | 2/27/1932 |
| Halston | 4/23/1932 |
| Dottie West | 10/11/1932 |
| Ellen Burstyn | 12/7/1932 |
| Raymond Berry | 2/27/1933 |
| Ralph Nadar | 2/27/1934 |
| Gloria Steinem | 3/25/1934 |
| Donald Sutherland | 7/17/1934 |
| Carl Sagan | 11/9/1934 |
| Diahann Carroll | 7/17/1935 |
| Vernon Jordan | 8/15/1935 |
| Roy Scheider | 10/11/1935 |
| Roy Orbison | 4/23/1936 |
| Bobby Charlton | 10/11/1937 |
| Judith Martin | 9/13/1938 |
| Lee Majors | 4/23/1939 |
| Howard Hessman | 2/27/1940 |
| Anita Bryant | 3/25/1940 |
| Katharine Ross | 1/29/1942 |
| Aretha Franklin | 3/25/1942 |
| Sandra Dee | 4/23/1942 |
| Harry Chapin | 12/7/1942 |
| Mary Frann | 2/27/1943 |
| John Ramsey | 12/7/1943 |
| Jacqueline Bisset | 9/13/1944 |
| Tom Selleck | 1/29/1945 |
| Radovan Karadzic | 6/19/1945 |
| Gene Upshaw | 8/15/1945 |
| Elton John | 3/25/1947 |
| Salmon Rushdie | 6/19/1947 |
| Camilla Parker Bowles | 7/17/1947 |
| Johnny Bench | 12/7/1947 |
| Nick Drake | 6/19/1948 |

# Jack of Clubs

| | | | | |
|---|---|---|---|---|
| Daryl Hall | 10/11/1948 | Andre Reed | 1/29/1964 |
| Joe Bouchard | 11/9/1948 | Sarah Jessica Parker | 3/25/1965 |
| Geezer Butler | 7/17/1949 | Alex Winter | 7/17/1965 |
| Tom Waits | 12/7/1949 | Luke Perry | 10/11/1966 |
| Anne Wilson | 6/19/1950 | Debi Thomas | 3/25/1967 |
| Tim Fort | 7/17/1950 | Edward Burns | 1/29/1968 |
| Peeter Madrus | 7/17/1950 | Debra Messing | 8/15/1968 |
| Princess Anne | 8/15/1950 | Jane Krakowski | 10/11/1968 |
| Al Franken | 5/21/1951 | Pepa | 11/9/1969 |
| Lucie Arnaz | 7/17/1951 | Scarface | 11/9/1969 |
| Wesley Magoogan | 10/11/1951 | Heather Graham | 1/29/1970 |
| Lou Ferrigno | 11/9/1951 | Head | 6/19/1970 |
| Mr. T | 5/21/1952 | Chris Jericho | 11/9/1970 |
| David Hasselhoff | 7/17/1952 | Chili | 2/27/1971 |
| Phoebe Snow | 7/17/1952 | Stella McCartney | 9/13/1971 |
| David Morse | 10/11/1953 | MC Lyte | 10/11/1971 |
| Oprah Winfrey | 1/29/1954 | Notorious BIG | 5/21/1972 |
| Kathleen Turner | 6/19/1954 | Ben Affleck | 8/15/1972 |
| Larry Bird | 12/7/1956 | Nick Lachey | 11/9/1973 |
| Judge Reinhold | 5/21/1957 | Fairuza Balk | 5/21/1974 |
| Nancy Spungen | 2/27/1958 | Natasha Henstridge | 8/15/1974 |
| Gia | 1/29/1960 | Sara Gilbert | 1/29/1975 |
| Greg Louganis | 1/29/1960 | Fiona Apple | 9/13/1977 |
| Valerie Bertinelli | 4/23/1960 | Garfield | 6/19/1978 |
| Steve Clark | 4/23/1960 | Sisqo | 11/9/1978 |
| Grant Shaud | 2/27/1961 | James King | 4/23/1979 |
| Dave Mustaine | 9/13/1961 | Chelsea Clinton | 2/27/1980 |
| Steve Young | 10/11/1961 | Ben Savage | 9/13/1980 |
| Grant Show | 2/27/1962 | Vanessa Minillo | 11/9/1980 |
| Paula Abdul | 6/19/1962 | Josh Groban | 2/27/1981 |
| Joan Cusack | 10/11/1962 | Michelle Trachtenberg | 10/11/1985 |
| Scott Johnson | 10/11/1962 | Bob Mackie | 3/25/2003 |

# Jack of Diamonds

You are the Jack of Diamonds! Songs have been written about you. You are the symbol, in most respects, of the gambler and hustler. Not that you necessarily play that role, but it is within you. You are playful to the max. What is life without a few good jokes? You worship your freedom in a way that no other card does. The United States is a J♦, by the way, and our country is founded on an ideal of personal and other freedoms. Likewise, you are committed to being free to do whatever you might. For many of you, this urge will preclude certain serious commitments, such as marriage. In fact, a lot of J♦ do get married. But many of the married ones struggle with the commitment to some degree.

Your card is called the salesman card. You have a creative financial mind that knows no bounds. You can always come up with an angle to buy and sell or otherwise promote something that will make you some fast money. But this creativity could be expressed in many areas for success. It is said that all J♦have an artistic gift but few actually express it. It is part of their karma and it is something that you might consider, either as a profession or at

# Jack of Diamonds

least as a hobby. Much good would come from such an endeavor.

You are dreamy and you care a lot about other people. You might even be a bit co-dependent because you like to help people so much. This is fine in your work or profession but will not do you much good in your personal relationships. Overall, you have good karma, in work, money, and in love. You are popular and know how to be with people around you successfully. Many of your best blessings come from the contacts you make.

All Jacks can distort the truth if they want. Your card, though, will tend to get caught more often than others. There is a karmic lock on you that ensures fairly swift payback.

In the highest sense, your life is about having a transformation in values, in learning the true value of things that will set everything in a place that is beneficial for you and those you love. You are the initiate of higher value. The things you want in life will always tell us the story of how you are doing in the process of making this transformation.

**Some of the best J♦ marriages happen with:**
K♣ Q♦, 4♥, 10♦, Q♣, J♣, and 9♦

**The hottest sex happens with:**
Q♥, A♠, 8♦, 7♣, 2♣, 6♣, 3♦, 4♣, 2♠, and 7♠

**Your marriageability is:**
Fair to not so good. Unless you can come to terms with your freedom issues, it is not something you would choose.

**Affirmation for you:**
I am a role model for transformation in values. I love my creativity and I use it to do work that I love and that helps others.

| Famous J♦ Birth Card people | |
| --- | --- |
| Jack Kerouac | 3/12/1922 |
| Virginia Kelley | 6/6/1923 |
| Eva Marie Saint | 7/4/1924 |
| Carroll O'Connor | 8/2/1924 |
| Don Rickles | 5/8/1926 |
| Joan Quigley | 4/10/1927 |
| Gina Lollobrigida | 7/4/1927 |
| Neil Simon | 7/4/1927 |
| Edward Albee | 3/12/1928 |
| Max von Sydow | 4/10/1929 |
| Al Davis | 7/4/1929 |
| George Steinbrenner | 7/4/1930 |
| Dian Fossey | 1/16/1932 |

# Jack of Diamonds

| | |
|---|---|
| Omar Sharif | 4/10/1932 |
| Sonny Liston | 5/8/1932 |
| Lamar Hunt | 8/2/1932 |
| Peter O'Toole | 8/2/1932 |
| Florence Henderson | 2/14/1934 |
| Esther Shapiro | 6/6/1934 |
| A.J. Foyt | 1/16/1935 |
| John Madden | 4/10/1936 |
| Levi Stubbs | 6/6/1936 |
| Marian Wright-Edelman | 6/6/1939 |
| Rick Nelson | 5/8/1940 |
| Paul Kanter | 3/12/1941 |
| Geraldo Rivera | 7/4/1943 |
| Kathy Lennon | 8/2/1943 |
| Carl Bernstein | 2/14/1944 |
| Jackie Martling | 2/14/1945 |
| Gregory Hines | 2/14/1946 |
| Liza Minnelli | 3/12/1946 |
| Francesco Scavullo | 1/16/1947 |
| Laura Schlessinger | 1/16/1947 |
| Teller | 2/14/1948 |
| James Taylor | 3/12/1948 |
| Robert Englund | 6/6/1949 |
| Debbie Allen | 1/16/1950 |
| Kathryn Harrold | 8/2/1950 |
| Lance Ito | 8/2/1950 |
| Steven Seagal | 4/10/1951 |
| Peter MacNicol | 4/10/1954 |
| Harvey Fierstein | 6/6/1954 |
| Sandra Bernhard | 6/6/1955 |
| Bjorn Borg | 6/6/1956 |
| Steve Harris | 3/12/1957 |
| Marlon Jackson | 3/12/1957 |
| Babyface | 4/10/1958 |
| Ice-T | 2/14/1959 |
| Brian Setzer | 4/10/1959 |
| Ronnie Lott | 5/8/1959 |
| Amanda Pays | 6/6/1959 |

# Jack of Diamonds

| | | | | |
|---|---|---|---|---|
| Apollonia | 8/2/1959 | | Graham Coxon | 3/12/1969 |
| Jim Kelly | 2/14/1960 | | Munky | 6/6/1970 |
| Courtney B. Vance | 3/12/1960 | | Andy Creeggan | 7/4/1971 |
| Steve Vai | 6/6/1960 | | Kate Moss | 1/16/1974 |
| Pam Shriver | 7/4/1962 | | Enrique Iglesias | 5/8/1975 |
| Enrico Colantoni | 2/14/1963 | | Edward Furlong | 8/2/1977 |
| Cynthia Stevenson | 8/2/1963 | | Aaliyah | 1/16/1979 |
| Melissa Gilbert | 5/8/1964 | | Mandy Moore | 4/10/1984 |
| Dave Rowntree | 5/8/1964 | | Lisa Simpson | 8/2/1984 |
| Mark Slaughter | 7/4/1964 | | Haley Joel Osment | 4/10/1988 |
| Mary Louise Parker | 8/2/1964 | | Cassidy Gifford | 8/2/1993 |
| Dave Navarro | 6/6/1967 | | | |
| Helen Baxendale | 2/14/1969 | | | |

# *Jack of Spades*

You are the Jack of Spades! You may be the most creative and resourceful card in the entire deck. You have the ability to be the most dishonest as well. Some call you the jokester, but there is much more to you than that. There is an innate freedom implied in your Birth Card that has you living outside of the normal laws and rules that govern the rest of us. Freedom is a key word for all Jacks, but for you it is the most important thing. You could be successful in any field, but you might find more fun and fulfillment in something artistic. Another aspect that is common for people of your card is the interest in either religion or spirituality. Your card is often called the "spiritual initiate" card, and often J♠ have an eternal interest in these matters. It is your path to someday ascend to the position of King. And to do this you must make the transformation from the playful and often irresponsible Jack to the place of authority, but also great responsibility. No hurry though—this is something that will happen when the time is right. There is a lot of fun and play to be had in the meantime!

You are one of the two one-eyed Jacks in the deck, the other being the J♥. This can make you subjective in your thinking, which means you can get things wrong if you already feel a certain way about

# Jack of Spades

them. It can also mean that you have trouble seeing other people's points of view. These two tendencies can cause trouble in relationships, even though overall you are very marriageable. Also, your freedom urge could be so strong as to preclude anything so binding as marriage. But most J♠ do get married. It is interesting that the J♠, which often has freedom issues, is so well connected to other cards that are all very marriageable. If any J♠ wants marriage, they are bound to find someone compatible.

You have an incredible mind and can solve any problem. Your life is really very blessed. If you have anything to complain about, it could only be something that you created on your own. You have the opportunity to inspire us all with your brilliance, fun-loving joy, and creativity. We can't wait to see what you will do next!

**Some of the best J♠ marriages happen with:**
Q♠, 8♦, 10♠, Q♥, 8♣, 2♦, 6♣, J♣, 10♥, 6♦, and 9♣

**The hottest sex happens with:**
A♥, 3♥, 8♠, 6♣, 4♠, 10♣, 6♥, 4♣, 7♣, 9♦, and Q♦

**Your marriageability is:**
Good. You just have to get clear about your version of freedom first.

**Affirmation for you:**
I am the Jack of Jacks, the master of creativity and resourcefulness. I continually use my gifts for good and strive to match my own spiritual ideals.

| Famous J♠ Birth Card people | |
| --- | --- |
| J.R.R. Tolkien | 1/3/1892 |
| Marion Davies | 1/3/1897 |
| Clark Gable | 2/1/1901 |
| Victor Borge | 1/3/1909 |
| George Martin | 1/3/1926 |
| Robert Loggia | 1/3/1930 |
| Boris Yeltsin | 2/1/1931 |
| Dabney Coleman | 1/3/1932 |
| Don Everly | 2/1/1937 |
| Garrett Morris | 2/1/1937 |
| Sherman Hemsley | 2/1/1938 |
| Bobby Hull | 1/3/1939 |
| Victoria Principal | 1/3/1945 |
| Stephen Stills | 1/3/1945 |
| John Paul Jones | 1/3/1946 |
| Rick James | 2/1/1948 |
| Bill Mumy | 2/1/1954 |
| Mel Gibson | 1/3/1956 |
| Princess Stephanie | 2/1/1965 |
| Sherilyn Fenn | 2/1/1965 |
| Brandon Lee | 2/1/1965 |
| Lisa Marie Presley | 2/1/1968 |
| Pauly Shore | 2/1/1968 |
| Ron Welty | 2/1/1971 |
| Danica McKellar | 1/3/1975 |

# The Queens

The Queen is a very powerful card. She is second in authority only to the King and in many ways is just as powerful, if not more powerful, than he. For this reason, a Queen person, regardless of gender, is aware of a certain power and responsibility she has in her life, one that can be used in positive ways or abused. The Queen is quite capable of ruling the kingdom, but would do it differently than the King. Her rule would be more service-oriented, and she would display more compassion. All Queens possess wisdom from having experienced so much in past lives. There are always some areas in life they will master with little effort. But those areas will usually not be personal relationships and marriage. Collectively, the Queens possess some of the most difficult love karma of any of the cards in the deck, especially the Q♦ and Q♣.

Queens are motherly by nature. Regardless of their occupation, they are mothering people through their work. They excel in helping others nurture and develop themselves. They have a natural desire to reach out to those in need of direction and support at certain stages in their evolution. They take great pleasure in knowing that they have contributed something to another's sense of well-being. They will feed you and offer you protection. The men and women of this card usually get along famously with children, whether or not they themselves have any children.

But one of their faults is that they often hold on to those they love and actually prevent them from leaving the nest when they are ready. This habit comes from their strong identity as mothers. If there is no one to mother, they feel as though their life has no purpose. After all, what is a mother if there are no children to raise? So, when their fears of losing their identity become stronger than their love for their children, they hold back the growth of their children and do exactly the opposite of what they intend.

One challenge of the Queen is to translate this maternal desire to a broader level, away from their own families and onto the world at large. Queens can make excellent counselors, teachers, and promoters of good.

They can play an instrumental part in helping large groups of people better their lives. They have a lot of natural leadership ability and are able to gather people together for a good purpose. The Queens that direct their loving energies toward those outside of their immediate family find much success and satisfaction from their interactions.

This same desire to mother others can cause innumerable problems in their intimate relationships. If they are looking for someone to mother or someone who could mother them, they set themselves up for a very difficult relationship. A co-dependent mire of unrealized dreams and needs is often the result of such a union. Queens invariably attract those who will take advantage of their need to be needed, or they themselves will be uncertain about where their true happiness lies. The Queen will sooner or later want to use some of her power to have romantic fun and adventure. In doing so, she will often create much uncertainty in her life.

The Queens represent some of the essential feminine archetypes. Whether male or female, they will exhibit many of these basic feminine qualities. The Q♥ is the dreamy Aphrodite, the goddess of love and pleasure, who has a love for humanity that is very spiritual in nature. She is the woman all men dream of. The Q♣ is very much a businesswoman and organizer. She is highly intuitive, quick-tempered and usually industrious. But she is also Mary, mother of Jesus, who makes great sacrifices on behalf of her children. She also possesses the highest spiritual gift—intuition. The Q♦ is the collector of things—usually money and relationships. She enjoys the things of the earth, much like the Q♥, but she is also very much involved in earning this wealth. She shares a higher sense of values with her children, who are not necessarily her biological children. These "children" may be people that she works with. The Q♠ is Martha of the Bible, the tireless worker who knows the value of service and work. She is an organizer supreme and makes a tough boss. But inside, she possesses the potential for the highest of spiritual accomplishments—mastery of the self.

# Queen of Hearts

You are the Queen of Hearts! You are the "mother card" ' and motherhood is what you are all about. This does not always mean that you will have children—many Q♥ don't. But whatever you are doing, you are nurturing those around you with the love you possess in abundance. This card is often called "the woman that all men dream of." If you are a female Q♥, you should know that you are in big demand and a prize! All Q♥ are sexy. Your card also is called the sex card. Let no one come between a Q♥ and his or her pleasures. So, there is a lot to say about you.

But you are also very success-oriented and have tremendous ambition. You are highly intelligent and could easily attain recognition for that part of your personality. You could actually excel in any area you choose, but you will be happier if that area can bring you recognition. You have innate leadership ability and easily take responsibility. Like cream, you always rise to the top.

You are marriageable. Relationships are very important to you. You will usually marry someone who is financially successful. There are Q♥ who are uncertain about their partners and

# Queen of Hearts

some will actually have affairs, especially the male Q♥. But the females rarely do and are faithful lovers and wives. Male Q♥ can become sexually obsessed at times—take Michael Douglas, for example. Well, women can too, but it is less frequent than with the men. You may or may not have children, but chances are you will. Either way, it will be a major topic in your life. Once a Q♥ has children, the upbringing and care of their children becomes their highest priority, at least as important as sex!

You are sensitive, beautiful, feminine, and very powerful. Anyone who crosses you will find that out. Your life will be what you decide it will be. So, what will you do?

**Some of the best Q♥ marriages happen with:**
K♥, 9♠, J♥, 10♣, J♠, and 6♠

**The hottest sex happens with:**
2♣, K♥, 9♥, 7♦, 4♦, 5♥, K♠, 8♥, and 7♠

**Your marriageability is:**
Excellent!

**Affirmation for you:**
I am the mother of love. I am here to serve others with all my beautiful gifts.

| Famous Q♥ Birth Card people | |
|---|---|
| Lyndon Johnson | 8/27/1908 |
| Mother Teresa | 8/27/1910 |
| Eleanor Powell | 11/21/1912 |
| Edith Piaf | 12/19/1915 |
| Martha Raye | 8/27/1916 |
| Phil Rizzuto | 9/25/1917 |
| Paul Rudolph | 10/23/1918 |
| Bob Montana | 10/23/1920 |
| Stan Musial | 11/21/1920 |
| David Susskind | 12/19/1920 |
| Frank Sutton | 10/23/1923 |
| Johnny Carson | 10/23/1925 |
| Ira Levin | 8/27/1929 |
| Barbara Walters | 9/25/1931 |
| Diana Dors | 10/23/1931 |
| Cicely Tyson | 12/19/1933 |
| Elizabeth Dole | 7/29/1936 |
| Peter Jennings | 7/29/1938 |
| Marlo Thomas | 11/21/1938 |
| Pelé | 10/23/1940 |
| Phil Ochs | 12/19/1940 |
| Juliet Mills | 11/21/1941 |
| Daryl Dragon | 8/27/1942 |
| Michael Crichton | 10/23/1942 |
| Tuesday Weld | 8/27/1943 |
| Michael Douglas | 9/25/1944 |
| Marcy Carsey | 11/21/1944 |
| Harold Ramis | 11/21/1944 |
| Richard Leakey | 12/19/1944 |
| Tim Reid | 12/19/1944 |
| Ian Badger | 11/21/1945 |

# Queen of Hearts

| | | | | |
|---|---|---|---|---|
| Goldie Hawn | 11/21/1945 | | Nicolette Sheridan | 11/21/1963 |
| Robert Urich | 12/19/1946 | | Jennifer Beals | 12/19/1963 |
| Barbara Bach | 8/27/1947 | | Bjork | 11/21/1965 |
| John Holliman | 10/23/1948 | | Martina McBride | 7/29/1966 |
| Marilyn Quayle | 7/29/1949 | | Yvonne Perry | 10/23/1966 |
| Paul Reubens | 8/27/1952 | | Troy Aikman | 11/21/1966 |
| Christopher Reeve | 9/25/1952 | | Eric Bobo | 8/27/1968 |
| Lorna Luft | 11/21/1952 | | Mike Johnson | 8/27/1968 |
| Ken Burns | 7/29/1953 | | Will Smith | 9/25/1968 |
| Patti Scialfa | 7/29/1953 | | Alex James | 11/21/1968 |
| Tina Brown | 11/21/1953 | | Catherine Zeta-Jones | 9/25/1969 |
| Ang Lee | 10/23/1954 | | Brooke Theiss | 10/23/1969 |
| Diana Scarwid | 8/27/1955 | | Ken Griffey Jr. | 11/21/1969 |
| Glen Matlock | 8/27/1956 | | Kristy Swanson | 12/19/1969 |
| Dwight Yoakam | 10/23/1956 | | Tony Kanal | 8/27/1970 |
| Michael Madsen | 9/25/1958 | | Tyson Beckford | 12/19/1971 |
| John Bjornstrom | 10/23/1958 | | Alyssa Milano | 12/19/1972 |
| Sam Raimi | 10/23/1959 | | Kaleena Kiff | 10/23/1974 |
| Weird Al Yankovic | 10/23/1959 | | Ryan Reynolds | 10/23/1976 |
| Heather Locklear | 9/25/1961 | | Jon Siebels | 8/27/1979 |
| Reggie White | 12/19/1961 | | Rachel Miner | 7/29/1980 |
| Bettina Huebers | 12/19/1962 | | Seamus Farrow | 12/19/1987 |
| Alexandra Paul | 7/29/1963 | | Daniel Jack Neeson | 8/27/1996 |

# Queen of Clubs

You are the Queen of Clubs! You are powerful and quick-minded. You are the most psychic card in the entire deck. You should trust your first impressions of people and situations—they are always right. You will always exert your authority in any situation you find yourself in. Though you are here to serve the world, you demand respect. You can handle responsibility just as any King and are fit to lead. But you are also compassionate and motherly. You are essentially here to feed your children the knowledge they need to grow and develop. You are not so kind to people who are slow, dull, or unintelligent, mostly because of your impatience and aggressive mind. Many Q♣ are fast drivers, though some realize the danger in that and intentionally slow down. You are one of the most distinguished cards in the deck and probably do not realize the importance of your intuitive gift. You are also very creative and artistic.

Your work can fall into many fields, though you will probably be happiest in something involving communications, learning, or teaching. You also have a natural gift for business—you have the ability to have a large, successful business, perhaps one that makes millions of

# Queen of Clubs

dollars. This is funny, because you also have a tendency to worry about money. Just remember that you can always make more! You demand respect from others in whatever work you do, even if that work is menial in nature. You are a Queen, after all.

The men Q♣ will not usually appear feminine, but inside, they are the sensitive type. And the women they meet really like that! But it is in the area of relationships that all Q♣ have their biggest challenges in life. This is one of the cards that has a plateful of love karma to deal with. And there is a basic uncertainty in the Q♣ nature that causes them to doubt their existing relationship or want variety. Some Q♣ birthdays, such as the Taurus and Libra ones, are practically unmarriageable.

There is so much mental power in this card—and the mind in every Q♣ is so powerful and active—that other areas of life can get overlooked. Q♣ should pay special attention to their feelings and their health, as they are usually at the bottom of their priorities and can suffer as the result. The neglected feelings contribute to relationship problems and many Q♣ die an early death because of the neglect

# Queen of Clubs

of their body. Either of these can be overcome if desired.

We owe a lot to the many Q♣ of our world. They have played such key roles in our society due to their many gifts. A quick glance down the list of people who share this card confirms this.

**Some of the best Q♣ marriages happen with:**
A♣, 10♠, 4♥, 2♥, K♣, and J♣

**The hottest sex happens with:**
9♣, 2♦, 3♦, K♠, A♥, A♦, 4♠, 7♥, 10♠, and 5♣

**Your marriageability is:**
Medium to not so good. Only the Gemini and Virgo Q♣ have strong marriage potential.

**Affirmation for you:**
I employ my intuition, high intelligence, and mental creativity to serve humanity. I am the "mother of knowledge."

| Famous Q♣ Birth Card people | |
|---|---|
| Babyface Nelson | 12/6/1908 |
| Clyde Barrow | 3/24/1909 |
| Joseph Barbera | 3/24/1911 |
| Ginger Rogers | 7/16/1911 |
| Jackson Pollock | 1/28/1912 |
| Sylvia Porter | 6/18/1913 |
| Jesse Owens | 9/12/1913 |
| E.G. Marshall | 6/18/1914 |
| Moshe Dayan | 5/20/1915 |

| | |
|---|---|
| Jackie Gleason | 2/26/1916 |
| Thelonius Monk | 10/10/1917 |
| Tony Randall | 2/26/1920 |
| Dave Brubeck | 12/6/1920 |
| Betty Hutton | 2/26/1921 |
| Otto Graham | 12/6/1921 |
| Vladimir Lenin | 4/22/1922 |
| Charles Mingus | 4/22/1922 |
| Christiaan Barnard | 11/8/1922 |
| Betty Page | 4/22/1923 |
| James Clavell | 10/10/1924 |
| Tom Wicker | 6/18/1926 |
| Fats Domino | 2/26/1928 |
| Aaron Spelling | 4/22/1928 |
| Claes Oldenburg | 1/28/1929 |
| Steve McQueen | 3/24/1930 |
| Harold Pinter | 10/10/1930 |
| Robert Novak | 2/26/1931 |
| Johnny Cash | 2/26/1932 |
| Susan Sontag | 1/28/1933 |
| John Brodie | 8/14/1935 |
| Alain Delon | 11/8/1935 |
| Alan Alda | 1/28/1936 |
| Jack Nicholson | 4/22/1937 |
| Astrid Kirchherr | 5/20/1938 |
| Bob Mackie | 3/24/1940 |
| Linda Gray | 9/12/1940 |
| Lynne Cheney | 8/14/1941 |
| David Crosby | 8/14/1941 |
| Richard Speck | 12/6/1941 |
| Roger Ebert | 6/18/1942 |
| Paul McCartney | 6/18/1942 |
| Jimmy Johnson | 7/16/1943 |
| Maria Muldaur | 9/12/1943 |
| Joe Cocker | 5/20/1944 |
| Barry White | 9/12/1944 |
| Steve Martin | 8/14/1945 |
| Wim Wenders | 8/14/1945 |
| Alan Rachins | 10/10/1945 |

# *Queen of Clubs*

| | | | |
|---|---|---|---|
| John Waters | 4/22/1946 | Julia Sweeney | 10/10/1961 |
| Cher | 5/20/1946 | Leif Garrett | 11/8/1961 |
| Susan Saint James | 8/14/1946 | Star Jones | 3/24/1962 |
| Danielle Steel | 8/14/1947 | Janine Turner | 12/6/1962 |
| Minnie Ripperton | 11/8/1947 | David Wells | 5/20/1963 |
| Mikhail Baryshnikov | 1/28/1948 | Annabella Sciorra | 3/24/1964 |
| Ruben Blades | 7/16/1948 | Charles Spencer | 5/20/1964 |
| Nick Lowe | 3/24/1949 | Alison Armitage | 2/26/1965 |
| Bonnie Raitt | 11/8/1949 | Jennifer Grant | 2/26/1966 |
| Barbi Benton | 1/28/1950 | Courtney Thorne-Smith | 11/8/1967 |
| Peter Frampton | 4/22/1950 | Sarah McLachlan | 1/28/1968 |
| Tommy Hilfiger | 3/24/1951 | Barry Sanders | 7/16/1968 |
| Mary Hart | 11/8/1951 | Catherine Bell | 8/14/1968 |
| Carol Kane | 6/18/1952 | Halle Berry | 8/14/1968 |
| Isabella Rossellini | 6/18/1952 | Jennifer Flavin | 8/14/1968 |
| Christie Hefner | 11/8/1952 | Parker Posey | 11/8/1968 |
| Michael Bolton | 2/26/1953 | Sice | 6/18/1969 |
| David Lee Roth | 10/10/1953 | Brett Favre | 10/10/1969 |
| Tom Hulce | 12/6/1953 | Lara Flyn Boyle | 3/24/1970 |
| Marilyn Chambers | 4/22/1954 | Pasemaster Mase | 3/24/1970 |
| Scott Hamilton | 9/12/1954 | Corey Feldman | 7/16/1971 |
| Peter Scolari | 9/12/1954 | Edward Kowalczyk | 7/16/1971 |
| Steven Wright | 12/6/1955 | Busta Rhymes | 5/20/1972 |
| Brian Benben | 6/18/1956 | Alyson Hannigan | 3/24/1974 |
| Jackee Harry | 8/14/1956 | Tara Reid | 11/8/1975 |
| Rachel Ward | 9/12/1957 | Colleen Haskell | 12/6/1976 |
| Ron Reagan | 5/20/1958 | Lindsay Price | 12/6/1976 |
| Tonya Tucker | 10/10/1958 | Daniel Johns | 4/22/1979 |
| Jello Biafra | 6/18/1959 | Nick Carter | 1/28/1980 |
| Magic Johnson | 8/14/1959 | Elijah Wood | 1/28/1981 |
| Kelly LeBrock | 3/24/1960 | Mila Kunis | 8/14/1983 |
| Sarah Brightman | 8/14/1961 | Jack Osbourne | 11/8/1985 |
| Rebecca Pidgeon | 10/10/1961 | | |

# Queen of Diamonds

You are the Queen of Diamonds! Sitting high in the suit of values and money, you demand respect from those around you. You know you are part of the royal family and you express that royalty most in the things you buy—and later show off. You like to look "expensive," and you do have expensive tastes. But you are not so good at managing money and have an inner sense of uncertainty about it, which contributes to your spending beyond your means at times, or simply feeling like there is never enough money. You are creative and business-minded and can make money selling your art or products. You enjoy having several things going at the same time. Having only one occupation or activity is much too boring for someone as creative as you. Just make sure that all your various activities serve a common goal, and that they support each other. Otherwise, you will find it difficult to make any definite progress along your path to wealth and fulfillment.

You are nurturing and loving, as long as others pay you the proper respect. You can be very mean-tongued at times and tend to be on the cranky side more often than most cards. You will have to work at developing a more positive

# Queen of Diamonds

attitude in general and in overcoming your sense of uncertainty about money. As a matter of fact, the Q♦ has work to do on almost every area of life, including relationships. You are special in that you are tested every step of the way in your life. You must follow the laws of life or pay the consequences, and usually it is "instant karma."

In the area of love, you are charming and can usually seduce whomever you like. You also enjoy variety, and for these reasons many Q♦ have difficulty remaining faithful to one person. Added to that is a fear that there will not be enough love. Multiple marriages are common for Q♦. You can be happily married, and if you are not, you are the only one to blame. Fortunately, you are also given the desire for inner exploration and the discovery of the truth. If you follow that, you will eventually unravel all the facets of yourself and be able to create the life you dream of.

Your potential is enormous. Some of the wealthiest people in the world have been Q♦. And perhaps your highest role is to impart to others a sense of higher values that will improve their lives.

**Some of the best Q♦ marriages happen with:**
K♣, A♦, K♦, J♦, 5♥, 8♦, and 5♣

**The hottest sex happens with:**
9♣, K♣, 2♠, 9♦, 7♣, 4♣, and J♥

**Your marriageability is:**
Not so great. Any Q♦ can get married. The trick is staying married.

**Affirmation for you:**
I nurture others, giving them a sense of higher values upon which they can build the life of their dreams.

| Famous Q♦ Birth Card people | |
|---|---|
| Chuck Yeager | 2/13/1923 |
| Anne Baxter | 5/7/1923 |
| Art Donovan | 6/5/1925 |
| Hugh Hefner | 4/9/1926 |
| Ken Russell | 7/3/1927 |
| Tom Lehrer | 4/9/1928 |
| Martin Luther King Jr. | 1/15/1929 |
| Pete Fountain | 7/3/1930 |
| Rupert Murdoch | 3/11/1931 |
| Kim Novak | 2/13/1933 |
| Emanuel Ungaro | 2/13/1933 |
| Jean Paul Belmondo | 4/9/1933 |
| John Unitas | 5/7/1933 |
| Dom DeLuise | 8/1/1933 |

# Queen of Diamonds

| | | | | |
|---|---|---|---|---|
| George Segal | 2/13/1934 | | Mario Van Peebles | 1/15/1957 |
| Sam Donaldson | 3/11/1934 | | Faye Resnick | 7/3/1957 |
| Bill Moyers | 6/5/1934 | | Joe Elliot | 8/1/1959 |
| Yves Saint Laurent | 8/1/1936 | | Chuck D | 8/1/1960 |
| Tom Stoppard | 7/3/1937 | | Henry Rollins | 2/13/1961 |
| Oliver Reed | 2/13/1938 | | Phil Campbell | 5/7/1961 |
| Fontella Bass | 7/3/1940 | | Mary Kay Bergman | 6/5/1961 |
| Gloria Allred | 7/3/1941 | | Tom Cruise | 7/3/1962 |
| Peter Tork | 2/13/1942 | | Thomas Gibson | 7/3/1962 |
| Kurtwood Smith | 7/3/1942 | | Hunter Tylo | 7/3/1962 |
| Jerry Garcia | 8/1/1942 | | Coolio | 8/1/1963 |
| Stockard Channing | 2/13/1944 | | Yeardley Smith | 7/3/1964 |
| Jerry Springer | 2/13/1944 | | Adam Duritz | 8/1/1964 |
| Andrea Martin | 1/15/1947 | | Paulina Porizkova | 4/9/1965 |
| Laurie Anderson | 6/5/1947 | | Cynthia Nixon | 4/9/1966 |
| Dave Barry | 7/3/1947 | | Lisa Lisa | 1/15/1967 |
| Betty Buckley | 7/3/1947 | | Chad Lowe | 1/15/1968 |
| Susan Atkins | 5/7/1948 | | Lisa Loeb | 3/11/1968 |
| Jan Smithers | 7/3/1949 | | Eagle-Eye Cherry | 5/7/1968 |
| Peter Gabriel | 2/13/1950 | | Traci Lords | 5/7/1968 |
| Bobby McFerrin | 3/11/1950 | | Kevin Hearn | 7/3/1969 |
| Jim Carroll | 8/1/1950 | | Mark Wahlberg | 6/5/1971 |
| Charo | 1/15/1951 | | Tempestt Bledsoe | 8/1/1973 |
| David Naughton | 2/13/1951 | | Robbie Williams | 2/13/1974 |
| Randy White | 1/15/1953 | | Andrea Barber | 7/3/1976 |
| Dennis Quaid | 4/9/1954 | | Eric Harris | 4/9/1981 |
| Amy Heckerling | 5/7/1954 | | Thora Birch | 3/11/1982 |
| Nina Hagen | 3/11/1955 | | Marston Glenn Hefner | 4/9/1990 |
| Joey Buttafuoco | 3/11/1956 | | Brandon Thomas Lee | 6/5/1996 |
| Montel Williams | 7/3/1956 | | Prince Jackson | 2/13/1997 |

# Queen of Spades

You are the Queen of Spades! Your card is often called the queen of work or the queen of labor. All the Spades are workers, and being the queen, you also place your work in a place of high importance in your life. But you should also see how incredible your mind is and how that mind should be used in the communications field. You could be an author or teacher or media celebrity. This is important: It is a tendency of people of your card to get mired in menial labor and to forget to pursue work that is more fulfilling and fun. So, look up and point yourself at a high dream for a creative, inspiring career. You will surprise yourself with how high you can go.

Yours is a rare card—only one birthday, so you will not find many celebrities in the list. Your card is also special because in a special spread we call the Spiritual Spread, it occupies the place of honor—the Sun position. And what that place indicates is that self-mastery, your birthright, is the highest spiritual accomplishment. Unlike the K♠, your partner card, you can rule the world through mastery of yourself. Nonetheless, you are powerful and fit to rule just as much as any King. So you

# Queen of Spades

will undoubtedly find yourself in positions of leadership and authority.

You are marriageable and could be very happily married. Any other area of life will compete with your work or be integrated into your work. It's a Spade thing. But it may be a challenge for you to receive from the opposite sex. This could cause you to marry someone who is not successful and be sort of stuck in hard work again. It is a tricky situation. Not all Q♠ will have this, but many will. Keep envisioning a life where there is abundance and ease. Let that be okay.

You are a Queen and regardless of your gender, you will have "children" around you that are yours to nurture and watch grow. You give them a work ethic that is pure and practical and connected to reality. And you are honored by watching them grow into productive, responsible adults.

**Some of the best Q♠ marriages happen with:**
K♠, J♠, 10♣, 9♦, 7♦, J♣, 5♦, J♦, A♦, and 2♣

**The hottest sex happens with:**

2♥, A♣, 9♠, 6♠, 2♣, K♥, 8♣, 7♠, K♦, 9♥, 7♦, 4♣, and 5♣

**Your marriageability is:**
Very good. No problem.

**Affirmation for you:**
I am the model of self-reflection and self-mastery. I achieve my highest expression through teaching or the sharing of knowledge.

| Famous Q♠ Birth Card people | |
| --- | --- |
| Sally Rand | 1/2/1903 |
| Isaac Asimov | 1/2/1920 |
| Jim Baker | 1/2/1936 |
| Roger Miller | 1/2/1936 |
| Wendy Phillips | 1/2/1952 |
| Gabrielle Carteris | 1/2/1960 |
| Tia Carrere | 1/2/1967 |
| Cuba Gooding Jr. | 1/2/1968 |
| Christy Turlington | 1/2/1969 |
| Taye Diggs | 1/2/1972 |

# The Kings

The King is the last card in each suit, representing the last stage of development. Within the King is the wisdom of having passed through every number below him in his evolution to the pinnacle of power. The King is the masculine archetype of leadership and power, accompanied by the wisdom of experience. All Kings know the right thing to do. However, they do not always act upon that wisdom, which is how we account for those Kings who are a discredit to their symbol. The problem lies primarily in the misuse of power, which is a very alluring and easily misused thing for all of us. You should also read about the Eights as you study the Kings, because they share this power. Hopefully, the King has already learned about the misuse of power during his or her evolution and will not abuse it again. But there are always enough variations that we will eventually run across a King who personifies all that is bad and undesirable in a powerful person.

All Kings have a certain amount of pride. Because they are natural born leaders, they tend to set themselves apart from the world at large and see themselves as part of a special group of leaders. Even those who do not directly recognize this quality within themselves will exhibit some pride or aversion to being given direction by others in spite of themselves. Many Kings do not recognize the power they already have and are using in their lives. Some actually believe they are somewhat powerless in their world, but a close examination of their lives always reveals that they are stubbornly persistent in doing things their own way. Usually others respect them or fear them, even if they themselves are unaware of it because of their damaged self-image. For many Kings, all they need to know is that they are a King, one who is meant to lead. Often, this by itself is all they need to get their minds in sync with who they really are.

Any King's power is defined primarily by their birth suit. The K♥ has power with people and personal relationships. They are charming and very intelligent. The K♣ has mental power that can be applied in a multitude of professions or situations. They make the fine distinctions that separate truth from untruth. The K♦ is the powerful and often ruthless business person. When they decide to take over, their isn't much they cannot accomplish on the material level, though their personal happiness may be lost in the process. The K♠ has the power of will backed by a deep wisdom. Their mind will never be swayed by others, since their own wisdom is constantly telling them the truth.

Female Kings are an interesting quirk in the cosmic plan. Here is a soul that has definite leadership ability, decisiveness, and usually a bit of aggressiveness to match. Women like Sharon Stone, Faye Dunaway, Jacqueline Kennedy Onassis, Janet Jackson, Queen Elizabeth II, and Bridget Fonda all personify women who are strong leaders of men. A King is not an easy card for anyone to be because of the tremendous responsibility implied. The women have the added burden of balancing their male and female sides in personal relationships. This hurdle alone can take most of a lifetime to conquer.

Being a King implies responsibility, and perhaps this is another of the real reasons that some Kings never achieve their potential. Responsibility can be either distasteful or fearful for some Kings, and they may make a decision early on to avoid this part of their life at all costs. When they do, they take off their crown and become either the Jack or Queen of their suit, throwing away most of their power and potential. Few K♠ are ready to wear their crowns. Since they are literally the King of Kings, their crown holds the most power, but also the most burden. Most K♠ feel more comfortable as a Jack or Queen. They make great artists, musicians, and actors, but few achieve the full potential of the most powerful card in the entire deck. However, the other Kings are also guilty of this same choice. Though it doesn't happen as often, other Kings will sometimes shy away from the responsibility of living up to their birthright. They just decide to have fun instead. In doing so, they throw away their power and then wonder why their lives don't seem to make them happy. All Kings have an inner voice that tells them they are fit to be leaders. Until they fulfill this aspect of their destiny, they cannot truly be at peace with themselves.

Other Kings will abuse their power, forsaking their inherent wisdom and giving in to their fears. They will bully, dominate, and use others but often claim that it is they who are being abused. These are the Kings that have lost their authority. However, this is not a common occurrence. Though we will find Kings who use their power unwisely, this is not the rule. Most Kings are aware of their power and have the wisdom and patience to know that it must be used with care and responsibility if it is to do any good to them or in the world. We can usually trust them to lead us to things that better our lives in many ways.

# King of Hearts

You are the King of Hearts! You are the charmer and seducer, and also the "father card." You have mastery over the area of people and relationships. You use that mastery every day, whether or not you see it. You are also highly intelligent. Many K♥ end up in jobs that require a lot of brainpower, such as research scientist or lab technician or computer analyst. But really, people is what you are all about. And if you do not have a lot of interaction in your job, you are probably not that happy.

Your mind is quick and aggressive. You could have an arguing or anger problem if not expressed positively, but you are generous and loving. And remember—you are the King! People must respect you and give you your due. As long as you are acknowledged by others to some extent, there will be no friction.

You can have whomever you want for a mate. You have the power to attract and seduce. And K♥ make great lovers. Some K♥ realize this and decide to play bachelor or bachelorette for a while, but usually they marry and get down to having children—one of their favorite activities. And many K♥ base their occupations around children. The K♥ is marriageable and family-oriented.

# King of Hearts

Though beautiful and elegant, female K♥ are very strong-willed. After a successful marriage, they often kick their husbands out and just go it alone. They really don't need a man all that much. And all K♥ take raising their children very seriously, often to the detriment of their partners.

You have the power to be successful in many occupations. You are the embodiment of maturity and responsibility in love. We are fortunate to be counted among your friends.

**Some of the best K♥ marriages happen with:**
A♣, 2♥, Q♥, 9♣, K♦, K♣, 2♠, and 3♣

**The hottest sex happens with:**
3♣, K♦, 10♥, 5♠, 5♦, 2♠, K♣, 8♦, Q♠, and 7♠

**Your marriageability is:**
Excellent!

**Affirmation for you:**
I am the father of love. My example inspires others to live a life based upon love and respect for others.

| Famous K♥ Birth Card people | |
| --- | --- |
| F. Scott Fitzgerald | 9/24/1896 |
| Ham Fisher | 9/24/1900 |
| Christopher Isherwood | 8/26/1904 |
| George Stevens | 12/18/1904 |
| Jim Davis | 8/26/1909 |
| Charles Hard Townes | 7/28/1915 |
| David Brown | 7/28/1916 |
| Judy Canova | 11/20/1916 |
| Betty Grable | 12/18/1916 |
| Susan Hayward | 6/30/1917 |
| Lena Horne | 6/30/1917 |
| Audra Lindley | 9/24/1918 |
| Timothy Leary | 10/22/1920 |
| David Begelman | 8/26/1921 |
| Jim McKay | 9/24/1921 |
| Dory Previn | 10/22/1925 |
| Robert F. Kennedy | 11/20/1925 |
| Estelle Parsons | 11/20/1927 |
| Jacqueline Kennedy Onassis | 7/28/1929 |
| Anthony Newley | 9/24/1931 |
| Martin Landau | 6/30/1933 |
| Geraldine Ferraro | 8/26/1935 |
| Jim Henson | 9/24/1936 |
| Pablo Elvira | 9/24/1938 |
| Christopher Lloyd | 10/22/1938 |
| Linda McCartney | 9/24/1941 |
| Robert Ballard | 6/30/1942 |
| Annette Funicello | 10/22/1942 |
| Florence Ballard | 6/30/1943 |
| Bill Bradley | 7/28/1943 |
| Catherine Deneuve | 10/22/1943 |
| Keith Richards | 12/18/1943 |
| Mike Bloomfield | 7/28/1944 |
| Jim Davis | 7/28/1945 |
| Rick Wright | 7/28/1945 |
| Joe Greene | 9/24/1946 |

# King of Hearts

| | | | | |
|---|---|---|---|---|
| Steven Spielberg | 12/18/1946 | | Branford Marsalis | 8/26/1960 |
| Sally Struthers | 7/28/1948 | | Brian Boitano | 10/22/1963 |
| Gordon Clapp | 9/24/1948 | | Brad Pitt | 12/18/1963 |
| Phil Hartman | 9/24/1948 | | Lori Loughlin | 7/28/1964 |
| Vida Blue | 7/28/1949 | | Steve Austin | 12/18/1964 |
| Richard Cowsill | 8/26/1950 | | Mike Diamond | 11/20/1965 |
| Robert Cowsill | 8/26/1950 | | Mike Tyson | 6/30/1966 |
| Gillian Armstrong | 12/18/1950 | | Chris Robinson | 11/20/1966 |
| Leonard Maltin | 12/18/1950 | | Tom Drummond | 6/30/1969 |
| Joe Kennedy | 9/24/1952 | | Adrian Young | 8/26/1969 |
| Patti Davis | 10/22/1952 | | Megan Ward | 9/24/1969 |
| Jeff Goldblum | 10/22/1952 | | DMX | 12/18/1970 |
| Tony Paloma | 11/20/1953 | | Elizabeth Berkley | 7/28/1972 |
| Elliot Easton | 12/18/1953 | | Sailor Moon | 6/30/1978 |
| David Alan Grier | 6/30/1955 | | Katie Holmes | 12/18/1978 |
| Ray Liotta | 12/18/1955 | | Macaulay Culkin | 8/26/1980 |
| Bo Derek | 11/20/1956 | | Christina Aguilera | 12/18/1980 |
| Mark Gastineau | 11/20/1956 | | Zachary Hanson | 10/22/1985 |
| Terry Fox | 7/28/1958 | | Stella del Carmen | |
| Kevin Sorbo | 9/24/1958 | |    Banderas Griffith | 9/24/1996 |
| Vincent D'Onofrio | 6/30/1959 | | | |

# King of Clubs

How nice it must be to be a King of Clubs! You are the king of knowledge, the master of distinction. Your keen mind analyzes everything successfully and correctly. Your assessments of things are generally right on the money, which is not something many cards can brag about. You are also a born leader and teacher. Being the master of the communications suit, you excel at most any job you apply yourself to. You like people and know how to communicate with them in a way that is harmonious and helpful, inspiring their cooperation and support. You will inevitably find yourself managing or leading others—it's part of your nature!

You are very partnership oriented when it comes to work. You prefer to work in concert with others, and many K♣ are destined to have a significant working partnership during an important phase of their life. This is unique among the cards. No other has this specific karma.

You are also one of the most marriageable cards in the deck, and many people of your card get married early and stay married. You are not generally promiscuous, though some male K♣ can be that way for a time until they are ready to

# King of Clubs

settle down—but they all settle down sooner or later. The choice of mate can be a problem for some K♣. The men often choose women of the Heart suit—women who are just like the man's mother, who is also often a Heart herself. What is intriguing about this is that Hearts is the rarest of suits, and the K♣ is the most common of the Birth Cards. How K♣ men find these Heart women is a mystery. But often their mates will be dreamy, elusive and sometimes co-dependent, just like mom.

Female K♣ will have challenges with either having children, being a mother, or will have some issue related to their sexuality. They make great wives but often choose men who are not so good.

K♣ are some of the most special people in the world. They contribute clarity of vision and inspiration to all they touch. They are honest and live by the truth, and they will never compromise it. They can be trusted and deserve our admiration. Throughout history K♣ have been our leaders, artists, and statesmen. Two of the Beatles were K♣ All make

# King of Clubs

their mark upon us, and it is always a positive contribution.

**Some of the best K♣ marriages happen with:**
A♦, Q♣, J♦, 2♣, 4♥, 6♣, 2♦, and J♠

**The hottest sex happens with:**
Q♦, 3♦, 10♣, 5♥, 8♠, 4♦, 9♦, and J♠

**Your marriageability is:**
Great!

**Affirmation for you:**
As the master of knowledge, I share my keen perception and its discoveries with people around me. I live what I teach and embody the higher principles I espouse.

| Famous K♣ Birth Card people | |
|---|---|
| Rembrandt | 7/15/1606 |
| John Wesley | 6/17/1703 |
| Wolfgang Amadeus Mozart | 1/27/1756 |
| Martin Van Buren | 12/5/1782 |
| Lewis Carroll | 1/27/1832 |
| John Muir | 4/21/1838 |
| George Armstrong Custer | 12/5/1839 |
| Auguste Renoir | 2/25/1841 |
| Annie Oakley | 8/13/1860 |
| Marie Curie | 11/7/1867 |
| Enrico Caruso | 2/25/1873 |
| Igor Stravinsky | 6/17/1882 |
| D.H. Lawrence | 9/11/1885 |
| Ho Chi Minh | 5/19/1890 |
| Dane Rudhyar | 3/23/1895 |

| | |
|---|---|
| M.C. Escher | 6/17/1898 |
| Alfred Hitchcock | 8/13/1899 |
| Erich Fromm | 3/23/1900 |
| Alastair Sim | 10/9/1900 |
| Zeppo Marx | 2/25/1901 |
| Walt Disney | 12/5/1901 |
| Ralph Bellamy | 6/17/1904 |
| Joan Crawford | 3/23/1908 |
| Ben Hogan | 8/13/1912 |
| Jim Backus | 2/25/1913 |
| Hedy Lamarr | 9/11/1913 |
| Anthony Quinn | 4/21/1915 |
| Billy Graham | 11/7/1918 |
| Donna Reed | 1/27/1921 |
| Al Hirt | 11/7/1922 |
| Tom Landry | 9/11/1924 |
| Malcolm X | 5/19/1925 |
| Queen Elizabeth II | 4/21/1926 |
| Fidel Castro | 8/13/1926 |
| Joan Sutherland | 11/7/1926 |
| Don Ho | 8/13/1930 |
| Little Richard | 12/5/1932 |
| Charles Grodin | 4/21/1935 |
| Alex Karras | 7/15/1935 |
| Ken Kercheval | 7/15/1935 |
| Calvin Trillin | 12/5/1935 |
| Troy Donahue | 1/27/1936 |
| Tom Courtenany | 2/25/1937 |
| Helen Prejean | 4/21/1939 |
| Lola Falana | 9/11/1939 |
| Brian De Palma | 9/11/1940 |
| John Lennon | 10/9/1940 |
| Nora Ephron | 5/19/1941 |
| Robert Hand | 12/5/1942 |
| Sally Jessy Raphael | 2/25/1943 |
| Newt Gingrich | 6/17/1943 |
| Barry Manilow | 6/17/1943 |
| Joni Mitchell | 11/7/1943 |

# King of Clubs

| | | | |
|---|---|---|---|
| Jan-Michael Vincent | 7/15/1944 | Danny Bonaduce | 8/13/1959 |
| Pete Townshend | 5/19/1945 | Kim Alexis | 7/15/1960 |
| Tommy Ray Franks | 6/17/1945 | Lolita Davidovich | 7/15/1961 |
| Leo Kottke | 9/11/1945 | Forest Whitaker | 7/15/1961 |
| Linda Ronstadt | 7/15/1946 | Dawnn Lewis | 8/13/1961 |
| Iggy Pop | 4/21/1947 | Virginia Madsen | 9/11/1961 |
| Betty Broderick | 11/7/1947 | Jean Sagal | 10/9/1961 |
| Jim Messina | 12/5/1947 | Liz Sagal | 10/9/1961 |
| Jim Plunkett | 12/5/1947 | Kristy McNichol | 9/11/1962 |
| Kathleen Battle | 8/13/1948 | Roy Dupuis | 4/21/1963 |
| Jackson Browne | 10/9/1948 | Brigitte Nielsen | 7/15/1963 |
| Patti LuPone | 4/21/1949 | Bridget Fonda | 1/27/1964 |
| Judy Tenuta | 11/7/1949 | Chris Henchy | 3/23/1964 |
| Arianna Huffington | 7/15/1950 | Debi Mazar | 8/13/1964 |
| Gary Frank | 10/9/1950 | Dana Plato | 11/7/1964 |
| Tony Danza | 4/21/1951 | Carrot Top | 2/25/1965 |
| Joey Ramone | 5/19/1951 | Scott Livingstone | 7/15/1965 |
| Jesse Ventura | 7/15/1951 | Moby | 9/11/1965 |
| Dan Fogelberg | 8/13/1951 | Tea Leoni | 2/25/1966 |
| Robert Wuhl | 10/9/1951 | Quinn Cummings | 8/13/1967 |
| Grace Jones | 5/19/1952 | Harry Connick Jr. | 9/11/1967 |
| Louie Anderson | 3/23/1953 | Carling Bassett | 10/9/1967 |
| Chaka Kahn | 3/23/1953 | Damon Albarn | 3/23/1968 |
| John Doe | 2/25/1954 | Midori Ito | 8/13/1969 |
| Mimi Rogers | 1/27/1955 | P.J. Harvey | 10/9/1969 |
| Scott Bakula | 10/9/1955 | Chi Cheng | 7/15/1970 |
| Steven Ford | 5/19/1956 | Savannah | 10/9/1970 |
| Marky Ramone | 7/15/1956 | Justin Jeffre | 2/25/1973 |
| Dennis Diken | 2/25/1957 | Brian Austin Green | 7/15/1973 |
| Jellybean Benitez | 11/7/1957 | Joshua Leonard | 6/17/1975 |
| Art Monk | 12/5/1957 | Keri Russell | 3/23/1976 |
| Andie MacDowell | 4/21/1958 | Jamie Sale | 4/21/1977 |
| Mike Singletary | 10/9/1958 | Randy Spelling | 10/9/1978 |
| Robert Smith | 4/21/1959 | Venus Williams | 6/17/1980 |
| Nicole Brown | 5/19/1959 | Frankie Muniz | 12/5/1985 |

# *King of Diamonds*

You are the King of Diamonds! You are the King of Money, the only one-eyed king in the deck, and you display an axe above your head. Let no man or woman think that you are not the ruler of rulers. You express power through values and know the worth of all things, as well as how to manipulate worth—and the things that others want—to meet your goals and objectives. You have a fortunate life path, and there are no obstacles (besides yourself) that could really stand in the way of your success. You are meant to rule, and somehow you will find your way to the top, be it sooner or later. You can be ruthless in the pursuit of your goals, and the K♦ is known to make enemies along the way. But who cares? It is all part of the path to your success. Not everyone will like you, but no one may rule you.

You have a blind eye, which means there are parts of situations that you really don't see. For some K♦, there is a blindness to your own faults. For others, it's a blindness to how your actions affect others. It is all part of the K♦ pattern. You can also be very subjective in your thinking. When you are riled up, your mind could betray you. It is always nice to have someone to bounce

# King of Diamonds

things off of just as a reality check. For some K♦, the biggest challenge is to find the power inherent in their birthday. This often requires taking the reins of their life chariot and living their life the way they want, disregarding the requests of family or friends. A king has to be a king.

You are very marriageable; you can settle down and be pretty happy married. There are some K♦ who are confirmed bachelors, such as George Clooney, but they are the exception to the rule. Female K♦ are so strong willed that it takes a special man to handle them. Look at Sharon Stone, Angelina Jolie, and Faye Dunaway for good examples of this. K♦ women will certainly not take any crap from a guy; so gentlemen, you have been warned. Anyone who hopes to marry a K♦ will have to know that the K♦ can only lead and probably not follow.

The world needs leaders, people who will stand up and take the heat for their stand in life. You are one of those people. We await your commands!

**Some of the best K♦ marriages happen with:**
A♣, Q♦, K♥, 6♥, 4♣, 2♣, 9♦, and 2♠

**The hottest sex happens with:**
3♠, 10♦, 8♣, 2♣, 2♦, 9♠, J♣, and 4♦

**Your marriageability is:**
Very good, if not excellent. This should not be a problem for you.

**Affirmation for you:**
As the King of Worth, I take the throne and lead others, showing all that having the things in life that we truly want is the way it is meant to be.

| Famous K♦ Birth Card people | |
|---|---|
| Orson Welles | 5/6/1915 |
| James Herriot | 3/10/1916 |
| Betty Ford | 4/8/1918 |
| Andy Rooney | 1/14/1920 |
| Franco Corelli | 4/8/1921 |
| Dan Rowan | 7/2/1922 |
| Franco Zeffirelli | 2/12/1923 |
| Dennis Weaver | 6/4/1924 |
| Medgar Evers | 7/2/1925 |
| Joe Garagiola | 2/12/1926 |
| Shecky Greene | 4/8/1926 |
| Ruth Westheimer | 6/4/1928 |
| Jacques Brel | 4/8/1929 |
| Imelda Marcos | 7/2/1929 |
| Dorothy Tutin | 4/8/1930 |
| Willie Mays | 5/6/1931 |
| Dave Thomas | 7/2/1932 |
| Bruce Dern | 6/4/1936 |
| Jack Jones | 1/14/1938 |
| Wayne Dyer | 3/10/1940 |
| Chuck Norris | 3/10/1940 |

# King of Diamonds

| | | | |
|---|---|---|---|
| Faye Dunaway | 1/14/1941 | Julian Lennon | 4/8/1963 |
| Peggy Lennon | 4/8/1941 | Prince Edward | 3/10/1964 |
| Holland Taylor | 1/14/1943 | Dave Parsons | 7/2/1964 |
| Gordon Waller | 6/4/1945 | Rod Woodson | 3/10/1965 |
| Catfish Hunter | 4/8/1946 | Edie Brickell | 3/10/1966 |
| Larry David | 7/2/1947 | Chris Titus | 3/10/1966 |
| Lawrence Kasdan | 1/14/1949 | Robin Wright Penn | 4/8/1966 |
| John Madden | 4/8/1949 | Emily Watson | 1/14/1967 |
| Sydney Biddle Barrows | 1/14/1952 | LL Cool J | 1/14/1968 |
| Douglas Adams | 3/10/1952 | Patricia Arquette | 4/8/1968 |
| Parker Stevenson | 6/4/1952 | Ron Goldman | 7/2/1968 |
| Tony Blair | 5/6/1953 | Jason Bateman | 1/14/1969 |
| John Schneider | 4/8/1954 | Dave Grohl | 1/14/1969 |
| Arsenio Hall | 2/12/1955 | Jim Creeggan | 2/12/1970 |
| Jerry Hall | 7/2/1956 | Angelina Jolie | 6/4/1975 |
| Sharon Stone | 3/10/1958 | Christina Ricci | 2/12/1980 |
| Roma Downey | 5/6/1960 | Michelle Branch | 7/2/1983 |
| Richard Hatch | 4/8/1961 | Taran Noah Smith | 4/8/1984 |
| George Clooney | 5/6/1961 | Lindsay Lohan | 7/2/1986 |
| Jimmy McNichol | 7/2/1961 | Sailor Lee Brinkley-Cook | 7/2/1998 |
| Izzy Stradlin | 4/8/1962 | Presley Walker Gerber | 7/2/1999 |
| Jeff Ament | 3/10/1963 | Ella Corinne Bening-Beatty | 4/8/2000 |

# King of Spades

You are the K♠ of Spades! You are one of the rarest of the cards in the deck—only one birthday has your Birth Card. Yours is the most powerful card in the entire deck. You are the king of work and the king of will. Your card also sits in its own place in the Crown Line of the entire deck, a place of honor and also a place of independence. You therefore are naturally a king and fit to rule. You are also very independent and will never allow others to have control over you. Whether male or female, you have one of the strongest wills of any card in the deck, along with wisdom gained through many lifetimes of experience. You bring all that to bear in this lifetime. But what will you do with all this power at your disposal? And how do you feel about the tremendous responsibility that comes with such power?

There is another side of you, and that side is adventurous and restless. You are not afraid to try most anything, and you enjoy your freedom and travel. This one element may prevent you from reaching your full potential, which requires both a commitment and a burden of responsibility. And this may not be your choice for most of your life. But it should be said here that you could accomplish anything—but that

# King of Spades

accomplishment could cause the sacrifice of your precious freedom.

Women of this card are strong-willed and able to stand up to any man. This, along with the aforementioned restless nature, can make marriage difficult. It takes a special man to bring out the feminine side of a female K♠, which is often overshadowed by their strong will and powerful demeanor. The male K♠ likewise love their freedom and often keep their options open. But if you, dear K♠, decide upon marriage, it certainly can be yours. It is just that many of your card will choose otherwise. And no one can sway your mind but you.

You have the ability to make a mark on the world, and, in a way, you have more potential than any other card in the deck. Yet that very potential may scare you away from doing much with your life. The world needs leaders such as you. Once you see that, perhaps you will come take your place and put on your crown!

**Some of the best K♠ marriages happen with:**
A♥, Q♠, 8♦, 6♣, 4♣, 2♦, 3♦, 10♠, 4♥, and 6♥

**The hottest sex happens with:**
3♥, Q♣, 10♠, Q♥, 3♣, and K♦

**Your marriageability is:**
Questionable, but only because you may never choose it.

**Affirmation for you:**
I have the power to change the world.

| Famous K♠ Birth Card people | |
| --- | --- |
| Paul Revere | 1/1/1735 |
| Betsy Ross | 1/1/1752 |
| E.M. Forester | 1/1/1879 |
| J. Edgar Hoover | 1/1/1895 |
| Barry Goldwater | 1/1/1909 |
| Hank Greenberg | 1/1/1911 |
| J.D. Salinger | 1/1/1919 |
| IdiAmin | 1/1/1926 |
| Famke Jansen | 1/1/1964 |
| Dedee Pfeiffer | 1/1/1964 |
| Verne Troyer | 1/1/1969 |